Practical Paranoia
OS X 10.11 El Capitan
Security Essentials

- ☑ The Easiest
- ☑ Step-By-Step
- ☐ Most Comprehensive
- ☐ Guide To Securing Data and Communications
- ☐ On Your Home and Office Macintosh

Marc L. Mintz, MBA-IT, ACTC, ACSP

D1468226

Practical Paranoia: OS X 10.11 Security Essentials for Home and Business
Marc Mintz

Editions: 1.0: 8/2015 • 1.1: 10/2015 • 1.2: 11/2015 • 1.3: 12/2015 • 1.4: 1/2016 • 1.4.1: 2/2016 • 1.4.2: 2/2016

Cover design by Ed Brandt

ISBN-10: 151693217X
ISBN-13: 978-1516932177

Dedication

To Candace,
without whose support and encouragement
this work would not be possible

Contents At A Glance

Contents In Detail

Contents In Detail

PRACTICAL PARANOIA
OS X 10.11
SECURITY ESSENTIALS

MARC L. MINTZ, MBA-IT, ACTC, ACSP

Introduction

Just because you're paranoid doesn't mean they aren't after you.
–Joseph Heller, *Catch-22*

Everything in life is easy–once you know the how.
–Marc L. Mintz

Who Should Read This Book

Traditional business thinking holds that products should be tailored to a laser-cut market segment. Something like: *18-25 year old males, still living at their parents home, who like to play video games, working a minimum-wage job.* Yup, we all have a pretty clear image of that market segment.

In the case of this book, the market segment is *all users of OS X computers.* Really! From my great-Aunt Rose who is wrestling with using her first computer, to the small business, to the IT staff for major corporations and government agencies.

Even though the military may use better security on their physical front doors–MP's with machine guns protecting the underground bunker–compared to a residential home with a Kwikset deadbolt and a neurotic Chihuahua, the steps to secure OS X for home and business use are almost identical for both. There is little difference between *home-level security* and *military-grade security* when it comes to this technology.

The importance of data held in a personal computer may be every bit as important as the data held by the CEO of a Fortune 500. The data is also every bit as vulnerable to penetration.

What is Unique About This Book

Practical Paranoia: OS X 10.11 Security Essentials is the first comprehensive OS X security book written with the new to average user in mind–as well as the IT professional. The steps outlined here are the same steps used by my consulting organization when securing systems for hospitals, government agencies, and the military.

By following the easy, illustrated, step-by-step instructions in this book, you will be able to secure your computer to better than National Security Agency (NSA) standards.

Hardening your computers will help your business protect the valuable information of you and your customers. Should your computer work include HIPAA or legal-related information, to be in full compliance with regulations it is likely that you will need to be using OS X 10.7, and I recommend OS X 10.11 or higher.

For those of you caught up in the ADHD epidemic, do not let the number of pages here threaten you. This book really is a quick read because it has lots of actual screenshots. Written for use in our *Practical Paranoia: Security Essentials Workshops* as well as for self-study, this book is the ultimate step-by-step guide for protecting the new OS X user who has no technical background, as well as for the experienced IT consultant. The information and steps outlined are built on guidelines from Apple, the NSA, and my own 30 years as an IT and Apple consultant, developer, technician and trainer. I have reduced dull background theory to a minimum, including only what is necessary to grasp the need-for and how-to.

The organization of this book is simple. We provide chapters representing each of the major areas of vulnerability, and the tasks you will do to protect your data, device, and personal identity.

Although you may jump in at any section, I recommend you follow the sequence provided to make your system as secure as possible. Remember, the bad guys will not attack your strong points. They seek out your weak points. Leave no obvious weakness and they will most likely move on to an easier target.

To review your work using this guide, use the *Mintz InfoTech Security Checklist* provided at the end of this book.

Theodore Sturgeon, an American science fiction author and critic, stated: *Ninety percent of everything is crap. https://en.wikipedia.org/wiki/Sturgeon%27s_law.* Mintz's extrapolation of Sturgeon's Revelation is: *Ninety percent of everything you have learned and think to be true is crap.*

I have spent most of my adult life in exploration of how to distill what is real and accurate from what is, well, Sturgeon's 90%. The organizations I have founded, the workshops I've produced, and the *Practical Paranoia* book series all spring from this pursuit. If you find any area of this workshop or book that you think should be added, expanded, improved, or changed, I invite you to contact me personally with your recommendations.

Why Worry?

In terms of network, Internet, and data security, OS X users must be vigilant because of the presence of malware *http://en.wikipedia.org/wiki/Malware* such as viruses, Trojan horses, worms, phishing, and key loggers impacting our computers. Attacks on computer and smartphone users by tricksters, criminals, and governments are on a steep rise. In addition to OS X-specific attacks, we are vulnerable at points of entry common to all computer users, including Flash, Java, compromised websites, and phishing, as well as through simple hardware theft. How bad is the situation?

- According to a study by Symantec, an average enterprise-wide data breach has a recovery cost of $5 million.

- According to the FBI, 2 million laptops are stolen or lost in the U.S. each year.

- Of those 2 million stolen or lost, only 3% ever are recovered.

- Out of the box, an OS X computer can be broken into–bypassing password protection–in less than 1 minute.

- The typical email is clearly readable at dozens of points along the Internet highway on its trip to the recipient. Most likely, that email is read by somebody you don't know.

- A popular game played by high school and college students is *war driving*: the act of driving around neighborhoods to find Wi-Fi networks, geographically marking the location for others to use and break into.

- The Cyber Intelligence Sharing and Protection Act (CISPA) *http://en.wikipedia.org/wiki/Cyber_Intelligence_Sharing_and_Protection_Act* allows the government easy access to all your electronic communications. PRISM *http://en.wikipedia.org/wiki/PRISM_ (surveillance_program)* allows government agencies to collect and track data on any American device.

The list goes on, but we have lives to live and you get the point. It is not a matter of *if* your data will ever be threatened. It is only a matter of *when,* and how often the attempts will be made.

Reality Check

Nothing can 100% guarantee 100% security 100% of the time. Even the White House and CIA websites and internal networks have been penetrated. We know that organized crime, as well as the governments of China, North Korea, Russia, Great Britain, United States, and Australia have billions of dollars and tens of thousands of highly skilled security personnel on staff looking for *zero-day exploits*. These are vulnerabilities that have not yet been discovered by the developer. As if this is not enough, the U.S. government influences the development and certification of most security protocols. This means that industry-standard tools used to secure our data often have been found to include vulnerabilities introduced by government agencies.

With these odds against us, should we just throw up our hands and accept that there is no way to ensure our privacy? Well, just because breaking into a locked home only requires a rock through a window, should we give up and not lock our doors?

Of course not. We do everything we can to protect our valuables. When leaving on vacation we lock doors, turn on the motion detectors, notify the police to prompt additional patrols, and stop mail and newspaper delivery.

The same is true with our digital lives. For the very few who are targeted by the NSA, there is little that can be done to completely block them from reading your email, following your chats, and recording your web browsing. But you can make it extremely time and labor intensive.

For the majority of us not subject to an NSA targeted attack, we are rightfully concerned about our digital privacy being penetrated by criminals, pranksters, competitors, and nosy people as well as about the collateral damage caused by malware infestations.

You *can* protect yourself, your data, and your devices from such attack. By following this book, you should be able to secure fully your data and your first device in two days, and any additional devices in a half day. This is a very small price to pay for peace of mind and security.

Remember, penetration does not occur at your strong points. A home burglar will avoid hacking at a steel door when a simple rock through a window will gain entry. A strong password and encrypted drive by themselves do not mean malware can't slip in with your email, and pass all of your keystrokes – including usernames and passwords – to the hacker.

It is imperative that you secure all points of vulnerability.

- NOTE: Throughout this book we provide suggestions on how to use various free or low-cost applications to help enforce your protection. Neither Marc L. Mintz nor Mintz InfoTech, Inc. receives payment for suggesting them. We have used them with success, and thus feel confident in recommending them.

About the Author

Marc Louis Mintz is one of the most respected IT consultants and technical trainers in the United States. His technical support services and workshops have been embraced by hundreds of organizations and thousands of individuals over the past 3 decades.

Marc holds an MBA-IT (Masters of Business Administration with specialization in Information Technology), Chauncy Technical Trainer certification, Post-Secondary Education credentials, and over a dozen Apple certifications.

Marc's enthusiasm, humor, and training expertise have been honed on leading edge work in the fields of motivation, management development, and technology. He has been recruited to present software and hardware workshops nationally and internationally. His technical workshops are consistently rated by seminar providers, meeting planners, managers, and participants as *The Best* because he empowers participants to see with new eyes, think in a new light, and problem solve using new strategies.

When away from the podium, Marc is right there in the trenches, working to keep client Android, iOS, OS X, and Windows systems securely connected.

The author may be reached at:
Marc L. Mintz
Mintz InfoTech, Inc.
1000 Cordova Pl
#842
Santa Fe, NM 87505
+1 888.479.0690
Email: *marc@mintzIT.com*
Web: *http://mintzIT.com* • *http://thepracticalparanoid.com*

Practical Paranoia Updates

Information regarding IT security changes daily, so we offer you newsletter, blog and Facebook updates to keep you on top of everything.

Newsletter

Stay up to date with your Practical Paranoia information by subscribing to our free weekly newsletter.

1. Visit *http://mintzIT.com*

2. Scroll to the bottom of the home page to the *Newsletter Signup* form.

3. Complete the form, and then click the *Sign Up* button.

Blog

Updates and addendums to this book also will be included in our free *Mintz InfoTech Blog*. Go to: *http://mintzit.com*, and then select the *Blog* link.

Facebook

Updates and addendums to this book also will be found in our *Practical Paranoia Facebook Group*. Go to *https://www.facebook.com/groups/PracticalParanoia/*

Practical Paranoia Book Upgrades

We are constantly updating *Practical Paranoia* so that you have the latest, most accurate resource available. If at any time you wish to upgrade to the latest version of *Practical Paranoia* at the lowest price we can offer:

1. Tear off the front cover of **Practical Paranoia**.

2. Make check payable to Mintz InfoTech for $30.

3. Send front cover, check, and mailing information to:
   Mintz InfoTech, Inc.
   1000 Cordova Pl
   #842
   Santa Fe, NM 87505

4. Your new copy of **Practical Paranoia** will be sent by USPS. Please allow up to 4 weeks for delivery.

Practical Paranoia Kindle Updates

We are constantly updating *Practical Paranoia* so that you have the latest, most accurate resource available. If at any time you wish to update to the latest Kindle version of *Practical Paranoia* at no cost:

1. Delete the copy of *Practical Paranoia* currently installed on your Kindle device.

2. Download the current edition of *Practical Paranoia*.

1. Vulnerability: Passwords

For a people who are free, and who mean to remain so, a well-organized and armed militia is their best security.

–Thomas Jefferson

Knowledge, and the willingness to act upon it, is our greatest defense.

–Marc L. Mintz

The Great Awakening

In June 2013, documents of NSA origin were leaked to The Guardian newspaper *http://en.wikipedia.org/wiki/NSA_warrantless_surveillance_controversy*. The documents provided evidence that the NSA was both legally and illegally spying on United States citizens' cell phone, email, and web usage. These documents, while causing gasps of outrage and shock by the general public, revealed little that those of us in the IT field already did not know/suspect for decades: every aspect of our digital lives is subject to eavesdropping.

The more cynical amongst us go even further, stating that *everything* we do on our computers *is* recorded and subject to government scrutiny.

But few of us have anything real to fear from our government. Where the real problems with digital data theft come from are local kids hijacking networks, professional cyber-criminals who have fully automated the process of scanning networks for valuable information, competitors/enemies and malware that finds its way into our systems from criminals, foreign governments, and our own government.

The first step to securing our data is to secure our computers and mobile devices. Remember, we are not in Kansas anymore.

Passwords

We all know we need passwords. Right? But do you know that *every* password can be broken? Start by trying *a*. If that does not work, try *b*, and then *c*. Eventually, the correct string of characters will get you into the system. It is only a matter of time.

Way back in your great-great-great grandfather's day, the only way to break into a personal computer was by manually attempting to guess the password. Given that manual attempts could proceed at approximately 1 attempt per second, an 8-character password became the standard. With a typical character set of 24 (a–z) this created a possibility of 24^8 or over 100 billion possible combinations. The thought that anyone could ever break such a password was ridiculous, so your ancestors became complacent.

This is funny when you consider that research has shown that the majority of passwords can be guessed. These passwords include: name of spouse, name of children, name of pets, home address, phone number, Social Security number, and main character names from Star Trek and Star Wars (would I kid you?). Most computer users are unaware that what they thought was an obscure and impossible-to-break password actually could be cracked in minutes.

It gets worse. A while back the first hacker wrote password-breaking software. Assuming it may have taken 8 CPU cycles to process a single attack event, on an old computer with a blazing 16 KHz CPU that would equate to 2,000 attempts per second. This meant that a password could be broken in less than 2 years. Yikes.

IT directors took notice.

So down came the edict from the IT Director that we *must* create *obscure* passwords: strings that include upper and lower case, numeric, and symbol characters. But in many cases this actually was a step backward. Since a computer user could not remember that their password was 8@dC%Z#2, the user often would manually record the password. That urban legend of leaving a password on a sticky note under the keyboard? I have seen it myself more than a hundred times.

Come forward to the present day. A current quad-core Intel i7 with freely available password-cracking software can make over 10 billion password attempts per second. Create an army of infected computers called a botnet to do your dirty work (*http://en.wikipedia.org/wiki/Botnet*), and you can likely achieve over a hundred trillion attempts per second, unless your system locks out the user after x number of failed log on attempts.

What does this mean for you? The typical password using upper and lower case, number, and symbol now can be cracked with the right tools in under than 2 minutes. If using just a single computer to do the break in, make that a week. Don't believe it? Take a look at the *haystack* search space calculator at *https://www.grc.com/haystack.htm.*

If we use longer passwords, we can make it take too time consuming to break into our system, so the bad guys will move on to someone else.

But you say it is tough enough to remember *8* characters, impossible to remember more?

This is true, but only if we keep doing things as we have always done before. Since virtually all such attacks are now done by automated software, it is only an issue of length of password, not complexity. So, use a passphrase that is easy to remember, such as, "Rocky has brown eyes" (which at 100 trillion attempts per second could take over 1,000,000,000,000,000 centuries to break – provided Rocky is not the name of your beloved pet and thus more guessable).

How long should you make your password, or rather, passphrase? As of this writing, Microsoft's Security Chief recommends a minimum of 14 characters. US-CERT currently recommends more than 14. Cisco recommends a minimum of 24. My recommendation to clients is a minimum of 14, in an easy-to-remember, easy-to-enter phrase.

In addition to password length, it is critical to use a variety of passwords. In this way, should a bad person gain access to your Facebook password, that password cannot be used to access your bank account.

Yes, pretty soon you will have a drawer full of passwords for all your different accounts, email, social networks, financial institutions, etc. How to keep all of them organized and easily accessed amongst all of your various computers and devices? More on that later in the *LastPass* section of this *Password* topic.

Assignment: Create a Strong User Account Password

Computer security starts with strong passwords. No password is as important as the password for your user account. This is the password used to log in to your computer, and to authorize major changes such as installing software. It is the first guard at the entrance of your computer, and therefore your data.

In this assignment, we will create a strong password for your user account.

1. Create an account password for yourself that is consists of at least 14 easy-to-remember and easy-to-enter characters.

2. Test how difficult it is to break your password by visiting haystack *https://www.grc.com/haystack.htm.*

3. If your password does not meet your or your organization's strength requirements, edit it until it does.

4. Record your new password in a way that you can find when you need it.

5. Exit the browser.

Change Your Old Password to the Strong Password:

6. Log in to your computer using your user account.

7. Click on *Apple* menu > *System Preferences* > *Users and Groups*.

8. Select the Chang*e Password* button:

- NOTE: When changing a user/login password, if at all possible, the change should be made while logged in with that user account. Doing so will simultaneously change the *Keychain* password to match. The Keychain stores usernames and passwords. When changing the user/login password in any other way, the Keychain password remains unchanged. If the user doesn't then know the password to the Keychain, it is impossible to ever open again, and all stored passwords will be lost. More on Keychain later.

9. By default your login password is set the same as your iCloud password. You will be asked if you want to *Use Separate Password…*, or to *Change iCloud Password…*

a. Synchronizing the iCloud and login password makes remembering both easier, and accessing your iCloud data from a new computer easier, but it also presents a roadblock to login should the Apple authentication servers be offline (as has happened at least once).

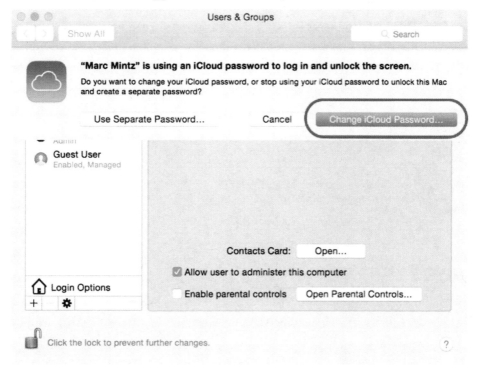

b. If you select Change iCloud Password, a browser opens to the My Apple ID page at Apple so that you may manage your ID.

c. If you select *Use Separate Password, the Create separate password for* "*<user name>*" window appears so that you may create a password. At the prompt, enter your *iCloud password, New password, Verify* your new password, and then select the *Use Separate Password* button:

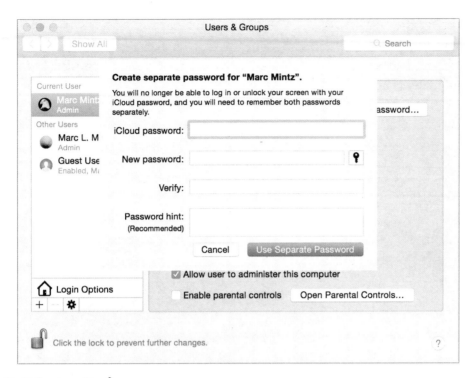

10. Quit System Preferences.

Your new, strong password now is in effect.

Keychain

In our grandparents' day, life was so much simpler. I'm not talking about politics or sociology, but, well… to give an example: My grandfather had four keys in his pocket at all times: one for home, one for the car, and the other two he could never remember what for.

In today's world, the realm of keys has expanded into the digital world. You now have keys or passwords for logging on to your computer, your phone, your tablet, your email, many of the websites you visit, Wi-Fi access points, servers, your frequent flyer account, etc. In my case, I have 857 passwords in use. I know because they are all neatly stored in a database so that I don't have to remember them.

Unfortunately for most of us, our "keys" are not very well organized, so when we need to access our mail from another computer, or order a book on Amazon, we are stuck.

By default, your Mac stores most usernames and passwords used to access Wi-Fi networks, servers, other computers, and websites. The built-in tools that store this information automatically can also be used to manually store any text-based data. This includes credit card information, software serial numbers, challenge Q&A, offshore banking information, etc.

Your Mac has two locations to store keys:

- Safari, which stores only the URL and password for websites visited with Safari.

- Keychain database, which stores username, password, and URL for websites which request authentication, Wi-Fi networks, servers, other computers you access, email accounts, and encrypted drives.

Keychain is what interests us here.

Let's take the case of visiting a website that requires a username and password, connecting to another computer or server, or performing some other action that triggers an authentication request. The following are the steps as they typically occur:

1. A prompt appears requesting a username and password.

   - Typical default authentication window for a server:

   - Typical authentication window for a website:

2. Enter your username and password. In most cases there is a checkbox to *Remember this password in my Keychain*. Enable that checkbox, and then click Enter or Continue.

3. The website takes you to the appropriate secured page or the other computer mounts a drive on your Mac.

Behind the curtain, your Mac has copied your username and password into the Keychain database, named *Login.Keychain*.

This database is located in your Home *Library/Keychains* folder. The database is military grade AES 256 bit encrypted, safe from prying eyes.

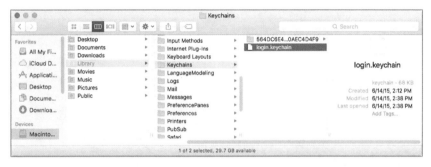

The next time you visit this same website or server, the steps change somewhat:

1. You surf to the website or select a server to access.

2. A prompt appears requesting a username and password.

3. Behind the scenes your web browser or Finder asks: "Has the Keychain stored the credentials for this site or server?"

4. A query is made of the Keychain database based on the URL of the site or the name of the server.

5. If Keychain has stored the username and password associated with the URL or server (it has), the credentials are automatically copied/pasted into the *username* and *password* fields.

6. Select *Enter*.

7. The website takes you to the appropriate secured page or the server share point mounts.

Note that you did not need to know your credentials–Keychain did it all for you.

OS X ships with a tool allowing the user full access to the database, named *Keychain Access*, located in the /Applications/Utilities folder.

Assignment: View an Existing Keychain Record

Perhaps a trusted visitor needs access to your Wi-Fi network, and you have forgotten the password to that network. The Keychain database has it stored, we just need to look for it. In this assignment, we will examine a record in the Keychain.

1. Launch *Keychain Access* (located in /Applications/Utilities/).

2. From the sidebar, in the *Keychains* field, select log in. This is the database that holds your secure information.

3. From the sidebar, in the *Category* field, select *All Items*.

4. In the center, main area of the window, double-click on the *target record*.

5. In this example, it is *Evernote*. The records *Attributes* window will open. At the bottom of the *Attributes* window you will see *Show Password*. Enable the checkbox. This will open the authentication window.

6. At the prompt, enter your Keychain password. By default, this is the same as your user account password. This will authorize Keychain to show you the password. Then click the *Allow* button.

7. The *Show Password* field will now display the needed password.

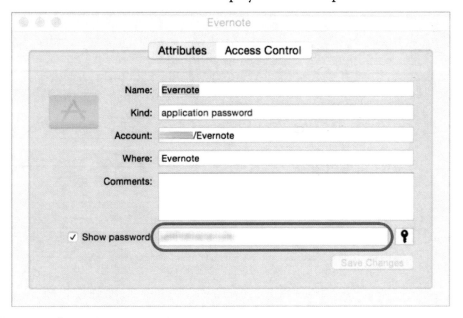

8. Quit Keychain Access.

Challenge Questions

A Challenge Question is a way for websites to authenticate who you claim to be when you contact support because of a lost or compromised password.

For example, when registering at a website you may see: *Question – Where did your mother and father meet?* Or: *Question – Who is the most important person you have ever met?*

The problem with this strategy is that most answers easily are discovered with an Internet search either of your personal information or a bit of social engineering.

The solution is to give bogus answers. For example, my answer to the first question, *Where did your mother and father meet?* may be: *1954 Plymouth back seat.* It would not be possible for a hacker to discover this answer, as it is completely bogus. My mother tells me it was really a 1952 Dodge.

Unless you are some type of savant, there is no way you will remember the answers to your challenge questions. But, there is no need to remember. We already have a built-in utility that is highly secure and designed to hold secrets such as passwords–Keychain Access!

Although Keychain can automatically record and auto fill usernames and passwords, it will require manually entering other data such as challenge Q&A.

Assignment: Store Challenge Q&A In the Keychain

In this assignment you will manually store the challenge Q&A for a pretend website, myteddybear.com.

1. Open *Keychain Access.app*, located in */Applications/Utilities.*

2. Select the Keychain Access *File* menu > *New Secure Note item…*

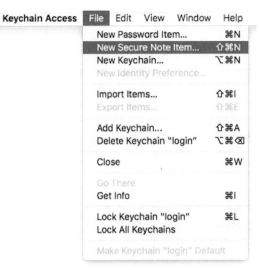

3. The Keychain *Item Name* window appears.

4. In the *Keychain Item Name* field, enter: *myteddybear.com Q&A*.

5. In the *Note* field, enter:
   Q: *Where did your parents meet? A: I don't know*
   Q: *What is the name of your first pet? A: Swims With Fishes*
   Q: *What is the name of your high school? A: Who needs an education*

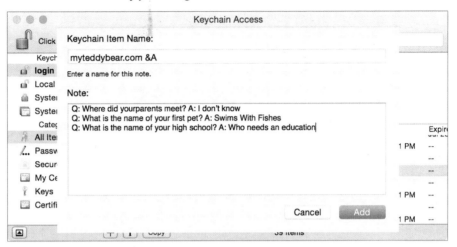

6. Select the *Add* button.

7. You will find your new Secure Note within all of your other Keychain items.

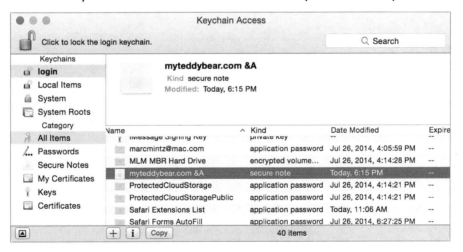

8. Quit Keychain Access.

Your challenge questions and answers are now securely stored.

Assignment: Access Secure Data From Keychain

There may come a time that you forget your password to myteddybear.com. A call to technical support with a request to either retrieve or reset your password is met with a challenge question. If you are like me, your synapses holding that memory have long died out.

But, no worries! You do remember that you have the habit of storing all of your important data securely in your Keychain.

In this assignment you retrieve your challenge Q&A for myteddybear.com.

1. Open Keychain Access.app, located in */Applications/Utilities.*

2. Click in the *search* field at the top right corner of the *Keychain Access* window.

3. Enter: *myteddybear.* As you type, only those records matching your search string appear, until only the proper record shows.

4. Double-click on the myteddybear.com record to open it. Your password is not initially displayed. This is intentional, doubly protecting your data.

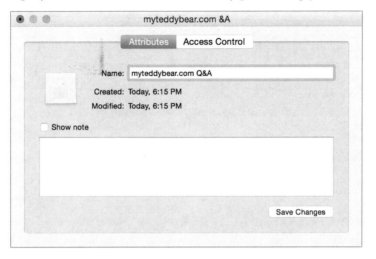

5. Enable the *Show note* checkbox.

6. You are prompted to enter your Keychain password. By default, this is the same as your log in password. Enter your Keychain password, and then click either the *Always Allow*, or *Allow*, button. By selecting *Always Allow*, you will not be asked to verify your Keychain password for this record in the future. If you select *Allow*, you have access to your data, but you will be prompted for your Keychain password in the future.

7. After selecting either *Always Allow* or *Allow,* you see your challenge Q&A.

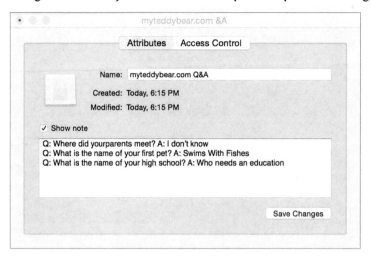

8. Close the window and Quit *Keychain Access.*

Harden the Keychain

The work we have done so far in Keychain Access is all that is necessary for almost every environment. Some situations call for even greater levels of security–think military bases, the computer used by the CEO, and my aunt Rose who needs to protect her secret recipe for kosher raisin noodle koogle.

There are two options to further protect the Keychain, which may be used separately or in tandem:

- Change your Keychain password to be different than your log in password

- Have your Keychain automatically log off after X minutes of inactivity.

By default your Keychain password matches your log in password. With this configuration, in the process of logging in to your computer the Keychain is automatically unlocked. If you give your Keychain a different password, it will remain locked after log in. Where you see this is when you attempt to access a website or connect with another computer and you have the authentication credentials stored in Keychain. Instead of auto filling as usual, you are prompted to enter the password for the Keychain. This unlocks the Keychain, allowing it to continue the auto fill process.

By default the Keychain remains unlocked as long as the user remains logged in. There is also the option to set the Keychain to automatically lock after a specified amount of inactivity time.

Let's say Keychain Access to automatically lock the Keychain after 5 minutes of inactivity. Upon log in, if the Keychain password is the same as the log in password, the Keychain will unlock and remain unlocked for 5 minutes. If you need an auto fill from data held in Keychain after that 5 minutes, you are prompted for the Keychain password. If within 5 minutes another auto fill is needed, the data is pulled from Keychain automatically. But when 5 minutes or more has passed, the Keychain will lock automatically.

Assignment: Harden the Keychain with a Different Password

By default the Keychain password is the same as the user login password. Under this condition, the Keychain automatically unlocks when the user logs in. An additional layer of security may be gained by giving Keychain a different password. If this is done, the Keychain remains locked at login. When called upon to provide a password, it prompts the user for the Keychain password so that it may unlock.

In this assignment, you give your Keychain a password different than your user account login password.

1. Open Keychain Access.app, located in */Applications/Utilities*. From the top of the sidebar, select the *login* keychain.

2.   Select the Keychain *Edit* menu > *Change Password for Keychain "login"*.

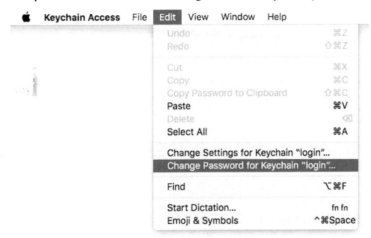

3.   This opens the Enter a new password for the *Keychain "login"* window. Enter the following:

- In the *Current Password* field, enter your current Keychain password. By default this is your user account log in password.

- In the *New Password* and *Verify* fields, enter your new strong password for Keychain. Write it down so it is not forgotten. I keep this in my Address Book / Contacts application.

4.   Select the *OK* button.

5. Select the Lock icon in the top left corner of the Keychain Access window. This locks the log in Keychain.

6. Quit Keychain Access.

Because your login Keychain now has a different password than your user account password, it will not automatically unlock when you log in to your computer. Attempting to access the Keychain through *Keychain Access* requires that you manually unlock it. Also, the first time that an autofill is attempted, you are prompted to enter the Keychain password.

7. If you do not wish to have a hardened Keychain, repeat steps 1–9, changing the password back to your user account password.

Assignment: Harden the Keychain with an Automatic Timed Lock

In this assignment, you give your Keychain a timeout to automatically lock after it has not been used for 1 minute.

1. Open Keychain Access, located in */Applications/Utilities*. From the top of the sidebar, select the *login* keychain.

2. Select the Keychain Access *Edit* menu > *Change Settings for Keychain "login."*

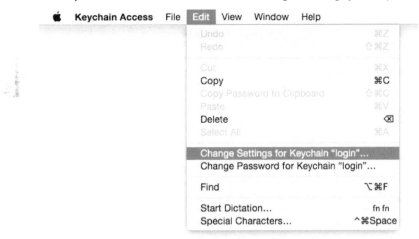

3. The *Login Keychain Settings* window will open. Configure as follows:

- Enable the *Lock after ___ minutes of inactivity* checkbox, and then set this to 1 minute.

- Enable the *Lock when sleeping* checkbox.

4. Select the *Save* button.

5. Quit Keychain Access.

6. Sit on your thumbs for 60 seconds–time enough for the Keychain to lock.

7. Open a browser and visit a website or connect to another computer on your network that you frequent with a password that otherwise auto fills. You find you now are prompted to enter the password for the Keychain it to open.

8. If you do not need a hardened Keychain, repeat steps 1–3, and then when the *Login Keychain Settings* window appears, disable the checkboxes. Then select the *Save* button.

9. Quit Keychain Access.

Your Keychain will now automatically lock, preventing anyone from accessing all of your passwords should you step away from your desk with your system awake and no screen saver in place.

Synchronize Keychain Across OS X and iOS Devices

Perhaps like me, you have a need to access most of these passwords and challenge answers anywhere, anytime. When I have my computer with me, no worries. But what if I don't? It would be a rare event indeed for me to be without my computer or my iPhone, so I keep my Keychain on my iPhone as well.

If you have upgraded to OS X 10.9 or higher and iOS 7 or higher, Apple has you handled. With the most recent incarnations of both operating systems, Apple has added *Keychain* to the iCloud synchronization scheme. This allows your Keychain database to be synchronized between all of your computers, iPhones, and iPads.

Assignment: Activate iCloud Keychain Synchronization

Synchronizing your Keychain with iCloud allows all of your OS X 10.9 and higher, and iOS 7 and higher devices share your keychain.

In this assignment you will enable iCloud Keychain synchronization on your iOS device(s) with iCloud.

This assignment assumes that you have configured Apple ID 2-step authentication. If you have not yet done this, please skip to chapter 15, *Assignment: Implement Apple ID Two-Step Verification.*

1. Open the *Apple* menu > *System Preferences* > *iCloud.*

2. Select the *Keychain* checkbox. The *Enter your Apple ID password to setup iCloud Keychain* dialog box appears.

3. Enter your Apple ID password, and then select the *OK* button.

4. If you have previously created a 2-step verification for your Apple ID, the *Keychain Setup* dialog box opens. You may select either the *Use Code…* or *Request Approval* button.

- If you click *Use Code…*, you will be asked to *Enter your iCloud Security Code* created when you setup 2-step verification. Enter the security code, and then click *Next*.

- If you click *Request Approval,* a request will be sent to the other devices currently approved on your account to approve this device. Enter your Apple ID password, and then click *Allow.*

5. Go back to *System Preferences,* and notice that the *Keychain* is now enabled.

6. *Quit* System Preferences.

Your Keychain on this computer will now synchronize automatically with your iCloud account.

LastPass

Another great solution to the problem of password management is *LastPass* at *http://www.LastPass.com.*

There are two important advantages of LastPass:

1. You no longer have to concern yourself with Internet passwords–the correct response becomes automatic. LastPass will keep your Internet passwords available in each of your browsers.

2. Stores and share your passwords with all of your devices–even across operating systems. It also securely stores manually entered data such as challenge questions.

LastPass provides the following solutions:

*   Provides free (ad supported) and premium (no ads) options

*   Automatically remembers your Internet passwords, fully encrypted

*   Auto fills web-based forms and authentication fields

*   Stores notes and challenge questions and answers (Q&A), fully encrypted

*   Synchronizes across multiple browsers

*   Synchronizes across multiple computers

*   Synchronizes across Android, BlackBerry, iOS, Linux, OS X, Windows

*   Automatically generates very strong passwords, which since you do not need to remember them, provide even greater online security.

Assignment: Install LastPass

In this assignment we will download and install LastPass on your OS X computer. It will synchronize across all of your various computers and devices, but only for 14 days. The free version works indefinitely across computers, but to synchronize with mobile devices beyond the 14-day trial requires upgrading to *LastPass Premium.*

1. Using your browser, surf to *LastPass* at *http://LastPass.com*. Select the *Download Free* button.

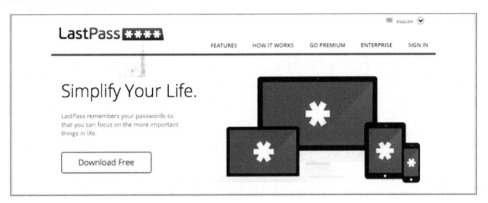

LastPass has a different download for each computer/browser platform. The website will automatically determine which platform combination you currently are on, and recommend the appropriate plug-in to download. As most OS X users use more than one browser, I recommend downloading the universal installer.

2. In the *Recommended LastPass Download* page, select the *Mac* link.

3. Scroll down to near the bottom of the page, to the *LastPass Universal Mac OS X Installer*, and then select the *Download* button.

4. Once the installer has downloaded, double-click to launch it.

5. When the LastPass installer opens, select the *Next* button.

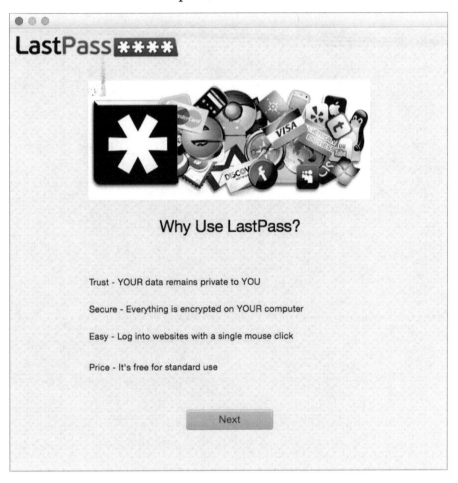

6. At the *Create your account or sign in* window, select *I do not have a LastPass account, create one for me*, and then select the *Next* button.

7. At the *Create Account* window, enter your information, and then select the
   Create button.

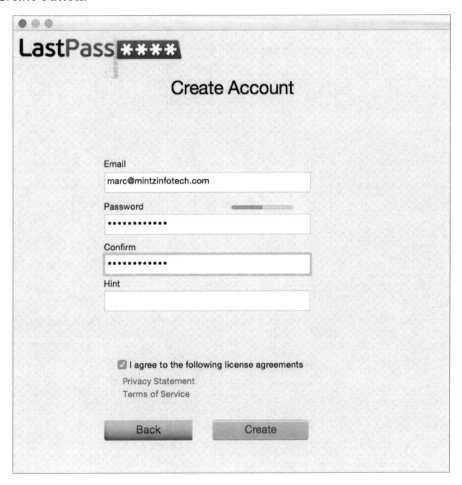

8. If you have a browser open, you will be prompted to close it, and then select the *Install* button.

9. Authenticate to complete the installation.

10. One last opportunity to back out (I can't imagine why you would want to!), and then select the *Install* button.

11. If you don't have Google Chrome installed, LastPass has now been installed in your browser(s). Skip to the next section: *Configuring Last Pass*. If you have Google Chrome installed, it will launch, prompting for authorization to install LastPass. Select the *Click to Install LastPass* button.

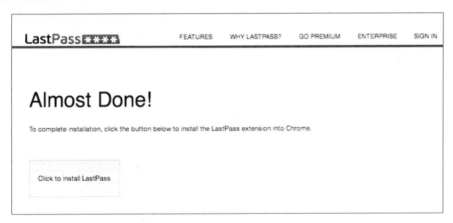

12. Select the *Add* button.

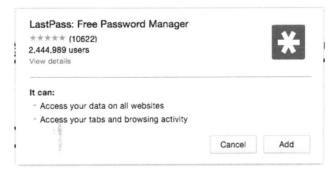

13. At the prompt, type *lp*, press TAB, and then enter in the desired URL.

14. At the prompt to log in to LastPass, enter your LastPass password, enable *Remember Email* and *Remember Password*, and then select the *Log In* button.

LastPass is now installed.

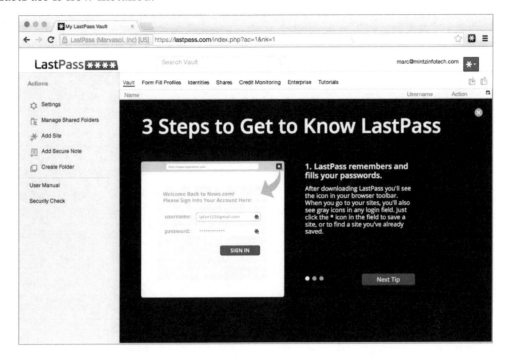

Assignment: Configure LastPass

In this assignment you will configure LastPass.

Once LastPass is installed, it must be configured. Open any of your browsers. You will find the *LastPass* button in the browser navigation bar.

Not logged into LastPass   *Logged into LastPass*

1. If you are not yet logged into LastPass, select the *LastPass* button, enter your credentials, and then select the *Log In* button.

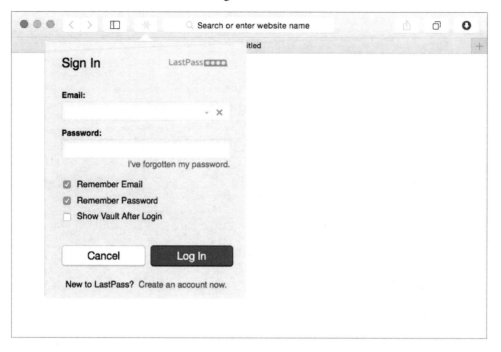

2. Select the *LastPass* button, and then select *My LastPass Vault*. This will take you to your LastPass account page.

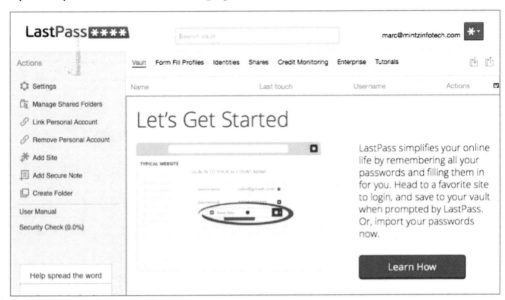

3. From the sidebar select *Settings*, and then from the tabs select *Form Fill Profiles*, and then select the *Create A Profile* button.

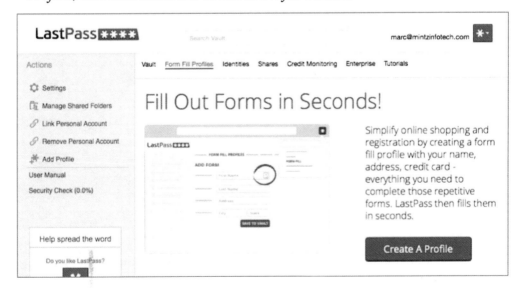

4. The *Add Form Fill* profile window opens. In the *Name* field, enter a name for this profile.

5. Select the *Personal* tab, enter the requested information, and then select the *Add Form Fill profile* button. You will be returned to the main window.

6. Select the *edit* button 🖉 to complete your profile.

7. Select the *Address* tab, enter the requested information, and then select the *Contact* tab. Repeat for all tabs, and then select the *Save Form Fill profile* button.

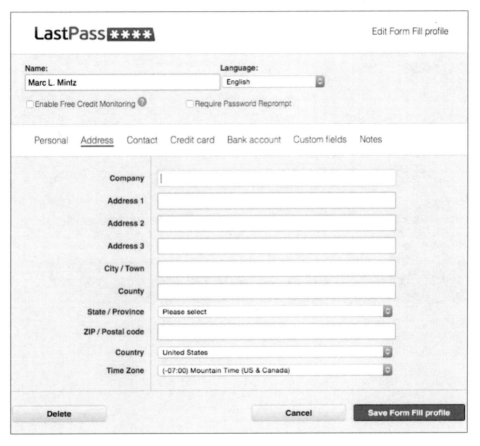

You have now successfully configured LastPass on your computer.

Assignment: Use LastPass to Save Website Authentication Credentials

Once you have LastPass installed, it's time to put it to use. In this assignment we will use LastPass to store the user name and password for Facebook.

1. Use your browser to visit Facebook *https://facebook.com.*

2. As this is the first time you have visited Facebook since installing LastPass, your log in credentials have not yet been stored in LastPass. Enter your Email or Phone and Password information, and then select the *Log in* button.

3. LastPass will detect that there is a form on this page, and present an option to remember your credentials. This will appear just under the navigation bar. Select the *Save Site* button.

4. The LastPass *Form Fill* web page for this site will open. Configure to taste (in most cases, no edits are necessary), and then select the *Save* button. This will return you to the Facebook page.

5. Quit your web browser.

Your Facebook account credentials are now stored in LastPass, so you do not need to remember them.

Assignment: Use LastPass to Auto Fill Website Authentication

When LastPass has saved user name and password information for a site, you will never need to manually enter that information again. For this assignment, we will revisit Facebook and allow LastPass to enter our credentials.

1. Launch your browser and surf to *Facebook* at *http://facebook.com*. Take note that your authentication credentials have been automatically entered for you by LastPass.

Done.

Review Questions

1. What are the minimum number of characters recommended for a password?

2. What is one website that can be used to test the strength of a password?

3. In which system preference can the login password be changed?

4. When changing a user login password, why is it best to do so only when logged in as that user account?

5. Where does OS X store most passwords?

6. What application is used to access the Keychain?

7. What are two ways to harden the security of the Keychain?

8. What System Preference is used to synchronize the Keychain between a user's OS X and iOS devices?

9. What are the minimum OS X and iOS versions needed to synchronize the Keychain?

2. Vulnerability: System and Application Updates

Every new beginning comes from some other beginning's end.

–Seneca, Roman philosopher, statesman, and dramatist

System Updates

The majority of computer users simply fail to update their systems. In most cases they give the reason that updates slow down the computers, or they are concerned about introducing instability to their computers.

It occasionally is true that updates may introduce instability–but it is far more likely that not updating will create greater instability.

More important is that many updates actually are about patching vulnerabilities and security holes in the system. Fixing these security issues is so important that US-CERT (Homeland Security division responsible for cyber terrorism and IT security) strongly recommends that all users update all computers within 48 hours of an update release.

There are fundamentally three reasons for updates and upgrades:

- **Bug fixes**. All software and hardware have bugs. We simply never will be rid of them. Developers do want to squash as many as possible so that you are so happy with their product and will continue to pay for upgrades.

- **Monetization**. Updates to operating systems and applications almost always are free, or included in the price of the original purchase. Upgrades typically are for fee. But developers will include significant new features in an upgrade to encourage the market to purchase, so the developers can afford to stay in business.

- **Security patches**. Although rarely talked about, one of the most important reasons for an update is to patch newly discovered security holes. Without the update, your computer may be highly vulnerable to attack.

It is for this last reason alone that I implore clients to be consistent with the update process. In fact, US-CERT (the division of the Department of Homeland Security tasked with protecting us from cyber terrorism) strongly recommends updating both OS and applications/apps within 48 hours of release in order to have the greatest protection from penetration and vulnerabilities.

To protect your computer from security holes in the operating system, it is critical to check for updates daily. Fortunately, we can automate this process.

Assignment: Configure Apple System and Application Update Schedule

In this assignment we will automate the process of updating the OS X operating system, as well as Apple software.

1. Open *Apple* menu > *System Preferences* > *App Store*. Configure as shown below:

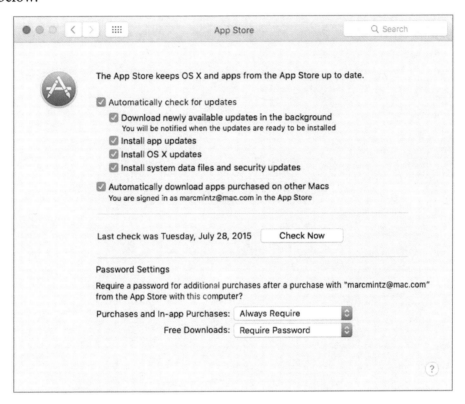

- Enable *Automatically check for updates.* That is why we are here!

- Enable *Download newly available updates in the background.* With this option active, the updates are downloaded without you knowing it. An alert will appear telling you updates are ready to be installed. Installation will start immediately upon you clicking *OK* or *Install.*

- Enable *Install system data files and security updates.* I cannot imagine why you would not want to have the most current OS X anti-malware installed.

- Enable *Automatically download apps purchased on other Macs*. If you own multiple OS X machines, and have the same Apple ID in use for the Mac App Store on each, this will automatically install applications on this Mac even if they were purchased on one of the others.

2. Close System Preferences.

3. When new system or Apple software updates are available, the *App Store Dock* icon will display a red dot with the number of updates available.

4. Select the *App Store* icon to launch the App Store Application. Select the *Updates* button in the navigation bar to display the available updates. Depending on your Internet connection speed, this may take several minutes to display.

5. Select the *Update All* button to download and install all available updates.

6. Quit the App Store application.

Your OS X system and Apple Store applications will now automatically alert you when updates are available.

Manage Application Updates with MacUpdate Desktop

OS X, Apple applications, and apps downloaded from the Apple App Store can be updated through the App Store app. Although some other applications have built-in automatic updating, it is still not the norm. Also, system preferences, plug-ins, and other software do not typically automatically update.

Recently, Adobe Flash and Oracle Java have been used by criminal elements to gain control over computers to access user data. Apple has taken the offensive by blocking older susceptible versions from running on OS X 10.7 and higher. There are many other software points that have been, can, and will be exploited. It is critical to keep all of your software up-to-date so that security holes can be secured.

As the typical user has over 100 applications, plug-ins, extensions, etc., by far the fastest, easiest, and most cost-effective way to do this is to automate the process using MacUpdate Desktop *http://www.macupdate.com/desktop* ($20/year license).

Assignment: Install and Configure MacUpdate Desktop

In this assignment we will download, install, and configure MacUpdate Desktop.

1. Open a browser to surf to the *Macupdate* home page at *http://macupdate.com.*

2. Select the *Desktop* button at the top of the page. The *MacUpdate Desktop 6* page opens.

3. Enter your First name, Last name, Email address, and create a Password. Select the *Download Now* button. Then select the *10-day free trial Download Now* button.

4. MacUpdate Desktop will begin to download. The default location is your Downloads folder.

5. Drag the MacUpdate Desktop.app into the Applications folder.

6. From the Applications folder, locate and launch *MacUpdate* Desktop. The app will open.

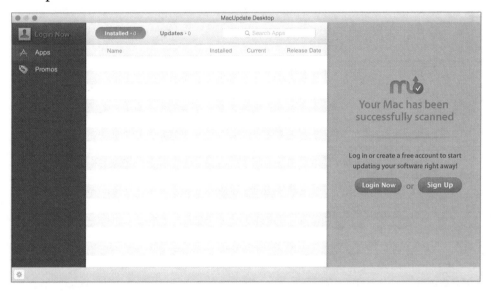

7. Click the *Login Now* button. The *Login to your MacUpdate account* dialog opens. Enter the *Email address* and *Password* used when downloading the app, and then click the *Login Now* button.

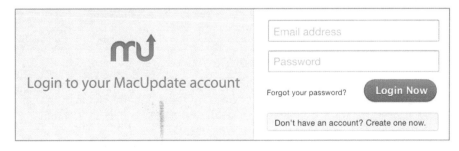

8. It will automatically scan your computer for all installed applications, check for any available updates, and then display them for you. Available updates will appear in red.

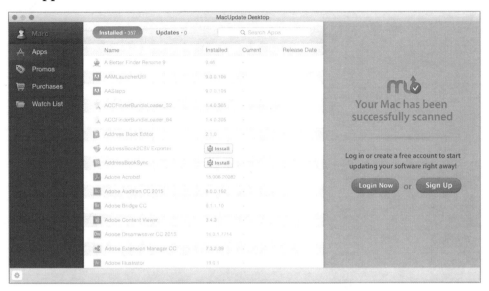

9. Select the *MacUpdate Desktop* menu > *Preferences*. Configure the main window as below:

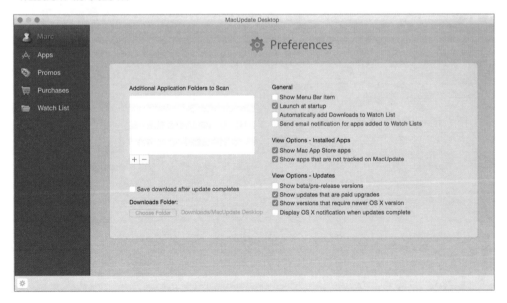

10. Quit MacUpdate Desktop to save your preferences.

You have successfully installed and configured MacUpdate Desktop on your computer.

Assignment: Application Updates with MacUpdate Desktop

Once you have MacUpdate Desktop installed and configured, it will notify you daily of available Apple and third-party application updates. In this exercise, we use MacUpdate Desktop to manually scan, download, and install updates.

1. From the *Applications* folder, launch MacUpdate Desktop. It will automatically begin scanning for available updates.

2. Select the *Macupdate* menu > *Preferences.* Configure as follows:

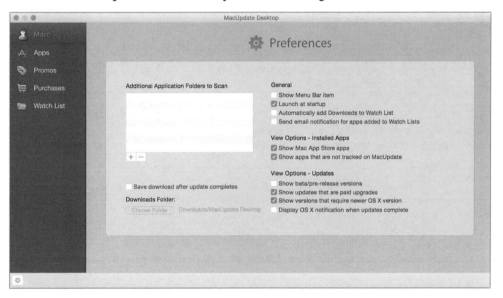

3. Close Preferences.

4. From the sidebar, select *Apps.*

5. Select the *Apps* menu > *Check for Updates.*

6. Select the *Updates* button in the navigation bar. This will filter out any applications that don't have updates. Then select the *Name* column to sort alphabetically:

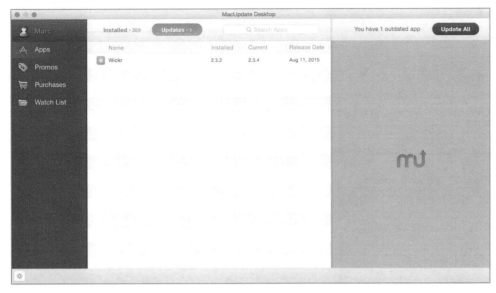

7. Select the *Apps* menu > *Update All* to, well, download and install all updates.

8. If you prefer to hand-select which updates to install, double-click the target update from the main window.

9. Most updates require authorization to install. At the prompts, enter an administrator name and password.

10. When all desired updates are complete, Quit MacUpdate Desktop.

Can it get any easier or faster than this?

Review Questions

1. US-CERT recommends installing updates within _____ hours of release.

2. Name the three fundamental reasons for updates and upgrades: _____ .

3. System and many application updates and upgrades can be configured from the _____ System Preference.

4. Apple and most 3rd-party application updates and upgrades can be automatically reviewed and downloaded using the _____ application.

3. Vulnerability: User Accounts

If money is your hope for independence you will never have it. The only real security that a man will have in this world is a reserve of knowledge, experience, and ability.

–Henry Ford

User Accounts

OS X allows six different types of user accounts, each with its own pros and cons, powers and limitations. Most of these may be designated from the *Users & Groups System Preference.*

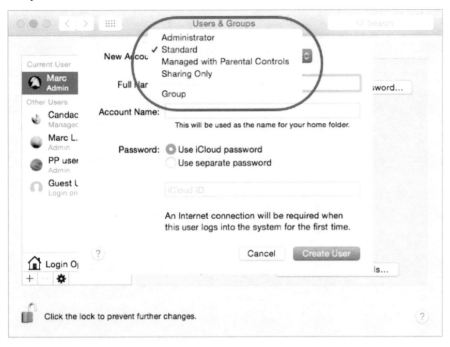

- **Root**. There is only one root account ever on any computer. Root is the ultimate lord over the system, with unquestioned power and control. If root does something dangerous–say, issues a command to erase the entire drive–the system will not even issue a *Danger, Will Robinson* alert, it will simply dutifully erase the drive. Root is present out of the box, but is disabled by not having a password assigned. It would be rare to ever need to enable the root user, as any administrator account can assume the powers of root.

- **Administrator**. There must always be at least one, and may be an unlimited number of administrators, or administrative user accounts, each having identical power over the computer. What makes an Administrator unique above the Standard, Sharing, and Guest user accounts are its abilities to: Create new user accounts, delete user accounts, modify the contents of restricted folders (System, Library, Applications), authorize the installation or removal of applications and system updates, and take on the powers of root from the command line by issuing sudo and su commands.

- **Standard**. There can be an unlimited number of Standard accounts. This is the recommended account level for most users working locally on the computer. Standard accounts can open and work without limitations with any application installed on your Mac. The advantage of working as a Standard account is that it is not possible to damage the operating system or applications.

- **Managed with Parental Controls**. This account is typically a Standard account that has had Parental Controls assigned to it. Parental Controls further restrict the powers of the account by limiting: Access to specific applications, access to specific websites or any adult site, who can communicate with the user via Apple Mail and Messages/iChat, the hours for which the user may stay logged in, etc. Although this account level was originally intended to protect children from the darker areas of the Internet, and the computer from the children, it is a powerful tool for use with employees (guess how many billions of dollars a year in wasted productivity are spent on Facebook?)

- **Sharing Only**. There can be an unlimited number of Sharing Only accounts. This type of account cannot log in locally to the computer. The only access is via the network and file sharing. It is highly useful if you need to work with someone else on the same network and share files with them. This allows them to access your computer and files over the network, but only those files.

- **Guest**. There is only one Guest account. With Guest enabled, anyone may access your computer, either locally or via file sharing over the network. The Guest only has access to folders and files that have been shared as either read or read & write for everyone. If a Guest logs in locally, any documents the Guest creates and saves in the Guest home folder are deleted upon log off. Unless you are certain of your file-sharing configuration, it is unsecure to allow Guest access.

Never Log In as an Administrator

Maybe it is the human condition. We want power, authority, and more power! This carries over into how we log in to the computer. Everyone wants to be the administrator of his or her computer! Apple enables this. When the owner of a new Mac boot up for the first time, that person is prompted to create a user account, which is by default an administrator account.

But this is bad juju.

If you have the bad luck of launching a malware attack on your computer (most often unknowingly) while you are logged in as an administrator, the malware will take on your user account power. This means the malware has full control and power over the computer–including all other user accounts. Yikes.

On the other hand, if you have the same lousy luck to launch a malware attack while logged in as a non-administrative user, the malware will typically take on your non-admin power. Under this scenario, the malware has full control over your home folder and nothing else.

I can hear the wailing from here: *But I need to be an administrator. How else will I be able to install software and updates, and perform maintenance?*

Fear not. In OS X you do not need to be logged in as an administrator to perform administrator tasks (adding/deleting user accounts, installing/updating the system and applications, and running system diagnostic and repair utilities). You can be logged in with any type of user account. You only need to authenticate with an administrator name and password when prompted.

To do this, you need to have an administrative user account on the computer, but log in with a non-admin (standard) user account. Then when you are prompted for an admin name and password while performing admin duties, just enter them.

Assignment: Enable the Root User

As mentioned earlier, the root user account is present right out of the box, but it is disabled. The way Apple has disabled the account is by not assigning a password. That's right–all that is needed to enable root is to assign the account a password!

Before jumping in and assigning a password, give thought to why you want to enable root. Any administrative account can assume the powers of root whenever needed. I've also seen far too many users send their data to the cornfield when logged in as root and then making a simple keystroke error.

However, if you would like to experiment with root powers, here we go…

1. Select *Apple* menu > *System Preferences* > *Users & Groups*.

2. Authenticate.

3. Select the *Login Options* button.

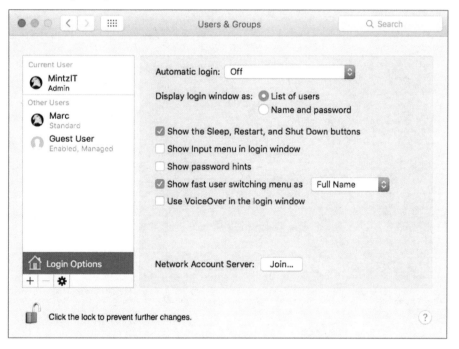

4. Select the *Network Account Server: Join or Edit button*.

5. Select the *Open Directory Utility* button.

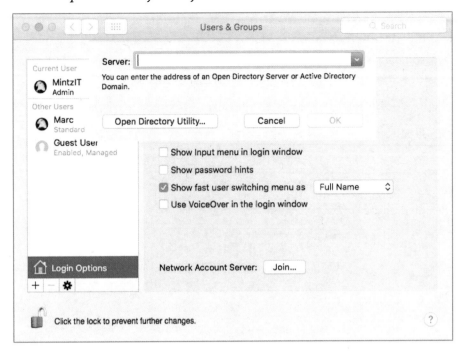

6. Authenticate.

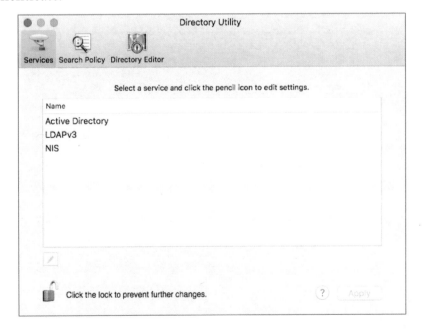

7. Select the *Edit* menu > *Enable Root User.*

8. Enter a strong password.

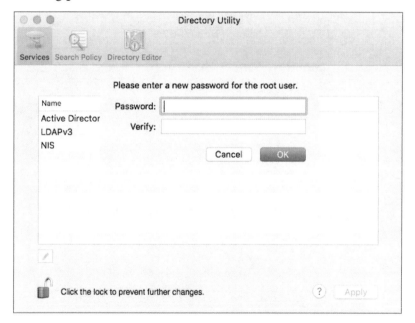

9. Quit Directory Utility.

10. Quit System Preferences.

Assignment: Login as the Root User

To see how the OS X landscape appears to root user, it's easiest to simply log in as root.

1. Log out of the current user account.

2. At the Login Window, log in as *root*. If you don't see the *root* user, select *Other...* From here you may enter the username "root", and the password you assigned for root.

3. Once at the Desktop, navigate to the */Users/<username>* folders. Notice that you are able to access any user folder with read and write permissions.

4. To log out, select the *Apple* menu > *Log Out*.

5. At the *Login Window,* log in with your standard account.

Assignment: Change the Root User Password

1. Select *Apple* menu > *System Preferences* > *Users & Groups*.

2. Authenticate.

3. Select the *Network Account Server Join* or *Edit button*.

4. Authenticate.

5. Select the *Edit* menu > *Change Root Password*.

6. Enter a strong password

7. Quit Directory Utility.

8. Quit System Preferences.

Assignment: Disable the Root User

1. Select *Apple* menu > *System Preferences* > *Users & Groups*.

2. Authenticate.

3. Select the *Network Account Server Join* or *Edit button*.

4. Authenticate.

5. Select the *Edit* menu > *Disable Root User.*

6. Quit Directory Utility.

7. Quit System Preferences.

Assignment: Create an Administrative User Account

In this assignment, you will create an administrative user account on the computer. In the next assignment, you will change your own account to a standard user account.

1. Log in to the computer with your normal administrator account.

2. Open *Apple* menu > *System Preferences* > *Users & Groups*. Click the *Lock* icon in the bottom left corner, and then authenticate with an administrator name and password.

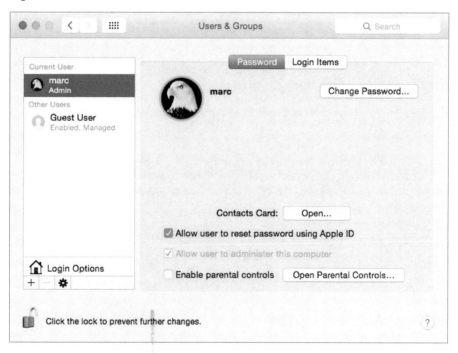

3. Click the + *(add user)* button at the bottom of the side bar. The *Create a New Account* window will open.

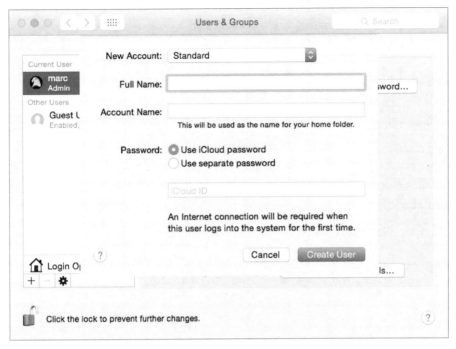

- From the *New Account* pop-up menu, select *Administrator.*

- In the Full Name field, enter "Administrator".

- In the Password field select either *Use iCloud password,* or, *Use separate password.*

- If selecting *Use iCloud password*, enter the iCloud ID.

- If selecting *Use separate password,* create and enter a strong password. Reenter in the Verify field.

- I'm not fond of entering anything in the Password Hint field, as this will be of assistance to hackers as well.

4. When done, click the *Create User* button. You are returned to the *Users & Groups* preference.

5. *Quit* System Preferences.

You have successfully created a new administrator account.

Assignment: Change from Administrator to Standard User

In the previous assignment, you created an administrative user account whose name and password can be used when needed. In this assignment, you change your own account to a standard user account, which will remain your regular log in account.

1. Select the *Apple* menu > *System Preferences* > *Users & Groups*.

2. Select your account in the side bar.

3. Disable the *Allow user to administer this computer* check box:

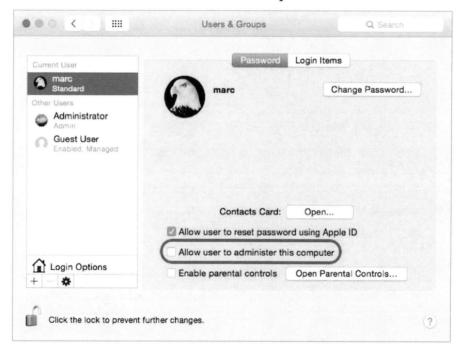

4. You receive a prompt informing you that the change will take place after a restart. Select the *OK* button.

5. Select *Apple* menu > *Restart*.

6. Log in with your everyday account (now a Standard account).

Whenever you need to perform administrative tasks, use the name and password of the new administrator account you have just created. No need to login as an administrator!

Application Whitelisting and More With Parental Controls

In 2014, Target, Home Depot, and other major retailers were hacked for their customer databases. Although there were multiple breakdowns in the security protocols of these organizations, one step would likely have prevented all of them–*Application whitelisting*. This same strategy should be used by both home and business systems to help secure computer systems.

Application whitelisting is a process that allows only authorized applications to run on a computer, blocking any executable that is not on the list. This is a vital ingredient to system security because even the very best anti-malware catches only 99.9% of the *known* bugs. And what if your computer is penetrated by *unknown* malware? Anti-malware is of marginal use here. However, if your computer has application whitelisting in place, the unknown malware are blocked from executing! In OS X, *Parental Controls* can be used to perform application whitelisting.

Parental Controls allow an Administrator to restrict access to specific applications and services to a non-administrative user account. As the name implies, this feature was originally intended as a way for parents to better manage their children's account. It also have its place in the business setting by restricting specific applications (disallowing Spotify, etc.), restricting access to specific websites (pornography, Facebook, etc.), or allowing access to the account only during work hours.

Once Parental Controls has been used to implement application whitelisting, it will be necessary for the administrator to be available for a brief time while the unintended consequences shake out. It is common for some permitted applications to require the use of a restricted application or process. An administrator will need to be available to provide authorization.

Once Parental Controls are established for a user account, the account is referred to as *Managed with Parental Controls,* or as a *managed* account. Only non-administrative accounts may be managed. If creating a new user account, it can be initially setup as *Managed with Parental Controls.* If the account already exists as a Standard account, it can be converted to managed. The *Guest* account can also have parental controls assigned.

Assignment: Configure a Managed with Parental Controls Account

For our assignment we will be configuring your own account to have the added security of application whitelisting. These same steps should be taken for all non-administrative accounts on your computer, and all computers in your household or business. Understand that best practices holds that *all* of your non-administrative accounts should have application whitelisting enabled–and that you never login with an administrative account.

1. On the computer hosting the user account to be managed, open *Apple* menu > *System Preferences* > *Parental Controls.*

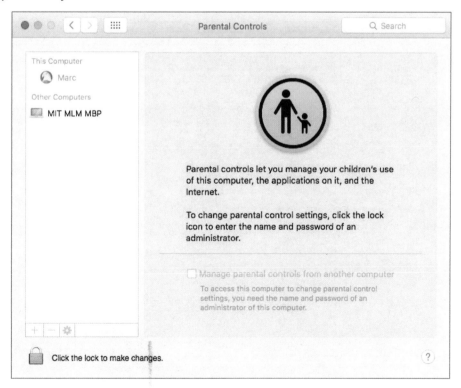

2. Select the *Lock* icon to authenticate as an administrator.

3. In the sidebar select the target account to manage.

4. If you want to manage parental controls from another computer on the same network, enable the *Manage parental controls from another computer* checkbox.

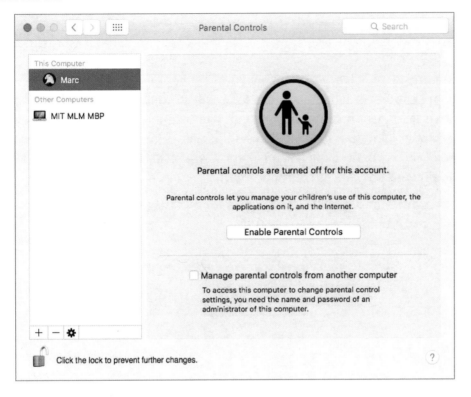

5. Select the *Enable Parental Controls* button. The *Parental Controls* System Preference pane opens. Unlock the pane.

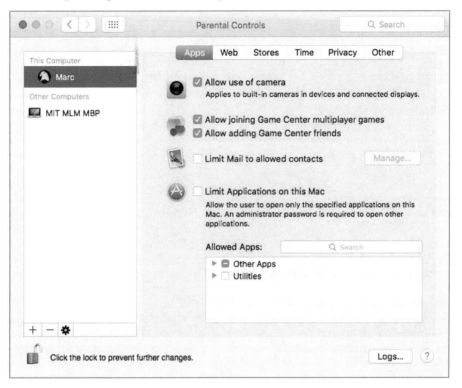

- *Allow use of camera* is self-explanatory.

- *Allow joining Game Center multiplayer games* is self-explanatory.

- *Allow adding Game Center friends* is self-explanatory.

- *Limit Mail to allowed contacts* helps to prevent unknown and unwanted people from exchanging email with the user. Selecting the *Manage* button opens a configuration window for this option.

- *Limit Applications* activates application whitelisting. It allows picking which specific applications the account will have access.

6. Expand *Other Apps*. Enable the checkbox for applications this account needs, but do not enable the *Other Apps* checkbox as this will allow any application to run. Keep in mind we are attempting to prevent unwanted malware from launching.

7. Enable the Utilities checkbox. A non-administrator is not going to create problems accessing these applications.

8. By selecting the *Logs* button, the administrator is able to view the activities of the managed user. Logs may be viewed from any other computer on the same network.

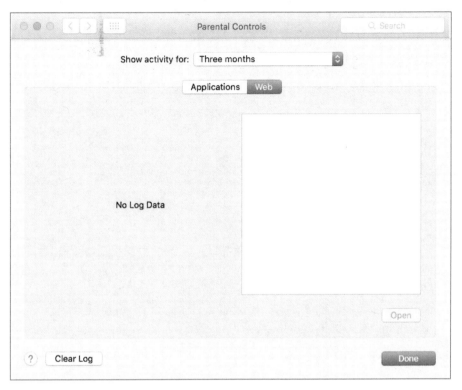

9. Select the *Done* button to return to Parental Controls.

10. Select the *Web* tab to view the managed web options.

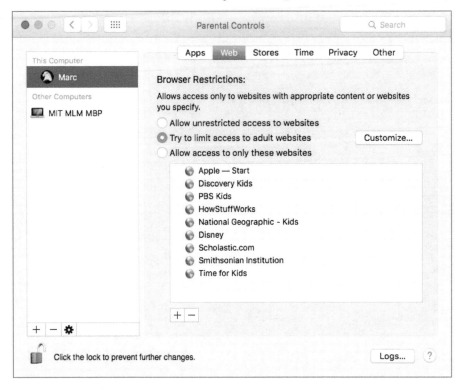

- *Allow unrestricted access to websites* eliminates any filtering of website access. Less than 5% of the businesses with which we hold an initial consult restrict web use. This is due primarily from leadership not understanding the consequences of doing so. According to a recent sarlary.com survey <http://www.salary.com/wasting-time-at-work-2012/>, 64% of employees visit non-work related websites *every day*. This is a costly misuse of company resources. It is also a significant source of malware infections. We do not recommend this option without a demonstrated business need.

- *Try to limit access to adult websites automatically* is our recommendation for business environments. Selecting the *Customize* button opens the configuration window. When done looking it over, select the *OK* button to return to Parental Controls.

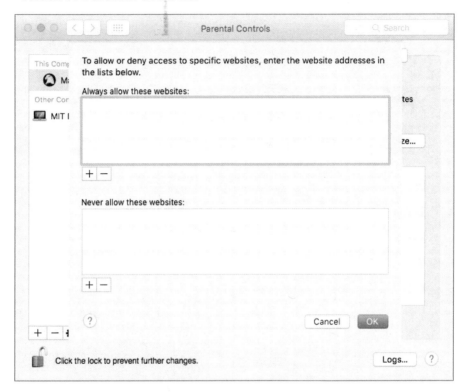

- *Allow access to only these websites* is the most restrictive, and may find its niche with young children.

- If the user attempts to visit a site that is restricted, they receive notice of such. If the user has access to administrative credentials, or if an administrative user is available, selecting the *Add Website* button will permanently unrestrict this website.

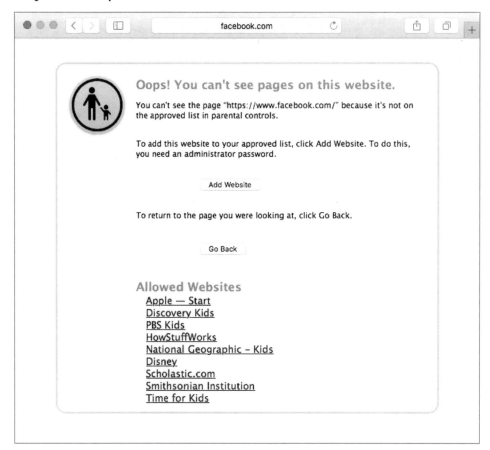

11. Selecting the *Stores* tab allows configuring access to all the various Apple commercial offerings.

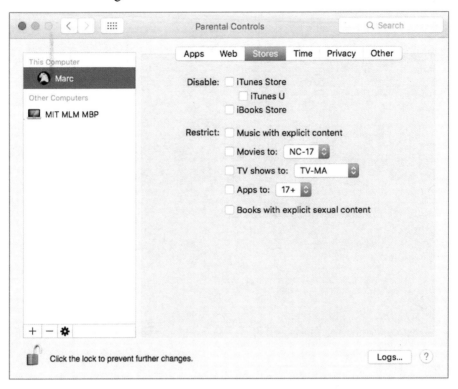

12. Selecting the *Time* tab allows configuration of when the account is able to use the computer:

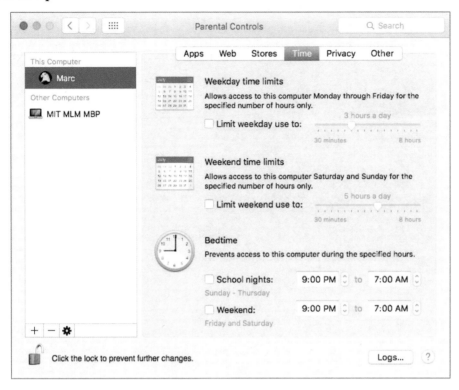

- As the end of their time approaches, an alert appears, allowing any administrative user to extend the managed user time for this session only:

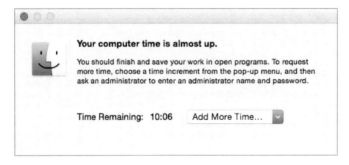

13. Selecting the *Privacy* tab allows configuration of privacy settings for this account.

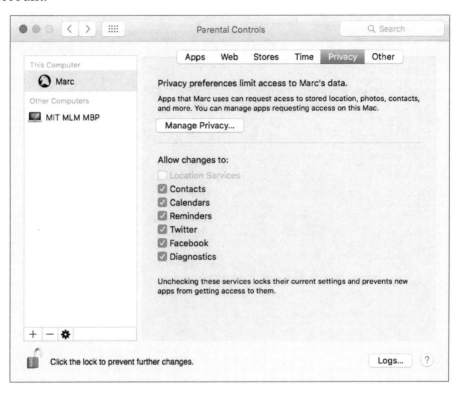

14. Selecting *Other* allows configuration of the odds and ends.

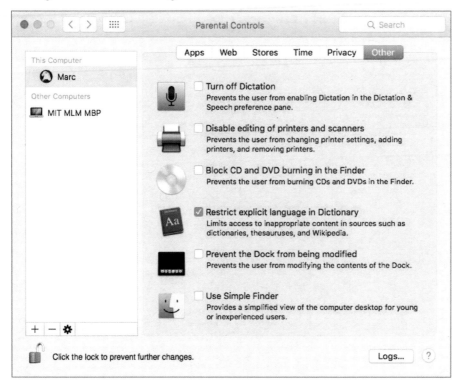

15. Quit System Preferences.

You have successfully created a Managed user account with Parental Controls.

Assignment: View Parental Controls Logs

If the managed user has an account on the same computer as the administrator, viewing the logs is just a couple of clicks away:

1. Log in as the administrator.

2. Select the *Apple* menu > *System Preferences* > *Parental Controls*.

3. Click the *Lock* icon and then authenticate as an administrator.

4. Select the targeted managed account.

5. Select the *Logs* button.

6. In the *Logs* window, you can choose to view the *Websites Visited, Websites Blocked, Applications,* and *Messages.* When selecting the specific log files, each event is listed individually, along with time stamps. In the case of websites, they will be grouped by category.

7. *Quit* Parental Controls.

8. Take your sweet time torturing the managed user with the knowledge you have gleamed about them.

Viewing the logs from another OS X computer on the same network is almost identical. The only difference is that when opening *Parental Controls* on your own Mac to view the logs of the managed user on the remote Mac, you will see the user account under *Other Computers.*

Review Questions

1. Name the six different types of user accounts available in OS X 10.11.

2. The maximum number of Root accounts available on OS X is _____ .

3. By default, is Root enabled or disabled?

4. Which user accounts may assume the powers of Root?

5. In what ways are Administrator accounts different than the Standard, Sharing, and Guest accounts?

6. How many Guest accounts are available on OS X?

7. Root may be enabled from the _____ System Preference.

8. The first user account to be created is a(n) _____ .

9. Application Whitelisting can be enabled with _____ .

4. Vulnerability: Storage Device

I am disturbed by how states abuse laws on Internet access. I am concerned that surveillance programs are becoming too aggressive. I understand that national security and criminal activity may justify some exceptional and narrowly tailored use of surveillance. But that is all the more reason to safeguard human rights and fundamental freedoms.

–Ban Ki-moon, Secretary General of the United Nations

Block Access to USB or FireWire Storage Devices

In some environments, it is appropriate to block access to USB and or FireWire storage devices. This may be required so that users cannot copy sensitive data. There are two ways to accomplish this:

- Disable the software controlling USB and FireWire storage devices. Advantages: Free, takes a minute to accomplish. Disadvantages: Difficult to undo, impacts all users equally.

- Install a utility to control access. We recommend DeviceLock *http://www.devicelock.com*. Advantages: Granular control over any storage device from thumb drive to iPhone, controllable user by user. Disadvantages: Must be run from a Windows computer to control both OS X and Windows clients.

Assignment: Disable USB and FireWire Storage Device Access

Within a few rarified, high-security environments, it is necessary to ensure that users are unable to use USB or FireWire storage devices. This can be accomplished by removing the drivers for such devices

1. Log in with an administrator account.

2. Navigate to the */System/Library/Extensions* folder.

3. Drag *IOUSBMassStorageClass.kext* and *IOFireWireSerialBusProtocolTransport.kext* to the Desktop.

4. Reboot.

5. Connect either a USB or FireWire storage device to the computer. Note that it will not mount, and that no user has access.

You have successfully blocked any user on this computer (including yourself, all administrators, and even root) from being able to "steal" data from this computer onto any USB or FireWire storage device.

Assignment: Re-enable USB and FireWire Storage Device Access

1. Log in with an administrator account.

2. Navigate to the Desktop (where the two files were moved in step 3 above.)

3. Drag *IOUSBMassStorageClass.kext* and *IOFireWireSerialBusProtocolTransport.kext* files to the */System/Library/Extensions* folder.

4. At the authentication prompt, enter an administrator name and password.

5. Reboot.

6. Connect either a USB or FireWire storage device to the computer. Note that it will now mount, and all users have access.

You have successfully returned your computer to default functionality.

FileVault 2 Full Disk Encryption

Strong passwords keep the network and Internet-based password attacks at bay, but should someone have physical access to your computer, it takes under 2 minutes to break in.

How?

One strategy is to boot the computer into Target Disk Mode *http://en.wikipedia.org/wiki/Target_Disk_Mode*. This is done by:

1. Power on an OS X computer.

2. Immediately after the power on tone, hold down the *T* key. This functionally turns off the computer system, making it nothing more than an external hard drive.

3. Connect the computer that is in Target Disk Mode to another computer via Thunderbolt *http://en.wikipedia.org/wiki/Thunderbolt_(interface)* or FireWire *http://en.wikipedia.org/wiki/Firewire*.

4. The computer in Target Disk Mode can now be accessed as if it were just a hard drive.

Another strategy is to boot the Mac into Single User Mode *http://support.apple.com/kb/PH10795*, and then trick the computer into thinking this is the first time it has ever been booted–and therefore forcing it to create a new administrator account:

1. Power on an OS X computer.

2. Immediately after the power on tone, hold down the cmd + S keys. Keep held down until you see a black screen with white text. This is called *Single User Mode*.

3. Enter: */sbin/mount -uw /*

   • This mounts the boot volume as writeable by the current user.

4. Enter: *rm /var/db/.AppleSetupDone*

    - This deletes a file that when not present, makes OS X think this is the first time it has booted.

5. Enter: *shutdown -r now*

6. The computer will reboot.

7. Upon reboot, thinking this is the first time the computer has been booted, it prompts the user to create what it thinks is the first user account–which is always an administrator.

8. Once at the desktop, this administrator can change the passwords of all users from the Users & Groups System Preference, and then gain access to all data!

Starting with Mac OS X 10.7 we now have FileVault 2 *http://en.wikipedia.org/wiki/FileVault*, which enables military-grade full disk encryption on the boot drive. With FileVault 2 configured, your drive has a secure wall around it that can only be penetrated by entering an account password.

Once FileVault 2 has been enabled, it may take 1–5 days for the encryption to complete. During this time you can continue working normally, although your computer may be sluggish as it is doing both your work and the encryption process.

Assignment: Enable and Configure FileVault 2

In this assignment you will enable full disk encryption using FileVault 2.

1. Open *Apple* menu > *System Preferences* > *Security & Privacy*, and then select the *FileVault* tab.

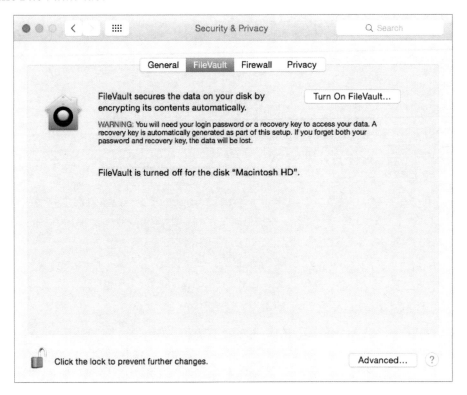

2. Unlock the *FileVault* lock icon.

3. Select the *Turn On FileVault…* button.

4. A dialog box appears to select using either your iCloud account or a recovery key to unlock the disk in the event your login password is forgotten.

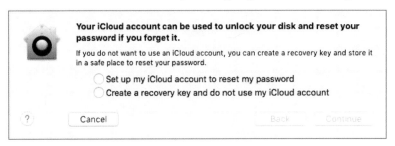

- Selecting *Allow my iCloud account...* allows you to use your iCloud account password to be used, and then select the *Continue* button.

- Selecting *Create a recovery key...* presents a randomly generated password. Store this key in a secure location. I recommend in your Address Book / Contacts application, and then select the *Continue* button.

5. If there are multiple user accounts on this machine, you are asked to enable the user accounts that are to be allowed to unlock the encrypted boot drive to boot up. For each of these accounts, click the *Enable User...* button, and enter the account password. (Users that have not been enabled can still access their accounts via *Fast User Switching* after the drive is unlocked by one of the authorized accounts.) Then click *Continue*.

6. Select the Restart button to restart the Mac and begin the encryption process.

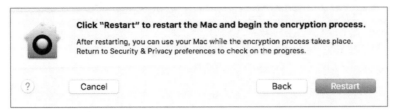

7. When your Mac returns to the Desktop, the *Security & Privacy* preference window will reopen, providing a progress indicator for the encryption process. You may close this window if desired.

The encryption process may take as little as an hour (small flash drive in a MacBook Air), or more than a day (4TB hard disk drive in an older, slower computer.) Though encryption will start again after the computer has been sleeping or turned off, to have it complete faster, set *Energy Saver* System Preferences to *Never Sleep*.

Enabling FileVault 2 is only half of the solution. The other half is to enable the Firmware Password. More on that later.

Review Questions

1. To disable access to USB and FireWire storage devices, the IOUSBMassStorageClass.kext and IOFireWireSerialBussProtocolTransport.kext files may be removed from which folder?

2. Explain the fundamental difference between the original FileVault, and FileVault 2.

3. FileVault 2 may be enabled from which System Preference?

4. Describe how to enable Target Disk Mode.

5. What does Target Disk Mode do?

6. Describe how to enable Single-User Mode.

7. What does Single-User Mode do?

5. Vulnerability: Sleep and Screen Saver

Do not take life too seriously. You will never get out of it alive.
–Elbert Hubbard, American writer, publisher, artist, and philosopher

Require Password After Sleep or Screen Saver

When you walk away from your computer, by default it will remain on. It is a trivial task for someone else to sit down in front of the computer and access all your data.

To help prevent this, configure your computer to lock down after a short period of inactivity, or upon command.

Assignment: Require Password After Sleep or Screen Saver

In this assignment, we will configure the computer to go into screen saver mode after 5 minutes of inactivity, and to require entering a password to remove the screen saver.

1. Open *Apple* menu > *System Preferences* > *Security & Privacy* > *General* tab.

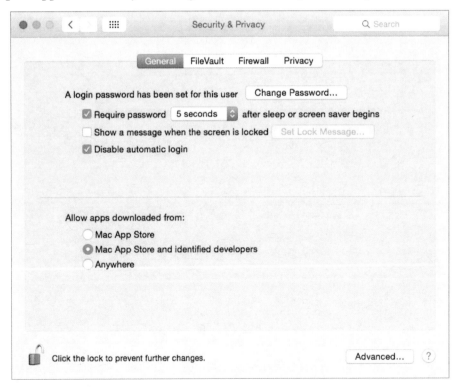

2. Click the Lock icon, and then authenticate as an administrator.

3. Enable and then set the *Require password ___ after sleep or screen saver begins* to 5 seconds. This provides a time buffer in the event your computer goes to sleep while you are at it. All you need do is move the mouse to wake it up within 5 seconds.

4. Enable *Disable automatic login*. How many nights of sleep will you loose should a thief take your computer, and all that is needed to access your data is to power it on?

5. Configure *Allow apps downloaded from*:

   • *Mac App Store*. This is the most secure setting. Apple performs diagnostics on apps sold through the App Store to verify being free from malicious code. It is also the most restrictive, as not all apps are available from the App Store.

   • *Mac App Store and identified developers*. Though less secure than the previous setting, it is better than the proverbial stick in the eye. This allows apps from developers that are a member of the Apple Developer Connection <http://developer.apple.com> to run on your computer. Though Apple has not vetted their software, at least you know they haven't been exiled by Apple for distributing malicious code.

   • *Anywhere*. This allows just any old junk to run on your computer. The only time this option should be selected is when you must run software that you know to be clean on your computer that is blocked by the other settings.

6. From the toolbar, select the *Show All* button, and then select the *Energy Saver* preference.

7. Set *Display sleep* to 5 minutes. This provides a minimal window of opportunity for someone to view your screen or gain access to your system should you step away from your computer.

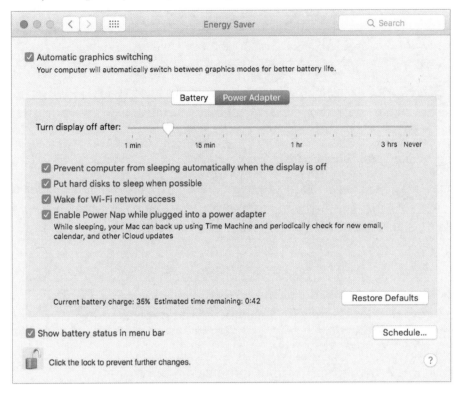

8. From the toolbar, select the *Show All* button.

9. Select the *Desktop & Screen Saver* preference, and then the *Screen Saver* tab.

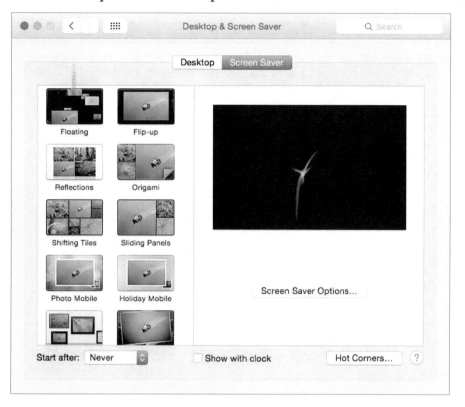

10. Select the *Hot Corners* button.

11. Select one of the four corners pop-up menus, and then select either *Put Display to Sleep* or *Start Screen Saver*. Either option will immediately put your computer into lock down mode the moment your cursor is pushed to that corner. Then select the *OK* button.

- NOTE: In the example below I held down the Control key while making my corner selection, which is reflected in the image.

12. Quit System Preferences.

13. Test your new setting by pushing your cursor into that corner. Leave the cursor there for 5 or more seconds, and then move the cursor. You should be presented with an authentication screen.

- NOTE: If following my example of holding down the Control key while creating the setting, you will need to hold down the Control key when moving the cursor to the corner.

14. Enter your password to unlock your computer and return to work.

You have successfully enabled lockdown of your system with sleep or screensaver.

Review Questions

1. Where can you configure requiring a password after sleep or screen saver?

6. Vulnerability: Malware

Behind every great fortune lies a great crime.

–Honore de Balzac, 19th-century novelist and playwright

Anti-Malware

Most people know this category of software as Antivirus, but there are so many other nasty critters out there (worms, Trojan horses, phishing attacks, malicious scripts, spyware, etc.) that the overarching term "Anti-Malware" is more accurate.

Depending on how one chooses to measure, there are from 500,000–40,000,000 malware *http://en.wikipedia.org/wiki/Malware* in the field that impact Windows. Currently there are fewer than 300 that specifically target OS X, but this number pales compared to the malware that impacts both Windows and OS X through scripts, Adobe Flash, Java, JavaScript, malicious websites, email phishing, etc.

OS X 10.7 and higher includes several automatically updating system-level architectures designed to help prevent malware from getting a foothold. Although Apple has done a good job here, they can do better. These invisible utilities only protect against known OS X malware, and Apple has been slow to update when new malware shows up.

Should we care about Windows malware? Yes. Not that Windows-specific malware will hurt you. Well, it will if you have Boot Camp or any virtual machine running another OS. But it is probable that at some point you will inadvertently pass windows malware along to a friend or business associate that is using Windows. Imagine how your relationship will change should an email from you take down a friend's computer, or a customer's entire network.

It is for these reasons that I strongly recommend the installation of quality anti-malware on all OS X machines. This raises the question of how to know that an anti-malware is quality software? We go by the results of independent testing organizations. One of the most recognized is AV Comparatives (AVC) *http://av-comparatives.org*. although no testing organization tests all of the 100+ anti-malware products on the market, AVC tests the major players at least a few times each year against a wide range of the current bugs. The results of their Windows anti-malware product tests are made public on their website *at http://www.av-comparatives.org/comparatives-reviews/*. The report on OS X anti-malware product tests is available at *http://www.av-comparatives.org/mac-security-reviews/*.

In their most recent testing of OS X anti-malware products, most of the tested software caught all of the OS X malware. So the deciding factors come down to ease of use, resource utilization (impact on computer performance), and ability to catch Windows malware.

For OS X home users without the need for the strictest security, we recommend Avira Free antivirus. Avira currently catches all OS X malware, and rates very highly in its ability to catch Windows malware. It has very low resource utilization, and has a clean and easy interface.

The only product we currently recommend for both OS X and Windows business users are Bitdefender. This is due to their first-rate ability to recognize and remove both OS X and Windows malware, simple interface, low impact on computer performance, they have both OS X and Windows versions, and can be centrally administered (although only from a Windows computer)–important for users running Windows on their Mac, as well as system administrators managing a mixed-platform environment.

For OX users running Windows in Boot Camp or in a Virtual Machine environment such as VMware Fusion or Parallels, you will also need a Windows anti-malware product. Though Microsoft provides a free option, by most independent testing reports, it is capable of catching only 80% of known malware. This is about the same as leaving for vacation after locking the front door, but leaving the back door wide open.

Turning to AVC for guidance, here is their chart on effectiveness of catching and removing malware from Windows:

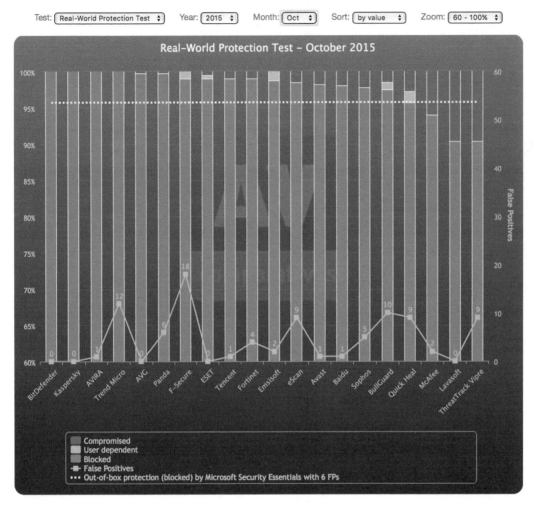

As of this writing, the top contenders for effectiveness at 100% are Bitdefender, Kaspersky, and Avira. But effectiveness isn't the only important measurement. In this same chart we can see false-positives. It's a sad day when a clean file is flagged as infected and then automatically trashed. Of the leading brands, only Bitdefender and Kaspersky, have zero false positives, with Avira at one.

Another vital measurement is performance–the impact the anti-malware has on overall performance of your computer. Anti-malware should use as little system resources as possible.

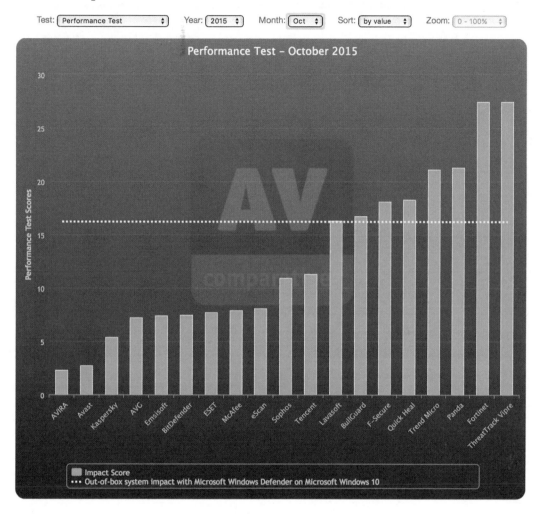

AV-Comparatives performs separate testing for OS X anti-malware products, located at *http://www.av-comparatives.org/wp-content/uploads/2015/07/avc_mac_2015_en.pdf*. For reasons only known to the organization, they do not conduct as thorough testing for the OS X products as they do for Windows. A summary of product testing is provided by AV-Comparatives below.

Product	Mac Malware Protection (105 recent samples)	Windows Malware Detection (1,000 most-prevalent samples)
Avast Free Mac Security	100%	100%
AVG AntiVirus for Mac	100%	100%
AVIRA Free Antivirus for Mac	99%	100%
Bitdefender Antivirus for Mac	99%	100%
ESET Cyber Security Pro	100%	100%
F-Secure SAFE for Mac	100%	28%
Intego Mac Premium Bundle X8	100%	50%
Kaspersky Internet Security for Mac	100%	100%
Kromtech MacKeeper	98%	97%
Sophos Anti-Virus for Mac	100%	100%

As with any research, don't use just one set of data points. The "winners" and "losers" will jostle for position on a monthly basis.

Assignment: Install and Configure Avira

In this assignment, you download, install, and configure Avira Free Antivirus.

1. Using your favorite web browser, download Avira Free Antivirus at *http://avira.com*.

2. Open the installer download, and then double-click to launch Avira_Free_Antivirus_for_Mac.pkg.

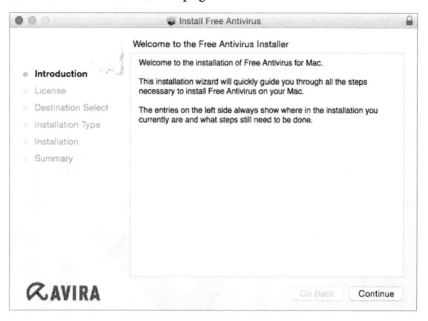

3. Select the *Continue* button.

4. Continue through the installation windows, and then when prompted, authenticate with an administrator username and password.

5. When installation completes, the Avira menu icon will appear: α , and the application will open.

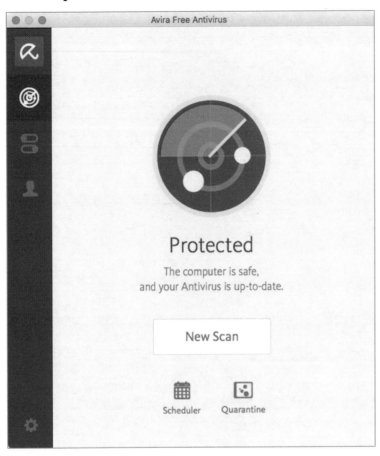

6. From the Avira application menu next to the Apple menu, select *Preferences*. The *Preferences* window will open. Select the *General* tab.

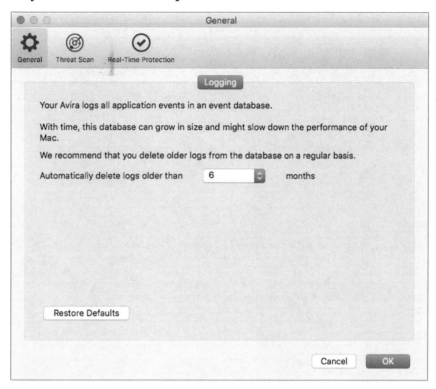

7. Set how long you would like to keep logs, and then select the *Threat Scan* tab, and then select the *Basic Settings* tab. The settings below are my recommendations. In a high-security environment, you may want to select *Detection Range* to *Scan all files.*

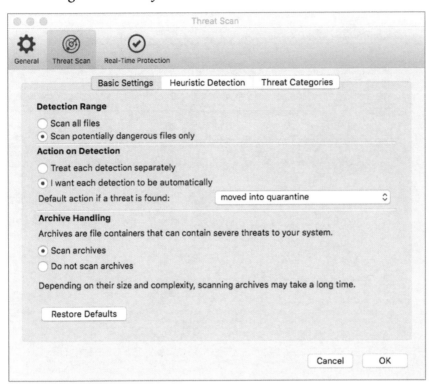

8. Select the *Heuristic Detection* tab, and then configure as below. In a high-security environment, you may want to change *Heuristic Detection Level* to *High.* The trade off is slower system performance.

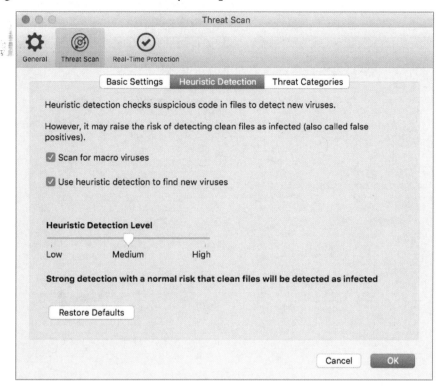

9. Select the *Threat Categories* tab, and then configure as below.

10. Select *Real-Time Protection* from the tool bar, and then select the *Basic Settings* tab. Configure as below. In a high-security environment, you may want to change *Detection Range* to *Scan all files*.

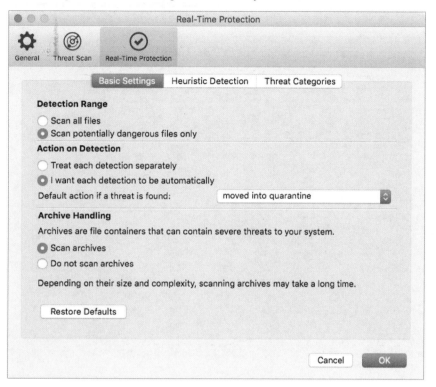

11. Select the *Heuristic Detection* tab, and then configure as below. In a high-security environment, you may want to change *Heuristic Detection Level* to *High*.

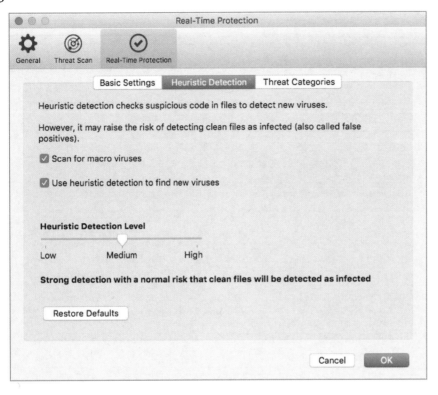

12. Select the *Threat Categories* tab and configure as below.

13. Select the *OK* button.

Assignment: Update Avira

When you installed Avira it may not have the most current virus definitions. Although Avira will automatically update daily, it is critical to start off with current definitions.

In this assignment, you will update the Avira virus definitions.

1. From the *Avira* menu icon, select *Update*.

2. The *Updating Free Antivirus* window appears, informing you of the download progress.

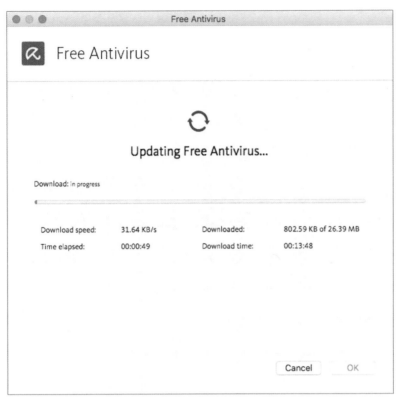

3. Once the update completes, select the *OK* button.

Assignment: Run a Virus Scan

After installing any anti-virus utility, it is vital to run an initial full scan of your system to ensure a healthy system. With any anti-virus that performs real-time scanning, you do not need to perform full system scans after the initial one.

In this assignment, you will run an initial full system scan for malware.

1. From the Avira menu icon, select *Open Avira.* The Avira main window appears.

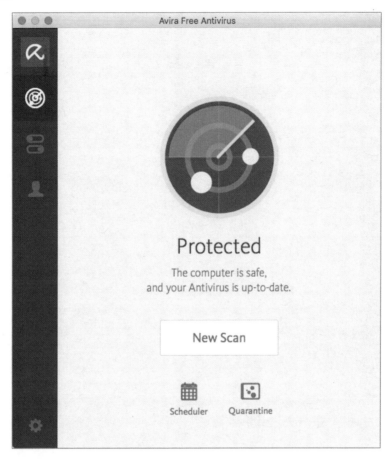

2. Select the *New Scan* button.

3. Select the *Change scan type* link.

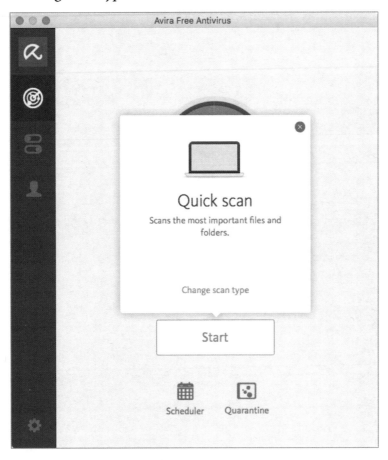

4. Select the *Computer Scan* radio button.

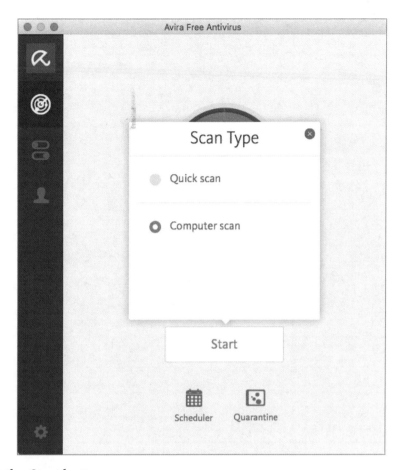

5. Select the *Start* button.

6. The *Scan in progress* window appears.

7. When the scan completes, select the *OK* button.

8. Close the *Avira* main window.

Your system is now malware-free and protected with real-time scans of new incoming email, and files that are opened.

Assignment: Uninstall Avira Anti-Virus

Should you decide to remove Avira Anti-Virus from your computer, follow these steps:

1. Open the *Avira-Uninstall.app,* located in */Applications/Utilities.* The uninstaller opens.

2. Select the *Yes* button.

3. At the authentication window, enter an administrator's name and password, and then select the *Continue* button.

Your Avira Anti-Virus has now been uninstalled from your computer.

Assignment: Install and Configure Bitdefender

In this assignment, you will download, install, and configure Bitdefender Antivirus for Mac.

Download Bitdefender Antivirus for Mac.

1. Using your favorite browser, visit *Bitdefender.com.*

2. In the navigation bar, click *Home Users > Bitdefender Antivirus for Mac*.

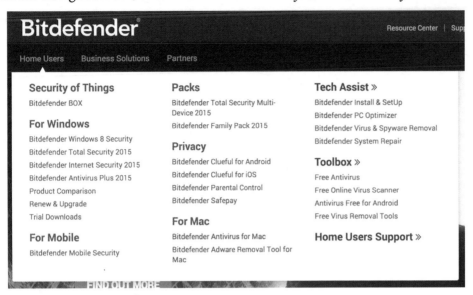

3. Select the *Download Now* link.

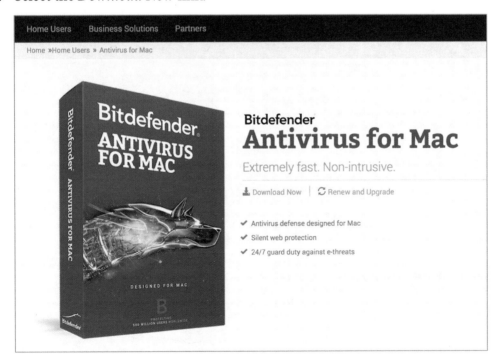

4. Enter your email address, and then click the *Submit* button.

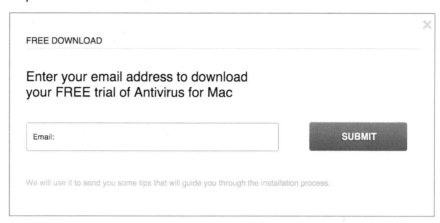

5. Check your email for the link from Bitdefender. Click the link to download
    the software.

6. Bitdefender Antivirus for Mac will download.

7. Double-click the downloaded installer. It will mount and open a virtual disk on your Desktop.

8. Open the *Antivirus for Mac.pkg* found inside the opened virtual disk. The *Install Antivirus for Mac* will launch. Follow the on-screen instructions to fully install.

9. Once installed, Bitdefender Antivirus for Mac will open.

10. To configure, select the *Antivirus for Mac* menu > *Preferences,* and then select *Scanner* from the toolbar. We recommend the following configuration.

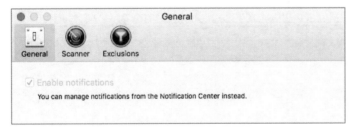

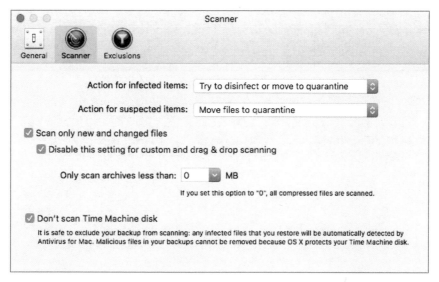

11. The default settings for *General* and *Exclusions* work well, so you may now close the *Preferences* window.

12. *Bitdefender Antivirus for Mac* includes *TrafficLight* to watch over your web browsing. It will alert if a site is potentially dangerous, and inform what is tracking your browsing. To enable *TrafficLight*, select the *Activate* button in the main window.

13. *TrafficLight* is an extension available for Safari, Google Chrome, and Firefox. Select the *Get extension* button for each browser you use.

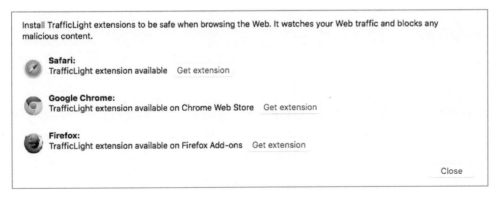

14. From the *TrafficLight* extension webpage, select the *Free Download* button.

15. For Safari, once downloaded, double-click the *TrafficLight* extension, and then select the *Install* button to install.

16. When visiting any website, the *TrafficLight* icon will show a red alert icon if the site is potentially dangerous, or if there is any tracking activity. Clicking on the *TrafficLight* icon will display more information.

- In this example, we are informed this is a safe page, and there is 1 tracker– Google Analytics.

- You can access the main window or preferences for Bitdefender at any time from the menu icon

Last step is to perform a full system malware scan. You normally would only need to do this once–right after the first installation of your antivirus software. When this step completes, Bitdefender will can new files, new emails, and files as they are opened.

17. From the Bitdefender main window, select *Full System Scan*.

18. When the scan completes, quit Bitdefender.

Congratulations! You have just built a wide moat to keep malware from your computer.

Review Questions

1. Apple started to include system-level anti-malware beginning with OS X
   _____ .

2. Name a website the independently researches and publishes anti-virus software effectiveness.

3. Name a few of the best anti-virus software for OS X in terms of both effectiveness and performance, according to this website.

7. Vulnerability: Firewall

If you could kick the person in the pants responsible for most of your trouble, you wouldn't sit for a month.

–Theodore Roosevelt

Firewall

Whenever a computer needs to communicate with the outside world–say, to print, receive or send email, or surf the web–it must *open a door* to that world. In the IT universe this is called *opening a port*.

Ports are numbered from 1–65,535, with one port number assigned to any one communication task. For example, when using your browser to visit Google, you enter *http://www.google.com* in the address field. This can be translated into English as: *Using the language of the Internet (http) I would like to communicate with a server named www, within a domain named google.com.*

The problem is that the www server at Google has 65,535 ports to which it may potentially need to listen. Invisible to the user, *:80* is been placed at the end of the address request. This translates into: *And please knock on port 80 (reserved for web server communications) so that www can respond to the web page requests that I send to it.*

To best secure your computer, it is important to only have those ports open that are necessary to perform your work.

The purpose of a firewall *http://en.wikipedia.org/wiki/Firewall* is to block unwanted attempts to get into or communicate with your computer from the network or Internet through your 65,535 ports. It is about as simple as anything gets on a computer, and once activated you likely will never need to know about it again.

To get into your computer or to communicate with it, a few ducks must be lined up.

- Your computer must be on a network with other computers (such as your local area network at home or office, or the Internet).

- You must have a port open. On OS X, ports are opened by enabling sharing services from the Sharing System Preference, and by some applications.

- Lastly, there has to be some process or application listening at the port that can respond. You can open port 80 on a web server, but if the web server application (typically Apache) hasn't been launched, no amount of your browser screaming at the server will elicit a response.

In OS X, activating the firewall puts guards at the gates to prevent unwanted visitors. The second step is to close those ports whose associated services you don't need. This is accomplished by disabling unnecessary services in *System Preferences > Sharing*.

Assignment: Activate the Firewall

In this assignment you enable the built-in firewall for OS X.

1. Open *Apple* menu > *System Preferences* > *Security & Privacy*.

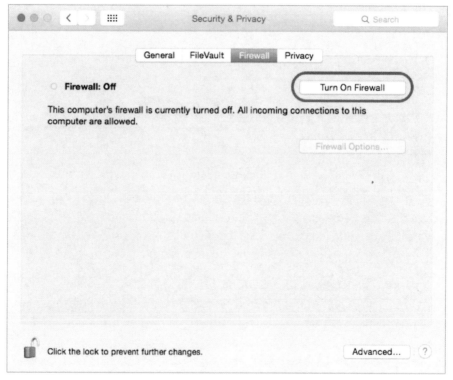

2. Select the *Firewall* tab.

3. Select the Lock icon to authenticate as an administrative user.

4. Select the *Turn On Firewall* button.

5. Select the *Firewall Options...* button to further refine the firewall.

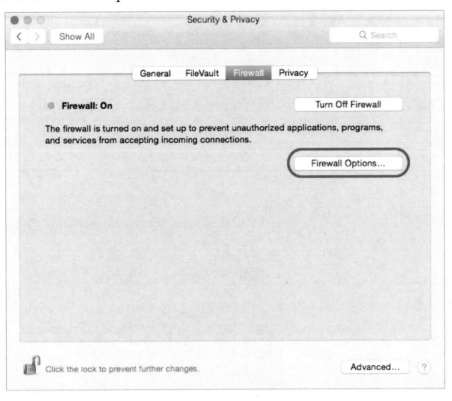

6. The *Firewall Options* window opens.

- *Block all incoming connections*: Enabling will effectively close down all but the most essential ports. You still will be able to reach out to initiate communications, such as to surf on a web browser or initiate a call on Skype, but you must do the initiating or others won't get in. Unless you are working in an unusual environment, this step is not necessary.

- In the white area, you see all of the ports that are open. Above the horizontal line are those ports you opened when enabling items in the Sharing System Preference. Below the line are those ports opened by launching applications that require communication outside of your computer. It is possible that some of these applications have no need for outside communications, in which case you can click on the Allow incoming connections, then select Block incoming connections.

- *Automatically allow signed software to receive incoming connections* is enabled by default. Applications that are "signed" have special coding that allows your Mac to determine if it has been damaged or modified from the original in any way. Apple has given its seal of approval to the original as being free of any intrusion software.

- *Stealth mode* can usually be left disabled. Enabling this checkbox will make your Mac unresponsive to Ping and other diagnostic tools. However, enabling this checkbox should have no impact on any aspect of your computer use.

7. Select the *OK* button.

8. Quit System Preferences.

Congratulations! Your firewall will now be on guard, preventing unwanted penetration of your computer.

Assignment: Close Unnecessary Ports

In this assignment we will examine our currently open ports, and close those that are not necessary.

1. Open *Apple* menu > *System Preferences.*

2. Select the *Sharing* preference. The *Sharing* System Preference pane opens.

3. As necessary, select the Lock icon and authenticate as an administrator.

4. If any of your sharing items are enabled, at least one port has been opened to allow communication for that item.

5. If any currently enabled item is not needed, disable its checkbox.

Next we check on which, if any, ports are opened via user-launched applications.

6. Select the *Show All* button.

7. Select *Security & Privacy* icon.

8. Select the *Firewall* tab.

9. Click the *Lock* icon, and then authenticate as an administrator.

10. Select the *Firewall Options...* button.

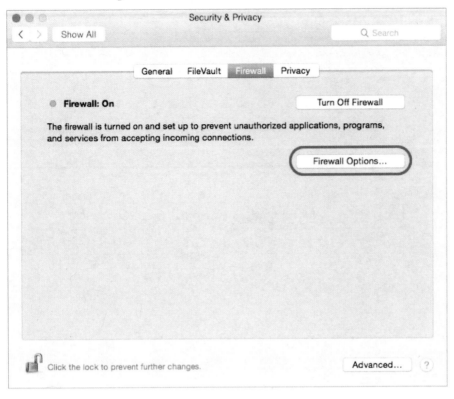

11. The Firewall Options window opens, displaying all open ports based on the name of the process or application that has opened them. In this example, above the line I have File Sharing (AFP, SMB) ports open.

- This screenshot reflects the *Sharing* preferences that I currently have open, *File Sharing*.

If any of the above the line ports should be closed:

12. Select *System Preferences > Sharing*, and then turn off the shared item.

Below the line are ports opened by some of the applications I have launched.

- BitTorrent (Internet file-sharing service)

- CrashPlanService (Internet backup service)

- iTunes.app (iTunes music store service)

- Keychain2Go.app (Password storage and synchronization service)

- Mono (Part of the ScreenConnect remote support service)

If any of these ports should be closed:

13. Select the *Allow incoming connections* pop-up menu, and then select *Block incoming connections*.

14. If changes have been made, select the *OK* button.

15. Quit System Preferences.

If any unnecessary port had been opened, you have now closed them, preventing unwanted access.

Review Questions

1. The OS X firewall is enabled by default. (True or False)
2. Where is the firewall enabled or disabled?
3. When selecting the firewall option to *Block all incoming connections*, are all ports disabled?

8. Vulnerability: Data Loss

Weather forecast for tonight: Dark.

–George Carlin

The Need for Backups

Data loss is a very real fact of life. It is not a matter of if you will experience data loss, just a matter of when, and how often. Only a small percentage of computer users back up on a regular basis. I suspect these are the folks who have experienced catastrophic data loss and never want a repeat.

There are many sources of data loss. The top contenders include:

- Computer theft

- Power surges

- Power sags

- Sabotage

- Fire

- Water damage. I personally have had 3 clients who have lost computers due to cats or dogs marking their territory, and my own cat took out a $4,000 monitor with nothing more than a hairball.

- Entropy / aging of the drive

- Malware

- Terrorist activities

- Criminal activities

- Static electricity

- Physical shock to the drive (banging the computer, dropping, etc.)

Best Practices call for three backups:

- **One full backup onsite**. This allows for almost immediate recovery of lost or corrupted documents, or full recovery of the OS, applications, and documents in the event of complete loss of the hard drive.

- **One full backup offsite**. This is your *Plan B* in the event of a catastrophic loss of both the computer and the onsite backup. This typically takes the form of fire or theft.

- **One Internet-based backup**. This is your OMG, what do I do now? fallback plan. Many people substitute the Internet backup for the offsite. A potential problem is that your Internet backup may take several days to weeks to download.

Onsite Full Backup with Time Machine

OS X comes with the most advanced backup software for any computer–Time Machine. Time Machine has several advantages over other options, including:

- Free

- Highly reliable and stable

- Low resource requirements

- Maintains document versioning. With each run Time Machine will back up the latest version of your documents, while maintaining all prior versions as well

- Runs in the background every hour without user intervention

- Works with Migration Assistant (part of the standard OS X installation) to replicate the last backup to another Macintosh.

- Does backup to a FireWire, Thunderbolt, or USB drive attached locally, to an Apple Airport Extreme Base station, or a computer running OS X Server

- Can create an encrypted backup to a locally attached drive (Mac OS X 10.7 and above), or to a drive attached to an Airport Extreme or OS X Server (OS X 10.8 and above)

As a general rule, the backup drive should be at least double the size of your data, preferably quadruple. This allows for future growth and the maintenance of long-term document versioning.

Although FireWire drives typically cost $20-$50 more than USB, and Thunderbolt $40 more than FireWire, that extra cost will be paid back with interest in the event you ever need to use the backup. FireWire drives outperform USB 2–4 fold, and Thunderbolt drives are a bit faster than FireWire. When recovering a Terabyte or more of data, speed will lessen the pain.

Onsite Full Backup with Carbon Copy Cloner

As great as Time Machine is, there is one critical area in which it fails–it does not create a bootable clone. A bootable clone is an exact duplicate of the original drive. This is where Carbon Copy Cloner comes in.

The need for a bootable clone backup becomes clear when you have a hard drive failure. Without a bootable clone, the recovery process looks like this:

1. Call a technician for assistance or rush to the store to buy a new drive.

2. Remove the old drive, install the new drive.

3. Install OS X.

4. Install all updates.

5. Use Migration Assistant to copy over the latest backup from Time Machine.

6. Get back to work–4 to 8 hours after the crash.

With a bootable clone, the recovery process looks like this:

1. Restart your Mac with the option key held down. This triggers the Start Manager, allowing you to select from which drive to boot.

2. Select the bootable clone drive as your boot drive.

3. Get back to work–5 minutes after the crash.

4. Call a technician for assistance. Let them know there is no rush.

5. At a time that is convenient (and not on overtime) the problem drive is replace and all data copied over.

So why use Time Machine? It is the fastest and easiest way to recover lost or damaged documents.

Internet-Based Data Backup

There are several great and unique advantages to Internet-based backups:

- If a small black hole opens up devouring your computer, backup and offsite backup, your Internet backup will always be waiting for you. Think disaster recovery after a multi-block explosion, terrorist activity that prevents access to either the computer or off-site location.

- Should you find yourself far away from your computer, as long as you have any computer, your data can be accessed.

- A few of the Internet-based options now include sharing access to any documents that have been backed up.

When looking for the right Internet-based backup service, in addition to cost, features, company and software stability, keep an eye out for document versioning. You want your service to keep at least one month of document versions. In the event that you accidentally delete a document, it will remain on the server for at least a month, or if a document corrupts, you want to be able to go back to a previous (presumably not corrupted) version.

My personal favorites include:

Backblaze at *http://www.backblaze.com*. Easy to use, very fast uploads, rock solid stable, 30-day document versioning, backs up all user accounts.

Carbonite at *http://www.carbonite.com*. Fast uploads, rock solid stable, limited document versioning, backs up all user accounts. 30-day document versioning, family and business accounts make it easier to administer multiple computers.

CrashPlan at *http://www.crashplan.com* for home and *http://www.crashplanpro.com*–my only choice for business. Fast upload, rock solid stable, document versioning, lifetime document versioning, individual and business accounts. Can meet your HIPAA or SEC compliance needs.

Assignment: Format the Backup Drive for Time Machine or Carbon Copy Cloner

Redundancy calls for two on-site backups. My preference is to use two tools, one for each backup–Time Machine and Carbon Copy Cloner.

In this assignment, we will format a drive for use with either. If you will be following my approach and have two backups, repeat this process with each of two drives.

1. Purchase an external hard drive that has at least four times the capacity of the data to be held on the host computer. We strongly recommend purchasing a drive with FireWire 800, USB 3, or Thunderbolt and USB 3. Although you pay up to $50 extra upfront, these drives are significantly faster than those with FireWire 400 or USB 2. That speed makes a huge difference as you are sweating blood trying to recover your data.

2. Connect the new drive to your computer.

3. Open Disk Utility, located in your */Applications/Utilities* folder.

4. Select the outdented hard drive name from the sidebar (the outdented name is the physical drive, while the indented name(s) is the partition or volume.) Then select the *Partition* tab.

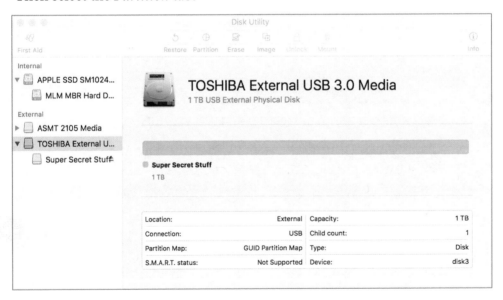

5. From the Toolbar, select *Partition*. The *Partition Device* pane will open. Configure as:

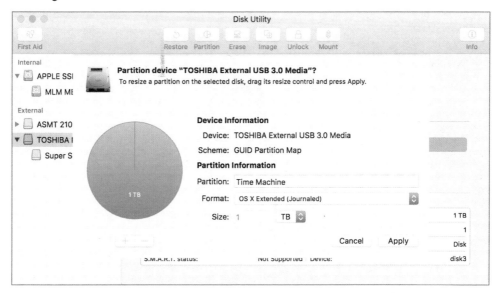

- *Partition*: Enter the name for this volume. To avoid confusion, keep it simple, with something like *Time Machine* or *Clone Backup*.

- *Format*: Use *OS X Extended (Journaled)*

- *Size*: Leave this at the default, which will be the entire drive.

6. Click the *Apply* button.

The formatting process will begin. Depending on the size and speed of the drive, and the speed of the computer, this may take from a few seconds to a few minutes. When complete, the drive is ready for use.

Assignment: Install and Configure Carbon Copy Cloner

In this assignment, you will download, install, and then configure Carbon Copy Cloner to create bootable clone backups of your boot drive.

1. Download and install Carbon Copy Cloner at *http://bombich.com*. This will be a time-limited full version. Should you wish to purchase CCC, you can do so from within the application.

2. Launch Carbon Copy Cloner. At the welcome window, select the *Trial* button.

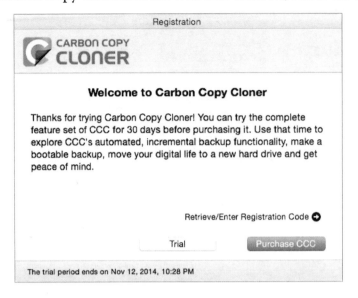

3. The main window opens. It's always a bright idea to configure an application's preferences before having it do heavy lifting. Select the *Carbon Copy Cloner* menu > *Preferences*. Configure each of the preference windows as below.

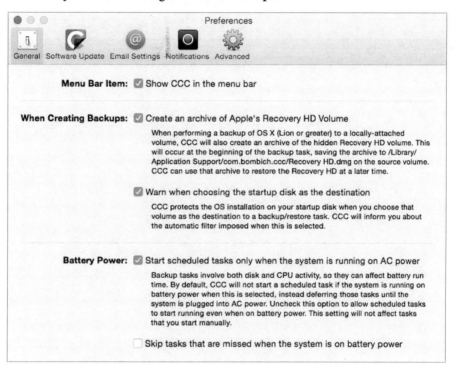

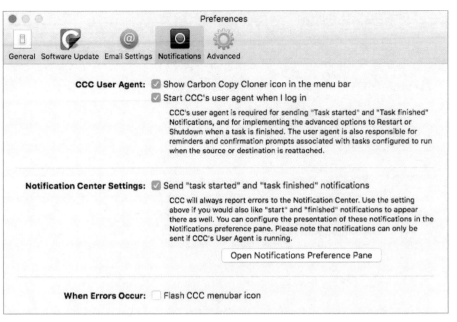

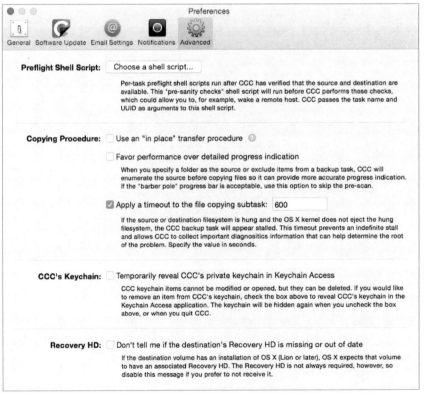

4. Close the *preferences* window.

5. Back at the main window, from the tool bar select the *Show Sidebar* button. The sidebar will slide out.

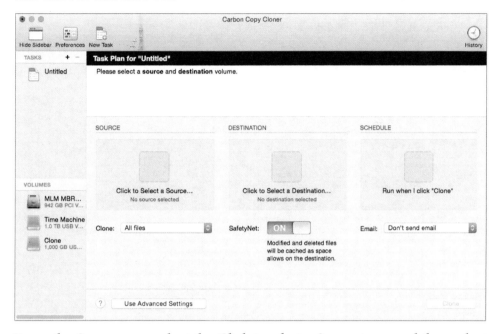

6. From the *Source* area, select the *Click to select a Source* icon, and then select your internal boot hard drive.

7. From the *Destination* area, select the *Click to Select a Destination* icon, and then select the Clone drive.

8. From the *Schedule* area, select the icon, configure as below, and then select the *Done* button.

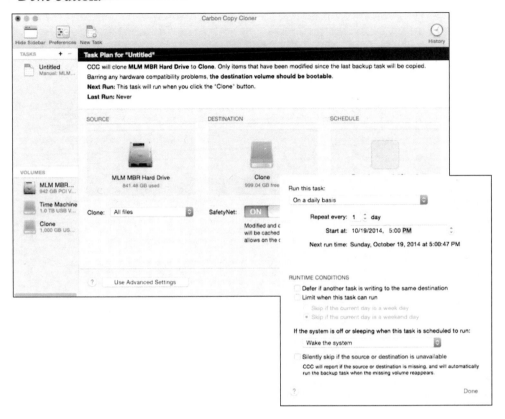

9. At the main window, in the sidebar, double-click on *Untitled* task, and then rename to *Daily Clone*.

10. Select the *Save* button. Your configuration should look like this:

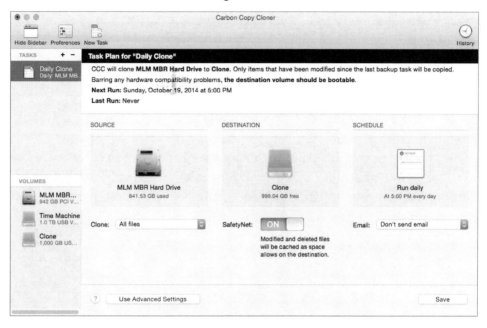

Assignment: Run the First Clone Backup

To test your Carbon Copy Cloner script, you will manually trigger the first backup. It is also necessary to have an initial backup in order to create a Recovery HD partition onto the drive (required to boot from an encrypted drive), and to then encrypt the drive.

Run the first clone backup.

1. From the *Carbon Copy Cloner* menu icon, select *Daily Clone > Run Now*.

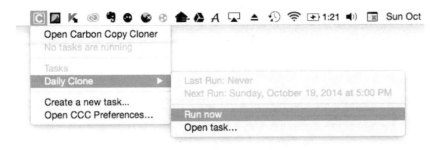

2. Depending on the speed of your computer and the size of the source drive, the first backup may take from 1-12 or more hours. Make certain that your computer will not go into sleep mode during the backup by selecting the *Apple menu > System Preferences > Energy Saver*. Although it is ok to have your monitor go to sleep, your system must not. Configure your preferences so the system will not sleep.

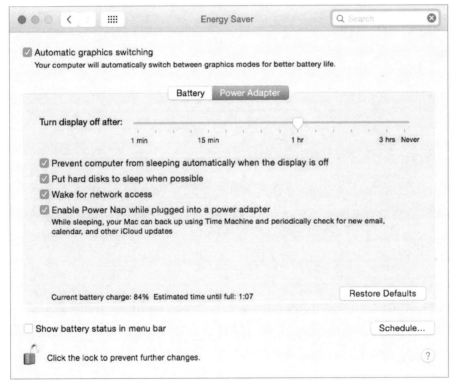

3. Close System Preferences.

Add a Recovery HD to your Clone Backup.

In order to have FileVault 2 encryption on a boot volume, it is necessary to add a hidden Recovery HD volume to the drive. The OS X installer performs this task behind the scenes when installing OS X onto a drive. But as we aren't "installing" OS X on the clone, we will have Carbon Copy Clone will do this for you.

4. Open Carbon Copy Cloner.

5. From the side bar, select the Clone volume. If you have added the Clone volume as the Destination volume, a window will appear recommending that you create a Recovery HD on this volume. Select the Create Recovery HD button.

6. This process takes only a minute. When complete, return to the main window.

Encrypt the Clone Backup

If an unauthorized person gains access to your clone backup, they will have full access to all of your data unless the data is encrypted. The process of encrypting the clone drive is identical to configuring FileVault 2 on the system drive.

7. Complete at least one full backup to the clone drive.

8. Restart your computer, booting from the clone drive.

9. Open *Apple* menu > *System Preferences* > *Startup Disk*.

10. Click the Lock icon and authenticate as an administrator.

11. Select the clone drive.

12. Click the *Restart…* button. Your computer will restart, booting into the clone backup.

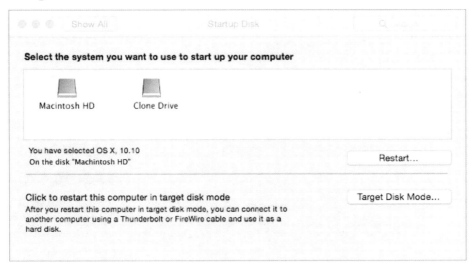

13. Once back at the desktop, we will start the encryption process for the clone drive by opening *Apple* menu > *System Preferences* > *Security & Privacy* > *FileVault* tab.

14. Click the Lock icon and authenticate as an administrator.

15. Click the *Turn On FileVault* button.

16. Follow the on-screen instructions.

17. Record the FileVault 2 Recovery Key in a secure location. I use the Address Book/Contacts application. The FileVault 2 Recovery Key is a secondary password used to decrypt and access your boot drive in the event the user does not remember their account password, or the account password does not work.

18. Click the *Restart* button. FileVault 2 will restart your computer to the clone drive.

19. When back on the desktop, open *Apple* menu > *System Preferences* > *Startup Disk*.

20. Select your normal system/boot drive, which is by default named *Macintosh HD*.

21. Click the Restart… button. The computer will restart, booting from your normal boot drive.

The encryption process for the clone drive will continue. Depending on the size of the drive, the speed of the computer, and if HDD or SSD, it may take from a few hours to a few days to complete the encryption. Although it is ok to let your computer sleep or turn off, this will delay the encryption process.

Assignment: Configure Time Machine

Although Time Machine is designed to auto-configure, that doesn't mean it has auto-configured correctly. To manually configure Time Machine:

1. Attach your Time Machine drive. If you have followed the steps above, it is already attached and mounted.

2. Open *Apple* menu > *System Preferences* > *Time Machine*.

3. Select the *Select Backup Disk…* button. All drives available to serve as backup drives appear.

4. Select the drive you wish to serve as your Time Machine, enable the *Encrypt backups* checkbox, and then select the *Use Disk* button.

5. At the prompt, enter a strong password for your Time Machine disk, and then select the *Encrypt Disk* button. Typically, this will be the same as your log in password (your log in password is strong, isn't it?!)

6. Quit System Preferences.

Time Machine will automatically start to back up to this drive within the hour.

Assignment: Integrity Test the Clone Backup

The step missed by almost every user is testing the integrity of the backups. This testing process should be performed every month. Not a bad idea to put it on your calendar for the first workday of the month.

Integrity testing requires that your backup has completed at least one full cycle. If you have just completed the previous exercise, allow 24 hours of uptime before moving on.

To test your bootable clone backup, you need to boot from it, and then verify it has been backing up by looking at the history.

1. Select the *Apple* menu > *System Preferences* > *Startup Disk*.

2. Select your clone drive.

3. Click the *Restart* button. Your computer will restart, then boot to the clone drive.

4. Verify that you have booted to the clone drive by selecting the *Apple* menu > *About This Mac*.

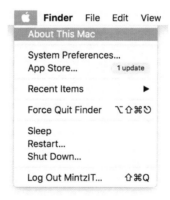

5. If the *Startup Disk* field lists the name of your clone drive, you know your clone is bootable and you are half way home.

6. Close the *About This Mac* window.

7. Open the clone drive.

8. Open the *CCC Archives* folder.

9. A date and time stamp will label each backup. If the most current date and time stamp is what it should be (as opposed to several days or weeks ago), you are good.

10. To restart your Mac into the default boot drive, select the *Apple* menu > *System Preferences* > *Startup Disk*.

11. Select your normal boot drive.

12. Click the *Restart* button. Your computer will restart, and then boot to the normal drive.

Congratulations! You have just verified the integrity of your clone backup.

Assignment: Integrity Test the Time Machine Backup

To test your Time Machine backup, you need to enter Time Machine, and then verify the existing backups. If you have a portable Mac, it is likely that you have two different backups–one on your Time Machine drive, and the other on your laptop itself. The local backups are created when Time Machine auto launches but does not find the Time Machine drive connected, so it backs up to the laptop drive itself. You can see the two backups in the Time Machine window. Backups to the Time Machine drive have purple tick marks, local backups have white tick marks.

1. From the menu bar, select the *Time Machine* icon > *Enter Time Machine* menu.

2. When in Time Machine, look to the right hand edge of your screen. If you see a series of tick marks that display date and time as the cursor moves over them, Time Machine has performed backups.

3. Verify the latest time stamp (at the bottom) is current.

Congratulations! You have verified your Time Machine backup is working properly.

Review Questions

1. Best Practices call for what backups?
2. What application is used to format a storage device, and where is it located?
3. What application can be used to create bootable clone backups?

9. Vulnerability: Firmware Password

I have six locks on my door all in a row. When I go out, I lock every other one. I figure no matter how long somebody stands there picking the locks, they are always locking three.

–Elayne Boosler, American comedienne

EFI Chip

Apple computers use a chip on the logic board for part of the boot process. It is named the Firmware chip. Intel-based Macs use the Intel EFI (Extensible Firmware Interface) chip as the firmware chip. This chip has the ability to be password protected. Once done, it is not possible to boot the computer from another source (such as Single User Mode, Target Disk Mode, or another startup disk), or use any startup modifier key without first entering the Firmware Password.

This puts gold plating on your computer security. It is also something to take very seriously. If your Mac was manufactured after January 1, 2010 and you forget your Firmware Password, the only way to unlock the chip is to physically take the computer to an Apple Store where you may be required to present documents proving your legal ownership over the computer. Macs made before this date can have their Firmware Password reset by the following:

1. Shut down the computer.

2. Remove or add RAM.

3. Power on, and then immediately hold down the cmd-opt-p-r keys until the computer reboots. This last process is called *Zapping the PRAM* (Parameter RAM chip.)

The Firmware Password now is erased. Not much security in these older units.

Assignment: Create a Firmware Password

In this assignment you create and install a password on your Firmware chip to add NSA-level security to your computer.

1. Shut down your Mac.

2. Power on.

3. Immediately after pressing the Power button, hold down the cmd-r keys until you see the dark gray Apple logo center screen.

4. At the *Recovery HD* window, select the *Utilities* menu > *Set Firmware Password*.

5. Enter a strong password.

6. Record your password in a secure location. I use the iPhone Contacts as this both synchronizes with my iPhone Contacts, and is accessible from any computer by visiting *http://icloud.com*.

7. Click the *OK* button, returning you to the main Recovery HD screen.

8. Restart your Mac by selecting *Apple* menu > *Restart*.

Congratulations! You have successfully locked down your data from all but perhaps NSA attempts.

Assignment: Test the Firmware Password

In this assignment we will verify that your firmware password is active.

1. Shut down your Mac.

2. Power on your Mac. Immediately after the startup tone, hold down the option key.

Without a firmware password, this startup modifier would put you into *Start Manager Mode*, allowing anyone full access to all of your data by booting from an external drive. But with a firmware password in place you should see a screen requesting the firmware password in order to proceed.

3. Enter your firmware password.

4. Select your normal boot volume and continue startup as normal.

Assignment: Remove Firmware Password

I consider having a firmware password in place as important as the user password. However, there may come a time when removing the Firmware Password is called for (selling the computer is all I can think of.)

In this assignment, you will remove your Firmware Password. If you wish to leave it enabled, skip this assignment.

1. Shut down your Mac.

2. Power on your Mac. Immediately after the startup tone, hold down the option key.

3. At the Firmware Password prompt, enter it.

4. Select the *Utilities* menu > *Set Firmware Password*.

5. Select the *Remove Firmware Password* button.

6. Enter the firmware password.

7. Select the *Remove* button.

8. Select the *Apple* menu > *Restart* to restart the Mac.

Review Questions

1. What is the name of the logic board chip can be password protected?

2. How is the Firmware password cleared on Macintosh computers manufactured prior to January 1, 2010?

3. To create a Firmware password, you must be an administrator. (True or False)

10. Vulnerability: Lost or Stolen Device

It takes considerable knowledge just to realize the extent of your own ignorance.

–Thomas Sowell, American economist, social theorist, political philosopher, and currently Senior Fellow at the Hoover Institution, Stanford University

Find My Mac?

Millions of computers are stolen each year. If you have followed the steps above to enable *FileVault 2* with strong passwords, as well as a Firmware password, nobody is going to break into your data.

But it would be nice to be able to get your Mac back.

Find My Mac is an option within iCloud accounts that locates your Mac on a web map, often to within 6 feet. You can pass this information along to your local police, allowing them to get a search warrant to the address and recover your property.

With FileVault 2 enabled, the thief won't be able to access your account or data, but if you leave the Guest account active, the thief will be able to boot your computer to the Guest account…All the while Find My Mac is broadcasting the thief's location.

For Find My Mac to function, the following must happen:

- An iCloud account has been activated.

- Find My Mac has been enabled for the computer.

- The computer is turned on.

- The computer is connected to the Internet via Wi-Fi. An Ethernet connection may work, but there is no guarantee for this.

Assignment: Activate and Configure Find My Mac

1. Select the *Apple* menu > *System Preferences* > *iCloud*.

2. If you have not created an iCloud account, select the *Sign In* button and follow the on-screen instructions to create an account.

3. Enable the *Find My Mac* checkbox. You will be prompted to *Allow* this function. Earlier OS versions did not present this prompt.

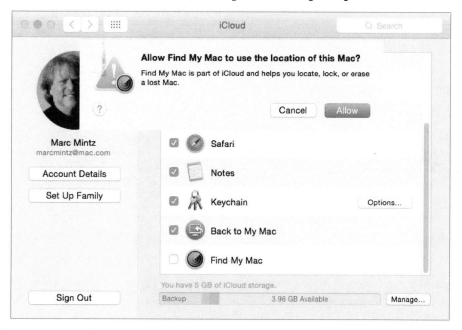

Next we need to allow the Guest account to log in.

4. Open *Apple* menu > *System Preferences* > *Users & Groups*.

5. Select the Lock icon and authenticate as an administrator.

6. From the side bar, select the *Guest User* account. Enable the *Allow guest to log in to this computer* check box. Do not enable *Allow guests to connect to shared folders*, as this could present a serious security issue.

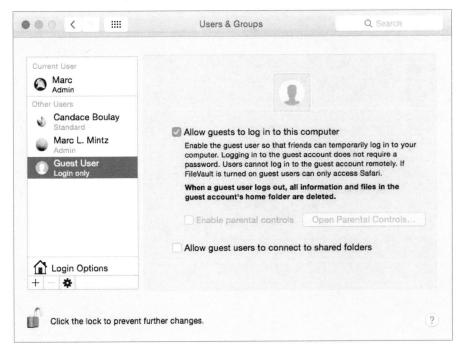

Next step is to ensure that a Guest is unable to modify any security-related System Preferences.

7. Select the *Show All* button.

8. Select the *Security & Privacy* icon.

9. Select the *Privacy* tab.

10. Select the Lock icon and authenticate as an administrator.

11. Enable the *Enable Location Services* checkbox.

12. Select the *Advanced* button.

13. Enable *Require an administrator password to access locked preferences*, and then select the *OK* button. This will stop a Guest, as well as other non-administrators, from changing critical system preferences.

Lastly, in the event that a Good Samaritan finds your computer, let's provide contact information so they can call you to return the computer.

14. Open *Apple* menu > *System Preferences* > *Security & Privacy*.

15. Select the *General* tab.

16. Select the *Set Lock Message…* button.

17. Enter the message to be displayed at the log in screen and screen saver. This will be displayed as one long line.

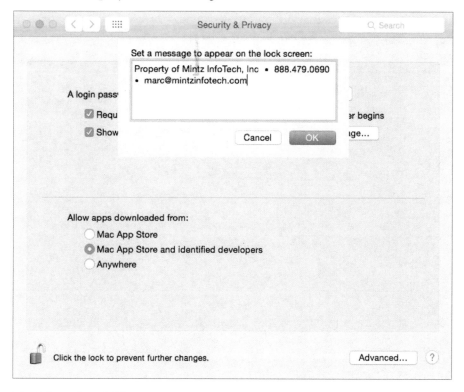

18. Select the *OK* button.

19. Quit System Preferences.

Find My Mac is now configured and active. In the event of loss or theft, you have a good chance of locating your computer.

Assignment: Use Find My Mac from a Computer

For the purposes of this assignment, let's assume someone has taken your Mac and we will use Find My Mac to locate it. As there are two ways this can take place depending on the device used, we have two assignments: Locating your stolen Mac using Find My Mac from another computer, and locating your stolen Mac using an iPhone or iPad and the Find iPhone app.

1. Turn your Mac on and log into the only account available to the thief–Guest.

2. Connect to the Internet. Wi-Fi will be more accurate with a location, but Ethernet will sometimes work as well.

3. On another computer (Windows or OS X), launch a web browser, visit iCloud at *http://icloud.com,* and then enter your Apple ID and password:

   - If you don't have another computer available, just perform this exercise on your own computer, logged in as Guest:

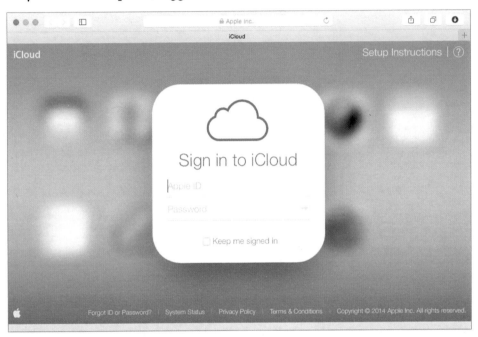

4. The iCloud desktop will appear. Select the *Find My iPhone* button.

5. At the prompt, enter your iCloud password again.

6. The Find My iPhone map appears.

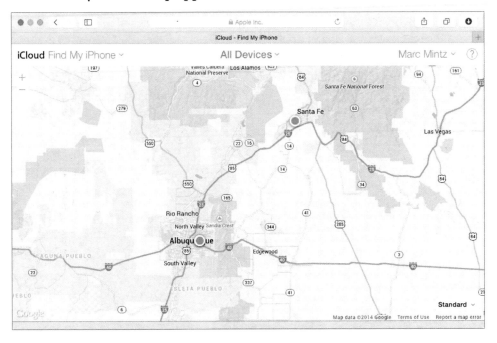

7. At top, select the *All Devices* menu. All of your registered devices with Find My Mac and Find My iPhone enabled will appear. If the device is powered on, it will have a green light next to it.

8. From the *All Devices field*, select the device to be located. Zooming into the map will provide a detailed location.

9. Once located on the map, a pop-up window with the name of your device will appear. If you wish, you have access to three options.

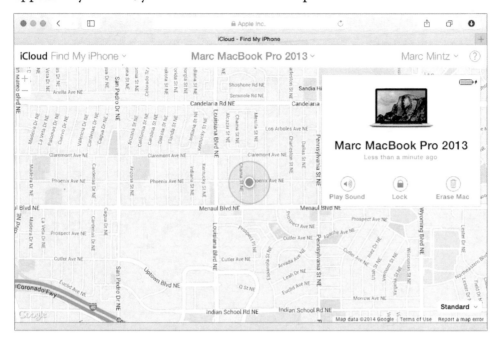

- *Play Sound*. This will play a "sonar" sound and display an alert window on the device.

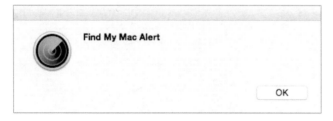

- *Lock*. This will lock down your system, preventing any use. I don't recommend either the Play Sound or Lock options, as it will notify the thief that you are tracking them. They may turn off the computer, blocking any future tracking, or worse; destroy the "tracking device."

- *Erase Mac*. If it is not possible to get prompt police intervention, you have valuable data on the computer, and the thief may have access to a server farm to perform a massive password hack attempt, you may want to consider simply erasing your Mac. After all, you do have a full current backup, don't you?

Assignment: Use Find My Mac From an iPhone or iPad

For this assignment we will assume the thief took your only Mac, and you don't have access to another computer. However, you do have access to an iPhone or iPad.

1. If you don't already have the *Find My iPhone* app installed on your device, visit the App Store and download it.

2. Open the *Find My iPhone* app.

3. Enter your *Apple ID* email address and *password*, and then select the *Go* key.

4. The *Find My iPhone* screen will open. Select the target device to locate.

5. The Find My iPhone map will open, displaying the exact last known location for the target device.

6. Select the device icon. The Info screen will open. From here you may have the device play a sonar sound (I use this at least once a week–my Yellow Lab is

obsessed with hiding my iPhone), lock it to prevent any access, or erase the drive.

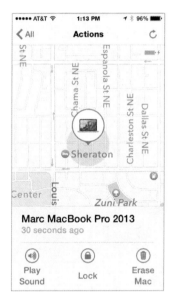

7. When done, exit the Find My iPhone app.

Hooray! You've found your lost/stolen device.

Review Questions

1. Find My Mac is enabled by default. (True or False)

2. Should the Guest account be enabled when Find My Mac is active, and why?

3. A lost Mac may be located via Find My Mac only with another OS X or iOS device. (True or False)

11. Vulnerability: When It Is Time To Say Goodbye

Don't cry because it's over. Smile because it happened.

–Dr. Seuss

Preparing a Computer for Sale or Disposal

The time comes when all good things must come to an end. This is just as true for your beloved Macintosh. But, your Mac holds all of your documents, passwords, pictures, web browsing history, etc. Not the items you would like someone else to see. Even if you are tossing your damaged computer into the trash, there is the very real probability that someone will find it, remove the drive, and harvest all your data.

So before selling, giving away, or trashing your Mac, all data on the drive must be made inaccessible. There are two options:

- Securely erase the drive

- Physically destroy the drive

If you have to comply with DoD, DoE, NSA, or other top security regulations, you may have to physically destroy the drive. For the rest of us, we have a built-in application to securely erase a drive.

Secure Erase a Storage Device

If the storage device (SSD, hard disk drive, or flash drive) has been encrypted using FileVault 2, all that needs to be done is to unencrypt the storage device using Disk Utility (located in /Applications/Utilities/) by performing a reformat without encryption, and you have securely erased the device.

If the storage device (hard disk drive only, not solid state devices) has not been encrypted, Disk Utility provides the tools to erase magnetic drives (hard disk drives) to Department of Defense standards. Even though these same tools can be run on a solid state drive (SSD and flash drive), they are not 100% effective, leaving some of your data accessible. For this reason the DoD and all other governmental agencies generally do not permit the erasure of SSD's prior to sale, instead requiring the SSD to be physically destroyed. However, for use outside of DoD, first encrypting the SSD/flash with FileVault 2, and then unencrypting will provide a high level of secure erasure.

Assignment: Secure Erase a Boot Drive

In this assignment, we will show the steps to secure erase a non-boot drive. Do not do this unless you intend to erase all of your data.

1. Restart your computer into *Recovery HD mode* by holding down the cmd+R keys immediately after restart.

2. At the *OS X Utilities* window, select *Disk Utility*.

3. From the sidebar, select the volume to be erased (indented names).

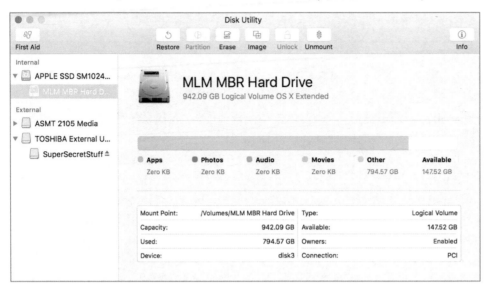

4. If the volume name is gray, this indicates FileVault 2 is enabled and the volume needs to be mounted. If the volume name is black, skip to step 11.

5. From the *Toolbar*, select the *Unlock* icon.

6. Enter the password for any user authorized to boot from this volume, and then select the *Unlock* button.

7. The volume will mount, and the volume name will now appear in black.

8. Select the *Erase* button.

9. From the *Format* drop-down menu, select *OS Extended (Journaled)*.

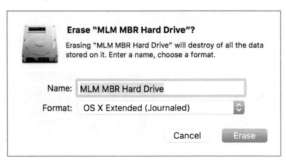

10. Click the *Erase* button.

Done! By removing the FileVault 2 encryption, the data on the drive is no longer readable.

11. From the toolbar, select the *Erase* button.

12. From the *Erase* window, select the *Security Options...* button.

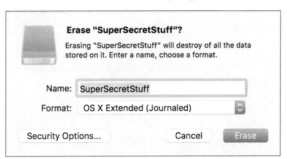

13. In the *Security Options* window, select your desired level of secure erase.

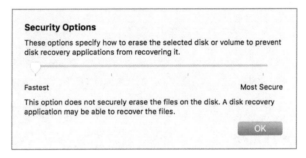

- *Fastest* only erases the directory structure, but leaves the data intact. It is trivial to recover data from such an erase procedure, but this only takes a few seconds.

- One tick to the right writes a single pass of zeros over the entire disk, directory and data. Depending on the disk size and speed, this may take from a few minutes to hours. Though this is considered secure, a determined hacker can recover your data.

- Two ticks to the right meets DoE compliance regulations for security with a 3-pass erase over the entire disk. This will take 3 times longer than the single pass of zeros. Highly sophisticated hackers might be able to recover your data.

- *Most Secure* meets DoD compliance regulations for security with a 7-pass erase over the entire disk. This will take 7 times longer than the single pass of zeros. It is highly unlikely anyone but the government will be able to recover data from this procedure. If you have the time, this is the step to take.

14. Select the *OK* button, and then click the *Erase* button to start the erase process.

Assignment: Secure Erase a Non-Boot Drive

In this assignment, we will show the steps to secure erase a non-boot drive. Do not do this unless you intend to erase all of your data.

1. Connect the non-boot drive to your Mac so that it mounts on the Desktop.

2. Open Disk Utility, located in /Applications/Utilities.

3. From the sidebar, select the volume to be erased (indented names).

4. If the volume name is gray, this indicates FileVault 2 is enabled and the volume needs to be mounted. If the volume name is black, skip to step 10.

5. From the Toolbar, select the *Unlock* icon.

6. Enter the password for any user authorized to boot from this volume.

7. The volume will mount, and the volume name will now appear in black.

8. From the toolbar, select the *Erase* button.

9. From the *Format* drop-down menu, select *OS Extended (Journaled)*.

10. Click the *Erase* button.

Done! By removing the FileVault 2 encryption, the data on the drive is no longer readable.

1. From the toolbar, select the *Erase* button.

2. Select the *Security Options* button.

3. From the *Secure Erase Options* window, select how to erase the drive.

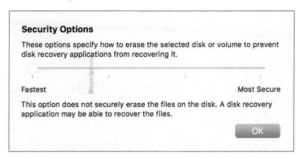

- *Fastest* only erases the directory structure, but leaves the data intact. It is trivial to recover data from such an erase procedure, but this only takes a few seconds.

- One tick to the right writes a single pass of zero's over the entire disk, directory and data. Depending on the disk size and speed, this may take from a few minutes to hours. Though this is considered secure, a determined hacker can recover your data.

- Two ticks to the right meets DoE compliance regulations for security with a 3-pass erase over the entire disk. This will take 3 times longer than the single pass of zero's. Highly sophisticated hackers might be able to recover your data.

- *Most Secure* meets DoD compliance regulations for security with a 7-pass erase over the entire disk. This will take 7 times longer than the single pass of zero's. It is highly unlikely anyone but the government will be able to recover data from this procedure. If you have the time, this is the step to take.

4. Select the *OK* button, and then select the *Erase* button to begin the process.

Review Questions

1. To secure erase a boot device requires booting into _____ .

2. When erasing a storage device, the *Fastest* option erases all directory information and data. (True or False)

3. If a storage device is using FileVault 2 encryption, it can be securely erased by reformatting without encryption. (True or False)

12. Vulnerability: Local Network

I am concerned for the security of our great Nation; not so much because of any threat from without, but because of the insidious forces working from within.

–General Douglas MacArthur

Ethernet Broadcasting

It is common wisdom that Ethernet is more secure than Wi-Fi. But as with most things we believe, this is not accurate.

There are two security issues with Ethernet: Broadcasting and Insertion. At the most fundamental level, what is happening when data travels through Ethernet is that electrons are traveling along a metal cable. There are two unintended consequences that occur whenever electrons go for a ride–heat generation, and the creation of an electromagnetic field. For our purposes, heat isn't an issue. But the electromagnetic field is.

Sending data through copper wire effectively turns that wire into a very large antenna that is broadcasting your data through radio waves. If you have the right receiver and translation software, you can easily capture every bit of data being sent and received along that cable.

This vulnerability is not something about which the average person or business would or should be concerned. On the other hand, if you or your business requires the utmost in security, it is mandatory to add encryption to your Ethernet network.

Speaking specifically about OS X, computer-to-computer communications are not encrypted, and so are not recommended. When using computer-to-OS X Server communications, then all communications are encrypted. For business, this means that users should not do file sharing between themselves, but instead copy any file to the OS X Server for others to copy back to their own computers.

Ethernet Insertion

You would notice if someone came into your home, plugged a computer into your network, and sat there watching data go by. But in the typical business, nobody would notice.

Ethernet and Wi-Fi networks can be protected from unwanted insertions by implementing the 802.1x protocol (often referred to as RADIUS) *http://en.wikipedia.org/wiki/IEEE_802.1X*. This protocol works with both Ethernet and Wi-Fi, mandating that anyone attempting to join the network authenticate with their own personal name and password. This is unlike the typical Wi-Fi authentication that uses the same password for everyone.

To implement 802.1x you need to have either an OS X, Windows, or Linux Server running within your network, or one of the many other 802.1x appliances that are available. Details on how to configure 802.1x are beyond the scope of this book. Please consult the following for more information:

OS X Server Administrator Guide at *http://help.apple.com/advancedserveradmin/mac/*

Jedda at *http://jedda.me/2012/11/configuring-basic-radius-os-108-server/*

Wi-Fi Encryption Protocols

Right out of the box almost all Wi-Fi base stations are insecure. Anyone that can pick up the signal can connect. This allows them not only to use your bandwidth to access the Internet, but also to see all of the other data–such as usernames and passwords–that are travelling on that network. All that is needed to secure your Wi-Fi is to add strong password protection with encryption.

Although cellular networks do use encryption, the protocol in use has been broken for many years, making it easy for a novice hacker to see all the data passing on it. In addition, it is common practice for police and other government law enforcement agencies to set up their own cellular towers with the purpose of harvesting data.

In order to prevent your data from being seen while on a cellular network or an unencrypted Wi-Fi network, it is necessary to use VPN (Virtual Private Network) encryption (more on that later.) If the Wi-Fi network is properly encrypted, you should have little concern over the security and privacy of your data.

Below you will find the brief on each of the Wi-Fi encryption protocols.

- **WEP** (Wired Equivalency Protocol) *http://en.wikipedia.org/wiki/Wired_Equivalent_Privacy* was the first encryption protocol for Wi-Fi. Introduced in 1999, it was quickly broken, and by 2003 was replaced by WPA and WPA2 (Wi-Fi Protected Access). Any Wi-Fi base station manufactured in the past 5 years will offer WPA and WPA2, in addition to WEP.

  There is only one reason to ever use WEP–you simply have no other option. Kids driving by your home can likely break into your WEP network before leaving the block.

- **WPA** (Wi-Fi Protected Access) *http://en.wikipedia.org/wiki/Wi-Fi_Protected_Access* superseded WEP in 2003. Although it is a great advancement, it too has been broken. As with WEP, the only reason to use WPA is that you have no other option.

- **WPA2** *http://en.wikipedia.org/wiki/Wi-Fi_Protected_Access* is the only protocol considered secure. WPA2 superseded WPA in 2004. Although in the past year WPA2 has been broken, it is very difficult to do, and with strong passwords or with 802.1x still provides military-grade protection for your wireless networks.

There are two encryption algorithms that can be used–*TKIP* and *AES* (technically known as CCMP, but virtually all vendors refer to it as AES.) TKIP has been compromised and is no longer recommended. If your Wi-Fi device allows the option of AES, use only that. If it only allows for TKIP, trash the unit and purchase a more modern device.

Routers: An Overview

The connection point between your Internet Service Provider (ISP) and your Local Area Network (LAN) is most likely a router. A router is a device designed to connect two different types of networks, and provide resources for them to interact.

Common brands of routers include: Cisco, Linksys, Netgear, D-Link, Apple, and the many unbranded devices that Internet Service Providers lease to their customers.

Some newer routers, especially those provided by ISPs are all-in-one units containing several, if not all of the components below:

- **Modem**. The hardware that decodes and modulates the signal from your Internet provider to your cable or telephone jack. This is most likely to be a separate component if more than one device exists for your Internet connection.

- **Router**. A component that runs a specialized program, which allows hundreds of different devices to interact on a network, usually sharing a single IP address to the Internet. Routers use *Network Address Translation* (NAT) to convert and direct Internet traffic from websites to your computer and from your computer to other computers and peripherals on the *Local Area Network* (LAN).

- **Firewall**. Software which inspects data traffic between the internet and internally connected devices

- **Network Switch**. A hardware component that allows multiple devices to be connected simultaneously and interact with the router

- **Access Point**. A hardware component that allows tens or hundreds of wireless (Wi-Fi) devices to connect to it.

Every router has at least some basic security controls built in, including the ability to filter out what it thinks are attempts to hack into your network, and the ability to forward specific types of data packets to a specific computer within your LAN, or to point specific types of data packets to a specific computer on the Internet.

Malware, hackers, criminals, and even some government agencies, sometimes attempt to alter these configurations so that either the malware or the perpetrators have an easier time harvesting your data. Because of this, it is wise to routinely inspect the condition of your router. How often is *routine?* Within larger or security-conscious organizations with high-value data, it is common to have a network administrator dedicated to maintaining watch over the status of network equipment. For a small business or household, once every few months wouldn't be too often.

Assignment: Determine Your Wi-Fi Encryption Protocol

You find yourself at a hotel with Wi-Fi and the need to access the Internet. You have the need to ensure that your data is not intercepted. How do you determine if the Wi-Fi network is using WPA or WPA2 instead of WEP? Just attempt to access the network, and the dialog box will tell what protocol is in use.

For this assignment, take yourself to a location that has an available Wi-Fi network. Your own home will do.

1. From the *Wi-Fi* icon in the menu bar, select the target network.

2. The authentication window will appear, requesting authentication and informing you of the security protocol.

   - If it does not appear, either the network does not use encryption, or your Keychain may be storing the password from a previous time you were connected.

If you have already connected to the Wi-Fi network and don't recall which security protocol it uses, you can find it from the Wi-Fi menu icon.

3. Hold down the *Option* key while clicking on the Wi-Fi menu icon. The Wi-Fi submenu will display with expanded information, including the encryption protocol in use, if any.

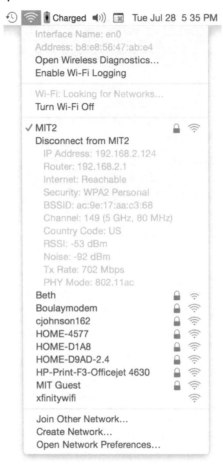

If the protocol is WPA2, life is all rainbows and unicorns. If it is anything else, *everything* you do on that network is clearly visible to others and I strongly recommend not using this network unless you have installed *VPN* software to encrypt your Internet traffic (more on this later.)

Assignment: Apple Airport Extreme Wi-Fi Encryption

Every Wi-Fi base station model has its own unique configuration method. We will detail how to configure your Apple Airport Extreme for WPA2 protection. For this exercise we assume you are on a network with an Apple Airport Extreme base station.

1. Open *Airport Utility.app*, located in your */Applications/Utilities* folder. Select the target base station.

2. The target base station information pane will appear. Select the *Edit* button.

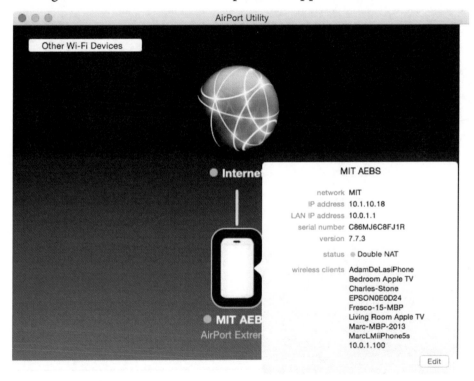

3. If so prompted, enter the administrator name and password for the base station.

4. Select the *Base Station* tab. Enter a strong administration password here.

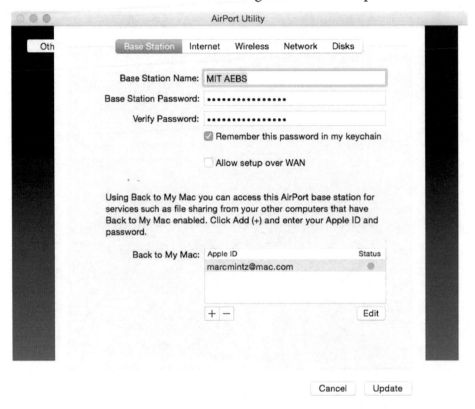

5. Select the *Wireless* tab and then configure as follows.

- From the Wireless Security pop-up menu, select *WPA2 Personal.* If you have older wireless equipment, you may need to change this to *WPA/WPA2 Personal* to offer compatibility with your older equipment. Keep in mind that doing so severely compromises your network security.

- In the *Wireless Password* and *Verify* Password fields, enter a strong password.

6. Click the *Update* button.

7. *Quit* Airport Utility.app.

Congratulations! All traffic across your Wi-Fi network is now securely encrypted.

Assignment: Non-Apple Wireless Router Wi-Fi Encryption

Although all Wi-Fi routers or base stations are configured differently, most follow a basic template. In this assignment we will be using an ASUS RT-AC3200. We will assume you are on a network with a similarly managed router.

Find the IP address of your Wi-Fi router.

1. Open the *Apple* menu > *System Preferences* > *Network*.

2. If needed, click the lock icon and authenticate as an administrator.
3. Select the *Advanced* button.

4. Select the *TCP/IP* tab.

5. About half way down on the left side you will find the *Router* address. This is your Wi-Fi base station or router IP address.

6. Close System Preferences.

Now, on to configuration:

7. Open a web browser.

8. In the URL or Address field, enter the IP address of the Wi-Fi base station or router.

9. At the *Authentication* window, enter the administrator user name and password. This will be the administrator of the router, not of your computer.

10. The router control panel will appear.

11. From the sidebar, select the *Wireless* button. This will display the options available with your Wi-Fi. Of interest to us now is the *Authentication Method* and *WPA Encryption*. Verify that your Wi-Fi is configured to use the *WPA2* protocol. If it isn't, select it now, and then enter your desired strong password to access the network.

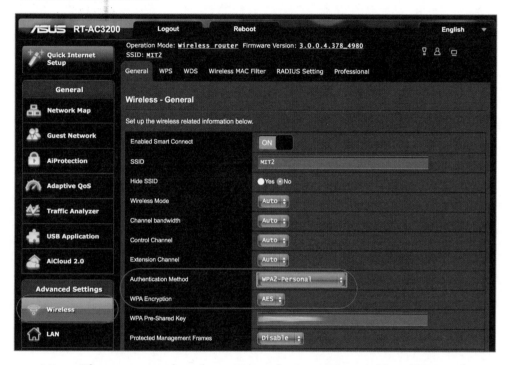

- Note: If your router has the option of using either *AES* or *TKIP*, select *AES*. The TKIP encryption scheme has been broken and is easily hacked.

- Note: Although the WPA2 Enterprise is the strongest security (even higher than WPA2), it requires network administrator skills and hardware that are outside the scope of this book.

12. If any changes were made, click the *Apply* button to save the changes.

13. Close the browser window to exit out of your router.

Congratulations! All traffic on your Wi-Fi is now securely encrypted.

Use MAC Address to Limit Wi-Fi Access

Every device that is capable of connecting to a TCP network has a unique *MAC Address* (Media Access Control) <http://en.wikipedia.org/wiki/MAC_address>. This address specifies the manufacturer of the device, and a device-specific number. Don't go to sleep on me yet! This MAC address can be used with most Wi-Fi base stations to limit what devices can connect to your network.

Although every Wi-Fi base station has a unique interface to filter by MAC address, they all operate on the same principle–either allow anyone with the proper password to gain access to the network, or allow anyone with the proper password *and* proper MAC address access to the network. In this way, you can easily lock down your Wi-Fi to only approved devices. So even if an employee knows the password, they are unable to connect their iPhone or personal computer to the Wi-Fi unless the MAC address for those devices are on the list.

Assignment: Restrict Access by MAC Address to Apple Airport

In this assignment we will configure our Apple Airport to allow only desired devices to connect.

1. Make a list of the devices to be permitted access to your Wi-Fi network. Include an identifying description and the MAC address of the device.

   - The MAC address of a Macintosh may be found in the *System Preferences > Network > Advanced...* button > *Hardware* tab.

- The MAC address of an iPhone may be found in the *Settings > General > About > Wi-Fi Address* field

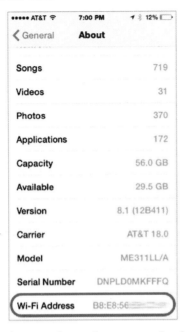

- The MAC address of a Windows device can be found with the ipconfig command in the command prompt.

- In Windows 8.1, right-click the Windows Taskbar button, and from the pop-up menu, select command prompt.

- The Command Prompt window appears.

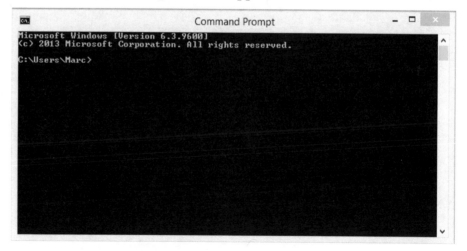

- Enter ipconfig –all. A listing of all network addresses for the device appears. The MAC address will show as the Physical Address.

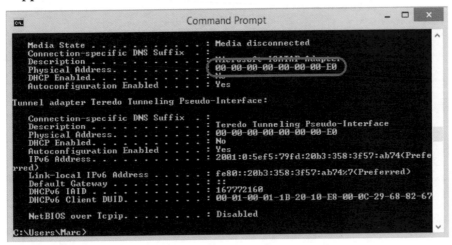

- Close the Command Prompt.

2. Launch *Airport Utility*. Located in the /Applications/Utilities folder.

3. Select your Airport base station, select the *Edit* button, and if necessary, authenticate for access.

4. Select the *Network* tab, enable the *Enable Access Control* check box, and then select the *Timed Access Control...* button.

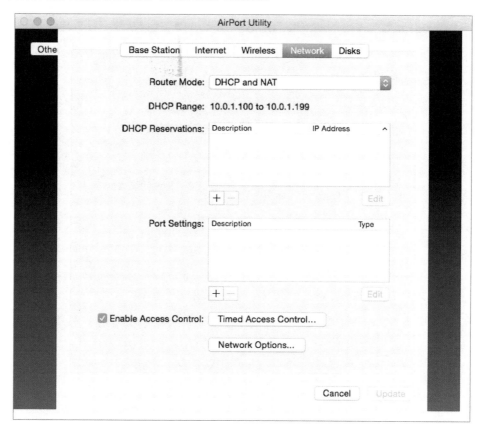

5. The *Timed Access Control* window appears.

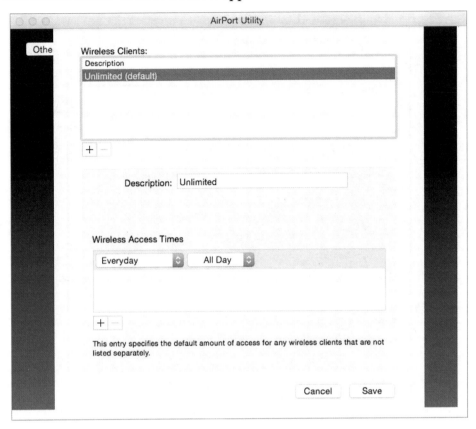

6. At the bottom left of the *Wireless Clients* field, select the + button. Configure as below:

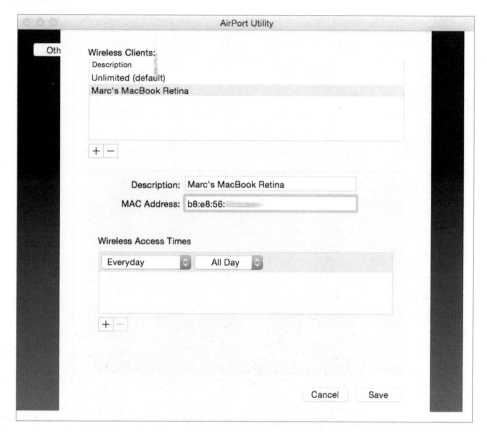

- *Description*: Enter a human-recognizable description of the device to be allowed access.

- *MAC Address*: Enter the MAC address of the device.

7. Repeat step 6 for every wireless device to have access to your network.

8. Select the *Save* button.

9. Any device not listed will be immediately dropped from your network.

10. Quit Airport Utility.

Congratulations! You have secured your wireless network so that only authorized devices are granted access.

Assignment: Restrict Access by MAC Address to a Non-Apple Router

In this assignment we will configure a non-Apple wireless router to allow only desired devices to connect. Although every wireless router or Wi-Fi base station is configured differently, they tend to use a similar template. In this example we will be using a Netgear R7000.

Find and record the IP address of your wireless router.

1. Open *Apple* menu > *System Preferences* > *Network*.

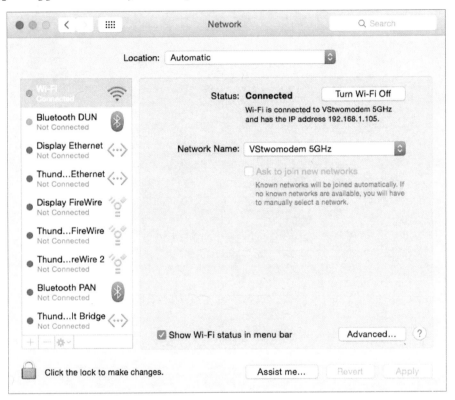

2. If necessary, unlock the preference.

3. Select the *Advanced* button.

4. Select the *TCP/IP* tab. The wireless router/Wi-Fi base station IP address will be found at the *Router:* field.

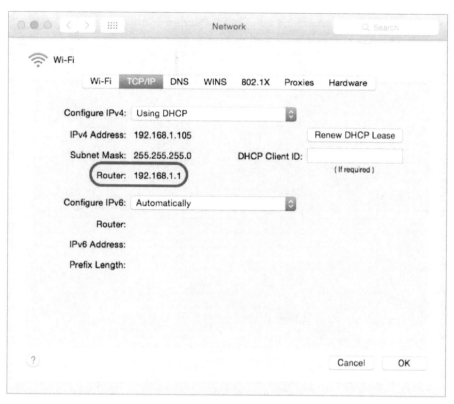

5. Quit System Preferences.

Make a list of the devices to be permitted access to your Wi-Fi network. Include an identifying description and the MAC address of the device.

6. The MAC address of a Macintosh may be found in the *System Preferences >
    Network > Advanced... button > Hardware* tab.

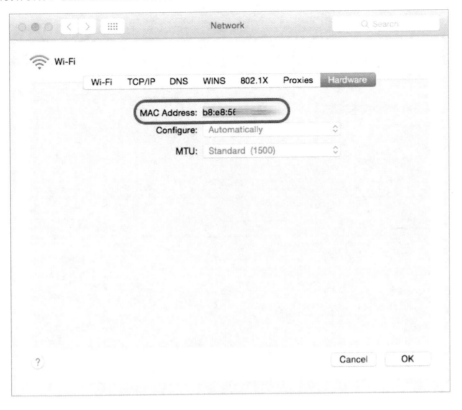

7. The Mac address of an iPhone may be found in the *Settings > General > About > Wi-Fi Address* field.

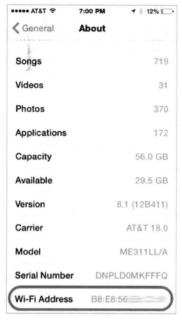

8. The MAC address of a Windows device can be found with the *ipconfig* command in the command prompt.

a. In Windows 8.1, right-click the *Windows Taskbar button,* and from the pop-up menu, select *command prompt.*

b. The *Command Prompt* window appears.

c. Enter *ipconfig –all*. A listing of all network addresses for the device appears. The *MAC* address will show as the *Physical Address*.

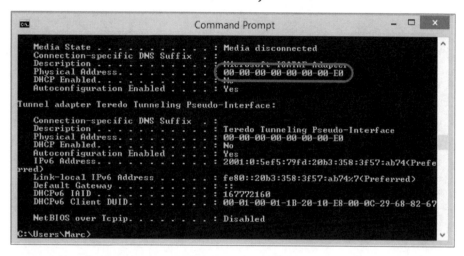

d. Close the Command Prompt.

9. Launch a web browser.

10. Enter the IP address of the wireless router.

11. In the *URL* or *Address* field, enter the IP address of the wireless router.

12. At the *Authentication* window, enter the user name and password of the router administrator. This is not the administrator of your computer.

13. The wireless router control panel will appear.

- Please keep in mind that all routers–even from the same company–have slightly different interfaces.

14. From the sidebar select *Wireless,* select the *Wireless MAC Filter* tab, enable the *Yes* radio button for *Enable MAC Filter,* and then se the *MAC Filter Mode* pop-up menu to *Accept.*

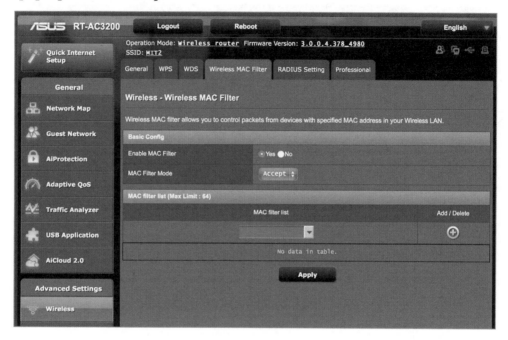

15. Clicking the disclosure triangle beneath the *MAC filter list* displays all of the devices currently connected to the router via Wi-Fi. Selecting any of these adds its MAC address to the *MAC filter list*. You may also manually enter a MAC address to this field.

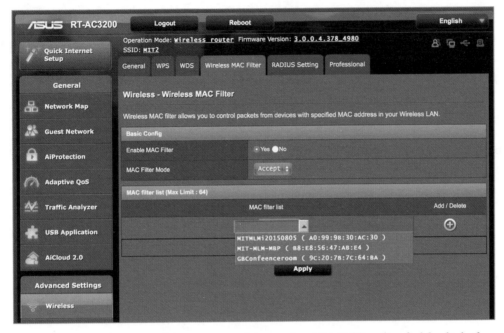

16. With a desired MAC address entered in to the *MAC filter list* field, click the *Add/Delete* button to add the device to the list.

17. Repeat the previous 2 steps for each devices to be allowed onto the Wi-Fi network.

18. Click the *Apply* button to save changes.

19. Close the browser window to exit out of your wireless router.

Congratulations! You have secured your wireless network so that only authorized devices are granted access.

Router Penetration

A more recent phenomenon is malware and hackers modifying router settings. Doing so allows for easy data harvesting from network traffic. Common areas of router penetration include:

- **Port forwarding:** Port forwarding is useful if you have a service such as a web server running that you wish to be accessible from the internet. However, if ports are being forwarded without purpose, the firewall is being bypassed and your internal computers may be visible from the internet.

- **DMZ:** Related to Port Forwarding is the DMZ, or De-Militarized Zone. DMZ is typically used to route *all* external traffic for a specific IP address, regardless of service request, to a specific computer. Unless there is a unique need, it should remain disabled.

- **RAM-Resident Malware:** Many router malware make their home in the RAM of the router. In this way they can take control of your data traffic without showing in the interface.

- **Firmware:** It is vital to keep the router firmware up to date. Just as with any software, router firmware will always have vulnerabilities. Over time, criminals (including some government organizations) discover how to use these vulnerabilities to their benefit. Keeping the firmware updated helps to stay a step ahead of this problem.

Router Security

The connection point between your Internet provider cable, DSL, fiber, radio, etc. and your Local Area Network (LAN) is most likely a *Router*. A router is a device designed to connect two different types of networks.

Every router has at least some basic security controls built in, including the ability to filter out what it thinks are attempts to hack into your network, and the ability to forward specific types of data packets to a specific computer within your LAN, or to point specific types of data packets to a specific computer on the Internet.

Malware often attempts to alter these configurations so that either the malware or the creeps behind the malware have an easier time harvesting your data. Because of this, it is wise to routinely inspect the condition of your router. How often is "routine?" Within larger organizations such as Apple, and other security-conscious organizations with high-value data, it is common to have a network administrator dedicated to maintaining watch over the status of network equipment. For a small business or household, once every few months wouldn't be too often.

Every router has a unique interface and may use different terms for the same configuration points. It would be wise to contact your Internet provider's technical support department to have them walk you through how your device should look. Take screenshots to use as reference in the future.

Assignment: Verify Apple Airport Port Security Configuration

In this assignment you will verify the integrity of your Apple Airport (Extreme or Express) base station.

Some malware will make its home in the router RAM. Also, over time router RAM may accumulate corruption. The fix for both issues is the same–power cycling.

1. After verifying that all users have disconnected from the Internet and have closed any connections to other devices on the network, pull the power cord from the back of the Apple Airport.

2. Wait a minute.

3. Plug the power cord back into the Apple Airport. It may take up to two minutes for it to be fully operational.

4. Open *Airport Utility,* located in */Applications/Utilities.* The main window opens. Click on the target base station (in this example, the *MIT ABS*.)

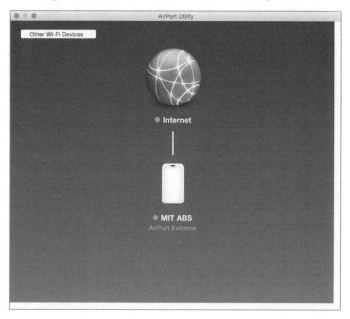

Verify there are no reported problems or firmware updates available.

5. In the pop-up window, to the right of *Status,* verify that there are no reported problems and that no update notification is present. If either condition exists, select the associated button to either resolve the issue or update firmware.

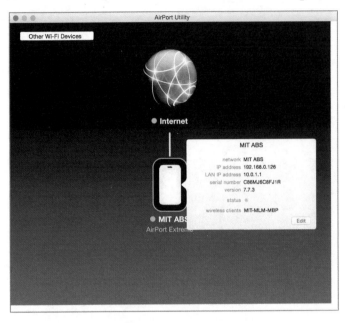

6. If there are no issues, select the *Edit* button.

Verify your DNS Servers are configured properly.

7. Select the *Internet* tab. Look in the *DNS Servers* fields and verify these are set to the IP address of the servers you wish to use. If you are uncertain, these may be set to:

- DNS Servers under the control of your Internet provider. You may contact them for the proper IP addresses.

- DNS Servers under the control of your organization. You may contact your IT department for the proper IP addresses.

- The IP address of your modem (not recommended, as you don't have certainty that the modem has not been compromised.)

- Any of the thousands of free and commercial DNS providers. In this example, we are using Google DNS.

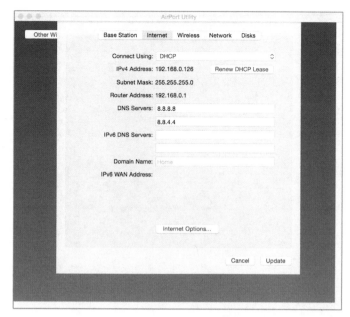

8. If changes to your *DNS Servers* has been made, select the *Apply* button.

Verify encryption is in place.

9. Select the *Wireless* tab.

10. Verify the *Wireless Security* field is set to *WPA2 Personal*, or if you know you have a RADIUS server within your environment, *WPA2 Enterprise*.

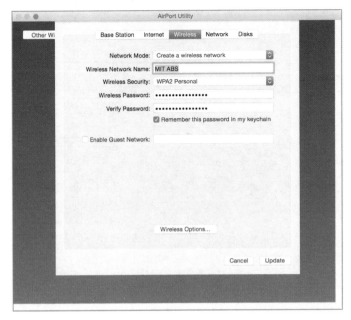

11. If changes have been made, select the *Update* button.

Verify port forwarding.

12. Select the *Network* tab. If there are any settings in the *Port Settings* area, verify there is a demonstrable business need for them, and that they are pointing to the proper devices. If not, remove them.

13. If any changes have been made, select the *Update* button.

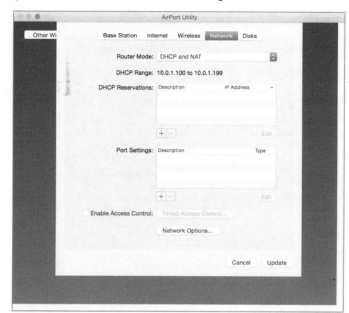

14. Quit Airport Utility.

You are in great shape. Be sure to repeat this check at least monthly.

Assignment: Verify Non-Apple Airport Router Security Configuration

In the example below I'm using an ASUS RT-AC3200. Although all routers have a somewhat different interface, most share the same functions.

Remove any RAM-resident malware

Some malware will make its home in the router RAM. Also, over time router RAM may accumulate corruption. The fix for both issues is the same–power cycling.

1. After verifying that all users have disconnected from the Internet and have closed any connections to other devices on the network, power off the router. If yours does not have an on/off switch, pull the power cord from the back of the router.

2. Remove the router batteries (if any).

3. Wait a minute.

4. Insert the router batteries (if any).

5. Power on the router. It may take up to 3 minutes for it to be fully operational.

6. Open a browser and enter the IP address of your router.

7. At the prompt, enter the administrator user name and password.

Verify router firmware is up to date.

8. Select *Administration* from the sidebar, and then select the *Firmware Upgrade* tab.

9. Scroll down to the *Firmware Version* field. The currently installed version number is listed.

10. To the right of this field is the *Check* button. Select it.

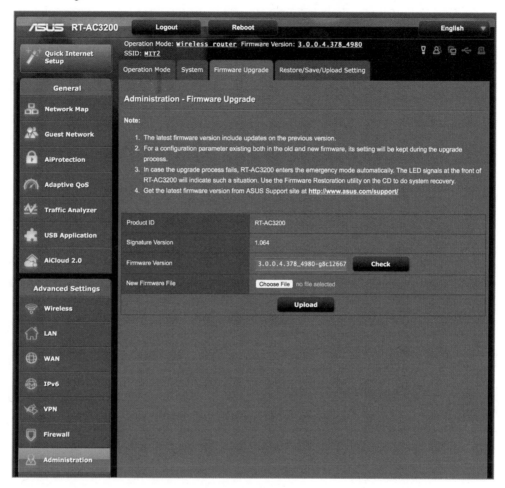

11. A dialog box will display, stating either the firmware is up to date, or a new version is available.

12. In this example, there is a more recent version, so we will select the *OK* button to download and install the update. If there is no new version available, exit the browser.

13. Note: During the download/install, the router will be offline, breaking Internet access for all on the network.

14. The firmware is downloaded.

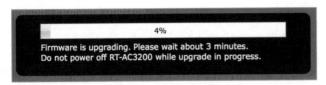

15. When the download/install completes, you may exit the browser.

Verify no unnecessary Port Forwarding.

16. In the sidebar select *WAN,* select the *Virtual Server/Port Forwarding* tab, scroll down to the *Basic Config* area. View if *Enable Port Forwarding* is set to *Yes.* If it is, verify there is a demonstrable business need for this feature to be on. More information will be found in the next step.

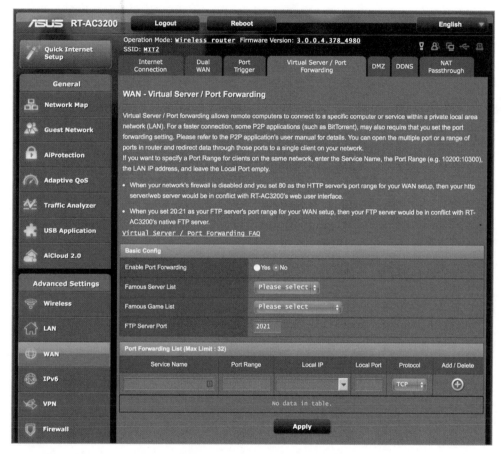

17. Scroll further down to the *Port Forwarding List* area. If Port Forwarding is turned on, this area will list which network services are being routed to which devices. Verify there is a demonstrable business need for this configuration. If not, then turn *Enable Port Forwarding* to *No.*

18. Select the *Apply* button.

Verify DMZ configuration.

Similar to Port Forwarding is *DMZ*. When *DMZ* is enabled, all inbound packets are routed to that device. This allows a single device on your network to be accessible from the Internet. This presents a very high level of vulnerability for that device. Unless there is a demonstrated business need for this function, and adequate steps have been taken to prevent unwanted penetration, turn *DMZ* off.

19. From the router control panel sidebar, select *WAN*, and then select the *DMZ* tab.

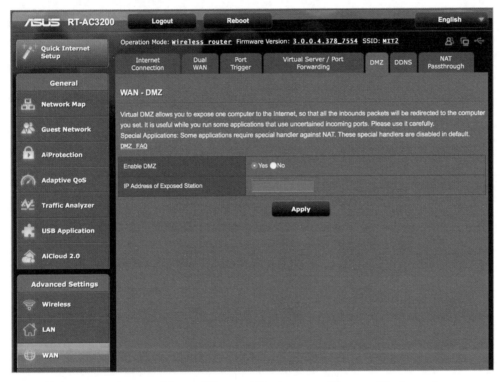

20. Scroll down to the *Enable DMZ* area. If it is set to *Yes,* verify there is a demonstrable business need for this function. The next step will provide additional information.

21. Below *Enable DMZ* is *IP Address of Exposed Station.* If *DMZ* is enabled, verify there is a true need for it based on this device. If not, set *Enable DMZ* to *No.*

22. If changes were made, select the *Apply* button.

23. Exit the browser.

Congratulations, your router is in great shape. Remember to perform this same checkup at least monthly.

Review Questions

1. OS X client to OS X client communications are encrypted. (True or False)

2. OS X client to OS X server communications can be encrypted. (True or False)

3. The WEP Wi-Fi encryption protocol should be used whenever possible. (True or False)

4. The WPA Wi-Fi encryption protocol should be used whenever possible. (True or False)

5. The WPA2 Wi-Fi encryption protocol should be used whenever possible. (True or False)

6. Of the two encryption algorithms–TKIP and AES–which should be used?

7. The network hardware that decodes and modulates the signal from your Internet provider to your cable or telephone jack is called a _____ .

8. The network hardware that allows hundreds or thousands of devices to interact between the local network and Internet is called a _____ .

9. The network hardware or software that inspects data traffic between the Internet and local network devices is called a _____ .

10. The network hardware that allows multiple devices to connect and interact with each other and the router is called a _____ .

11. The network hardware that allows tens or hundreds of wireless devices to connect to a network is called a _____ .

12. The network connection speed between an OS X computer and Wi-Fi Access Point can be found by _____ .

13. A _____ address includes a unique manufacturer code and a unique device code.

13. Vulnerability: Web Browsing

Distrust and caution are the parents of security.

–Benjamin Franklin

HTTPS

Due to an extraordinary marketing campaign, everyone knows the catchphrase: *What happens in Vegas, stays in Vegas.* With few exceptions, web surfers think the same thing about their visits.

Most websites use HTTP (Hypertext Transport Protocol) to relay information and requests between user and website and back again. HTTP sends all data in clear text–anyone snooping on your network connection anywhere between your computer and the web server can easily see everything that you are doing.

Typically, the only exceptions you will come across are financial and medical sites, as they are mandated by law to use HTTPS (Hypertext Transport Protocol Secure). HTTPS uses the SSL (Secure Socket Layer) encryption protocol to ensure that all traffic between the user and server is military-grade encrypted.

- NOTE: With the recent changes in Google SEO guidelines that give a higher priority to HTTPS sites, it will soon become common for sites to use encryption.

Although it is unlikely that you would ever be in the position to enter your password or bank account into an unsecure web page, you are almost guaranteed to enter your identity information, such as full name, address, phone number, and social security number. It is effortless for an identity thief to copy this information.

Anytime that you visit a web page that is secured using https, it will be reflected in the URL or address field of your web browser.

In the following example, I visit Wikipedia.org by entering *http://www.wikipedia.org* in my browser address field:

In the next example, I visit Wikipedia again, but this time I enter *https://www.wikipedia.org* in the address field:

Note how the address field reflects that I am now connected securely by displaying https and the *Lock* icon. Each browser will indicate security slightly differently–some displaying just the https, some just the lock.

Now that I am connected securely to Wikipedia, snoops will not be able to see my actions. However, they still can see that I am connected to Wikipedia. If you would like to shield yourself completely, continue reading to our chapter on using a Virtual Private Network (VPN.)

Having to remember to connect via HTTPS for each web page is an impossible task. First, you have other, more important items to store in your synapses. Second, many websites do not have an HTTPS option, resulting in many error pages and wasted time during the day.

There are two options to resolve this:

- Automate the attempt to connect to sites via HTTPS

- Encrypt your entire online session using VPN

Using VPN is covered in a later chapter. Automating the attempt to connect via HTTPS is both easy and free. All it requires is a freeware plug-in, *HTTPS Everywhere.*

HTTPS Everywhere is available for Firefox, Opera, and Chrome. Unfortunately, this currently leaves Safari users without the option. If you are happy to use either of these two browsers instead of Safari, there is no reason not to install HTTPS Everywhere!

Assignment: Install HTTPS Everywhere

HTTPS Everywhere is available for Firefox, Opera, and Chrome. For this example we will be using Firefox.

1. Open Firefox.

2. Select the *Tools* menu > *Add-ons.*

3. Select *Get Add-ons* from the sidebar.

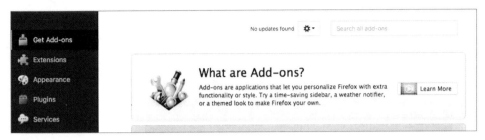

4. In the *Search* field, enter *https everywhere,* and then press the *Return* key. Matching items will appear below.

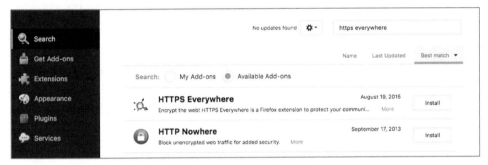

5. Select the *Install* button to the right of *HTTPS Everywhere.* HTTPS Everywhere will download.

6. When the download completes, select the *Restart Now* link.

7. Firefox will restart.

8. The *SSL Observatory* window will open. Select *Yes.*

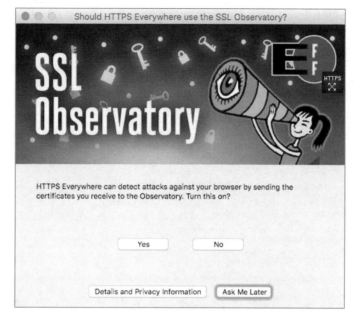

9. Select the *Tools* menu > *HTTPS Everywhere* > *SSL Observatory Preferences.*

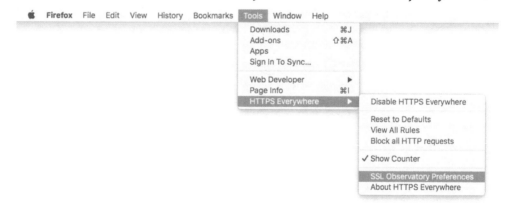

10. The *SSL Observatory Preferences* window opens. Select the *Show advanced options.* Configure as below, and then select the *Done* button:

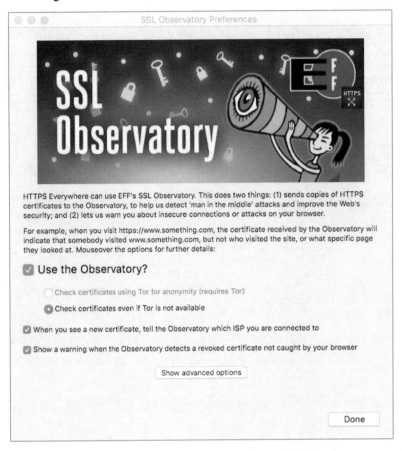

From now on, if a website has an HTTPS option (not all do), then you will be routed automatically to that page instead of the default unsecure page. If the site does not have an HTTPS option, the default unsecure page will load.

Safari Private Mode, Firefox Private Browsing, and Chrome Incognito

Private Mode (Safari), *Private Browsing* (Firefox), and *Incognito Mode* (Chrome), a feature that prevents any normally cached data from being written to the hard drive while using a browser. This data includes browsing history, passwords, user names, list of downloads, cookies, and cached files. This is an essential tool if you work on a computer where your account is shared (what's with that?.), or if there is the possibility that someone else will examine your browsing habits.

Assignment: Safari Private Browsing

Before we secure your website travels from roaming eyes out on the Internet, we should first be secure from the roaming eyes on the home front. If you have secured your computer to this point, including: Strong password, nobody else has access to your account, your *System Preferences > Security & Privacy* are set to *Require password after sleep or screen saver begins*, it is unlikely that you also need to implement *Safari Private Browsing*. But just in case…

1.   From the *Safari File* menu, select *New Private Window*.

2. A new Safari window will appear. Sites that are visited from within this window will leave no trace in the *History,* and cookies are not shared with any other browsing windows.

Assignment: Firefox Private Browsing

If you prefer Firefox to Safari, then let us enable its private browsing.

1. Launch Firefox.

2. Select the Firefox menu (3 lines) > *New Private Window.*

3. A new *Private Window* opens, informing that you are now, well, browsing privately.

    • NOTE: A Firefox *Private Window* will display a mask icon in the left side of a private tab, and in the top right corner of a private window.

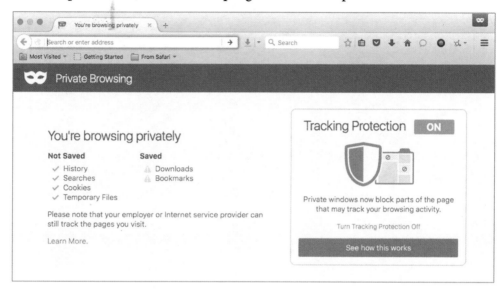

Assignment: Google Incognito Mode

If your preference leans toward Google Chrome, you can enable its *Incognito Mode*.

1. Launch Google Chrome.

2. Select the *File* menu > *New Incognito Window*.

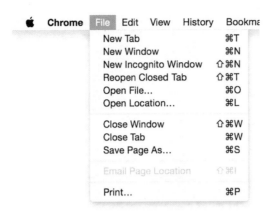

3. A new *Incognito Window* opens, informing that you have now, gone incognito.

- NOTE: A Chrome *Incognito Window* will display the incognito icon in the top right corner, and the title bar will turn dark.

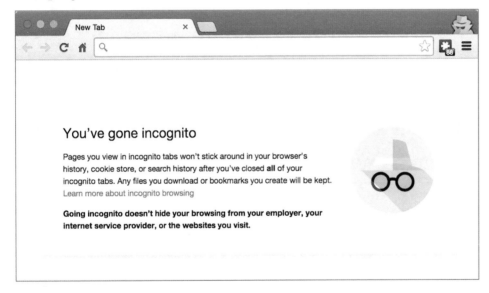

Secure Web Searches

With most web browsers, when performing a search, the search criteria and sites visited are collected and stored by the search engine. The Cookies assigned from one website can communicate with other sites and webpages you open. Also, most search engines record your searches and build a profile of your search history so that your search results will be unique and tailored to your interests.

Not so with the *DuckDuckGo* search engine. DuckDuckGo's policy is that it keeps no information on user searches, nor does it track search queries via IP addresses. Subsequently, all search results are identical for everyone.

Starting with OS X 10.10, Safari offers the option to make DuckDuckGo your default search engine. This is a big step towards providing a better level of privacy on the Web.

Assignment: Make DuckDuckGo Your Safari Default Search Engine

In this assignment, you will change the default Safari search engine from Google to the secure search engine DuckDuckGo.

1. Open Safari.

2. Open the *Safari* menu > *Preferences*.

3. Select the *Search* icon from the Toolbar.

4. From the *Search Engine* pop-up menu, select *DuckDuckGo.*

5. Close the Preferences window.

From now on, your default search engine for Safari will be *DuckDuckGo*, hiding your search activities.

Assignment: Make DuckDuckGo Your Firefox Default Search Engine

In this assignment, you will change the default Firefox search engine to the secure search engine DuckDuckGo.

1. Open Firefox.

2. Select the *Firefox* menu > *Preferences*.

3. Select *Search* from the sidebar, and then select *DuckDuckGo* from the *Default Search Engine* pop-up menu.

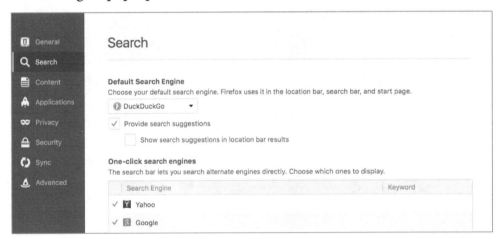

4. Close the Preferences window.

From now on, your default search engine for Firefox will be *DuckDuckGo*, hiding your search activities.

Assignment: Make DuckDuckGo Your Chrome Default Search Engine

In this assignment, you will change the default Chrome search engine to the secure search engine DuckDuckGo.

1. Open Chrome.

2. Select the *Window* menu > *Extensions,* scroll to the bottom of the *Extensions* window, and then select *Get more extensions.*

3. From the sidebar, select *Extensions,* in the search field, enter *DuckDuckGo,* and then press the *Return* key. *DuckDuckGo Home Page* listing will appear.

4. To the right, select the *ADD TO CHROME* button.

5. Close the Preferences window.

From now on, your default search engine for Chrome will be *DuckDuckGo,* hiding your search activities.

Clear History

You just realized that: 1) Your mother is coming over, 2) you have been naughty on the web all day, 3) you did not turn on Safari Private Browsing, and 4) your mom will feel insulted if you insist that an account for her must to be created instead of accepting her protest: "Oh, baby, I only need to check my AOL email. Just let me get on your account for a minute."

Is it time to panic?

Not yet! You can erase your entire (steamy) Safari history in one click.

Assignment: Clear the Safari History

In this assignment you will clear your entire browsing history in Safari. Be forewarned, there is no recovery from this action. If you wish to keep your history, pass on this assignment.

1. Open Safari, and then select the *History* menu > *Clear History...*

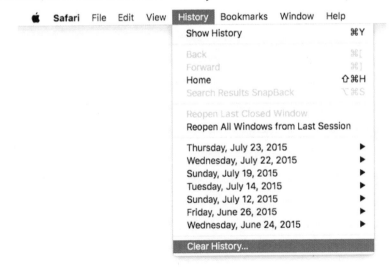

2. A dialog box opens asking for what time frame you wish to clear your history. Make your selection, and then select the *Clear History* button.

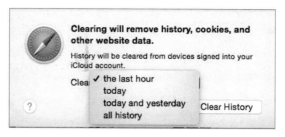

The Safari history is now cleared as you defined.

Assignment: Clear the Firefox History

In this assignment you will clear your entire browsing history in Firefox. Be forewarned, there is no recovery from this action. If you wish to keep your history, pass on this assignment.

1. Open Firefox.

2. Select the *History* menu > *Clear Recent History…* The *Clear All History* window opens.

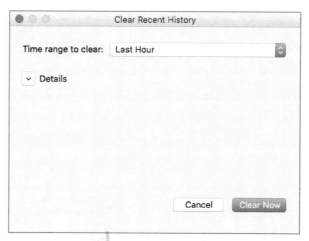

3. Select the *Details* disclosure button to expand your options.

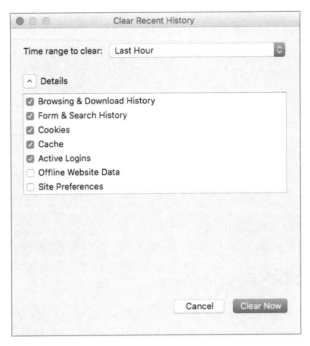

4. Select the *Time range to clear,* which history items are to be cleared, and then click the *Clear Now.*

5. Close the *Clear Recent History* window.

The Safari history is now history.

Assignment: Clear the Chrome History

In this assignment you will clear your entire browsing history in Chrome. Be forewarned, there is no recovery from this action. If you wish to keep your history, pass on this assignment.

1. Open Chrome.

2. Select the *Chrome* menu > *Clear Browsing Data*... The *Clear Browsing Data* window opens.

3. Select which items are to be cleared, and then click the *Clear Browsing data* button.

Done!

Adobe Flash and Java

Both Adobe Flash and Oracle Java are used by many websites to create a more animated or interactive web experience. The functions of both may soon be absorbed by HTML 5. Until that day comes, many of us will require both products in order to have fully-functioning website behaviors.

However, the power these products offer is a double-edged sword. They can also be used to take control of your computer. And very often are. There is a vicious cat and mouse game played by hackers who have discovered how to bend Flash and Java to their wills, and Adobe and Oracle patching these vulnerabilities.

The end result for users is they have a choice to make:

- Do not install Flash or Java, which renders some sites unusable.

- Install Flash and Java, and be vigilant with updates.

- Install Flash and Java, but don't be vigilant with updates. This renders their system highly vulnerable.

I suspect if you are one who ops for the last option, you aren't taking this course.

Either of the other two options are legitimate strategies. Both Adobe and Oracle have tried to make updates automatic, but we have found this process to be less than perfect. Many times we have found systems with out of date versions, even with their preference settings on *Automatic Updates.*

Associated with the vulnerabilities caused by out of date Flash and Java, are malicious or compromised web pages that prompt the visitor to update Flash, Java, or some audio/video codec. In most cases, if you follow the links provided on the site all that gets downloaded is malware.

If a site prompts you do install software, visit the website of the recommended software and download from there, not from the requesting site.

Assignment: Configure Adobe Flash Automatic Updates

In this assignment you will install Flash and configure it for automatic updates.

Install Adobe Flash.

1. Open *Apple* menu > *System Preferences.* If you see the Flash icon, it is already installed. If so, skip to the next section *Configure Flash for Auto-Updates.*

2. Open a browser, and then surf to *http://www.adobe.com/.*

3. Click the menu icon (3 lines) > *Adobe Flash Player.*

4. Click the *Install Now* button.

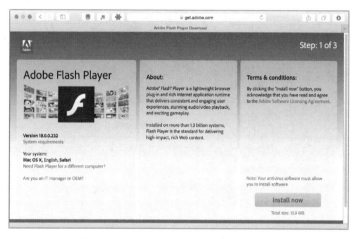

5. The Flash installer will download and open.

6. Double-click the installer, and then follow the on-screen instructions to complete installation.

Configure Flash for Auto-Updates.

7. Open *System Preferences* > *Flash Player.*

8. Select the *Updates* tab, select the *Allow Adobe to install updates (recommended)* radio button, and then click the *Check Now* button. This (at least in theory), verifies your system has the latest version of Flash, and authorizes Flash to automatically update.

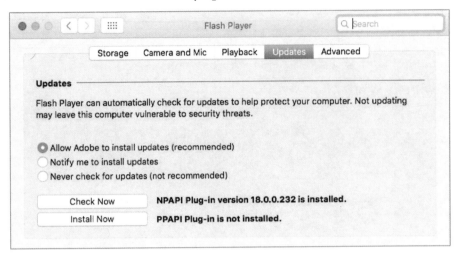

Manually check for Flash updates.

9. Open *System Preferences > Flash Player*.

10. Select the *Updates* tab.

11. Click the *Check Now* button. If an update shows as available, follow the on-screen instructions to download and install.

Assignment: Configure Oracle Java for Automatic Updates

In this assignment, you will install Java and configure it to automatically update.

Install Oracle Java.

1. Open *Apple* menu > *System Preferences*. If you see the Java icon, it is already installed. If so, skip to the next section *Configure Java for Auto-Updates*.

2. Open your browser to surf to *http://www.java.com/*.

3. Click the *Download* button.

4. Click the *Agree and Start Free Download* button.

5. Once the Java installer has downloaded, launch it, and then follow the on-screen instructions to complete installation.

Configure Java for Auto-Updates.

6. Select *System Preferences > Java.*

7. Select the *Update* tab, and then enable the *Check for Updates Automatically* checkbox.

At this point, both your Flash and Java are up to date, and configured to automatically update. However, there is a decent chance that they will not do so. It is wise to perform a manual update check at least monthly.

Manually check for Java updates.

8. Open *System Preferences > Java.*

9. Select the *Update* tab.

10. If updates are available, select the *Update Now* button, and then follow the on-screen instructions to download and install.

Web Scams

Over the past couple of years, a new type of scam has become popular. Instead of directly compromising the user computer, web sites are either compromised, or are deliberately designed to be malicious.

When a user visits such a site, they may receive a pop-up window stating something to the effect of: *Your computer has been found to be infected with XX viruses. Please call Apple at XXX-XXX-XXXX to have this infection removed.*

Upon calling the provided toll-free phone number (which, of course, is not really Apple, but that of the scammer), with your permission, they will install remote control software. After looking around your computer, they will assure they can remove the malware for only $$$.

There are two problems here. First, they have installed remote control software that allows the criminal access any time they wish. This gives them access to your usernames, passwords, banking, and other information. The second is that they now have your credit card information.

What to do if this happens to you?

1. Don't call!

In most cases, the malicious website has modified your web browser preferences to make the malicious page your home page.

2. Open your browser *preferences* (in this example, Safari) > *General*. If the *Homepage* field is not what you have set, delete the entry.

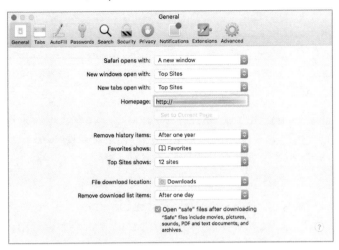

3. If you are not able to access your preferences to delete the homepage setting, open *System Preferences* > *General*, and enable *Close windows when quitting an app*.

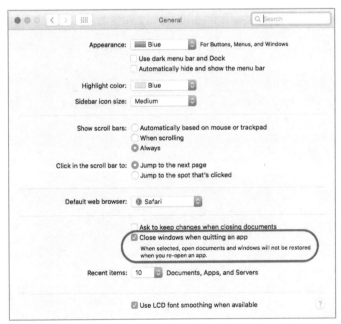

4. Quit Safari.

5. Open Safari to test. You should no longer have the malicious page open. Done!

Tor

Tor *http://en.wikipedia.org/wiki/Tor_(anonymity_network)* is a technology developed by the US Department of the Navy that enables anonymous web browsing. It has long since been released to the open source community for the public to use in the form of the *Tor Browser*. Many people within the security community are strong supporters of Tor, including Edward Snowden. Entire books have been written on just Tor. I'm not so sadistic as to subject you to that. What we are going to do is cut to the core of Tor, and learn the basics of how to surf the web anonymously.

The advantages of Tor include:

- Strong anonymity for all activity on the Internet.

- Can be used with Tails at *https://tails.boum.org*, which is a bootable, self-contained, flash drive that can run on most Windows, Linux, and Apple computers that leaves no trace behind

- The bootable Tails flash drive can be immediately disconnected from the host computer, causing the computer to erase memory of all trace of your session, and reboot.

These features make Tor ideal for those in oppressed countries, journalists working undercover, and anyone who may need to use someone else's computer and leave no trace behind.

Tor works by encrypting your packets as they leave your computer, routing the packets to a Tor relay computer hosted by thousands of volunteers on their own systems, many of which are co-located at ISPs. The relay knows where the packet came from, and the next relay the packet is handed to, but that is all. The user computer automatically configures encrypted connections through the relays. Packets will pass through several relays before being delivered to the intended destination. Tor will use the same relays for around 10 minutes, and then different relays will be randomly selected to create the next path for 10 minutes.

Alas, there is no free lunch. The encryption process and the relay process combine to create *latency*, which mean a delay in processing. Most users will experience around a four-fold performance degradation. So, if accessing a web page without Tor normally takes 3 seconds, it may take 12 seconds with Tor.

Something that Tor proponents tend to minimize is that Tor was developed by the U.S. Department of the Navy for military use, and then made available to the open source community. It is no secret that the U.S. government (and very likely other governments) host relays with the purpose of being able to monitor traffic over Tor. Several high-profile arrests have been made because of this tactic.

Even though Tor does as good a job as anything to keep you anonymous on the Internet, you must take precautions to protect your identity. These steps include:

- Don't enable JavaScript when using Tor. This has been used to track users within the Tor network.

- Don't reveal your name or other personal information in web forms.

- Don't customize the Tails boot flash drive. This will create a unique digital fingerprint that can be used to identify you.

- Connect to sites that use HTTPS so your communication is encrypted point to point.

For many security-conscious users, Tor becomes their only tool for defense. However, Tor by itself is a partial solution at best. It can protect your anonymity while surfing the web. At the very least, this still leaves email and messaging to be secured. A bigger issue is what to do when you need to use a computer and leave no trace behind on that system. This is where *Tails* comes into play.

Tails is a Linux Debian fork designed with two primary purposes in mind:

- Provide a highly secure operating system in a format that can be booted from either DVD or thumb drive on almost any PC or Apple computer, and

- Include the tools and applications necessary to provide a secure, anonymous Internet experience

What this means is that you can create a thumb drive that has an operating system capable of booting almost any computer, whereby you can then run Tor for secure anonymous Internet activity, send and receive email that is securely encrypted with GPG/PGP, and message with others in complete privacy. Then, when you remove the Tails thumb drive, there is absolutely no record of your activity on either the computer *or* the thumb drive!

For those of you chomping at the bit to just use Tor, we will start there. When your curiosity has been satisfied, please take the next step to learn Tails at *https://tails.boum.org.*

Assignment: Install Tor for Anonymous Internet Browsing

Tor is a stripped down, simplified web browser, designed to provide an encrypted, anonymous browsing experience. In this assignment, we will download and install Tor.

1. As a first step, we need to know our public IP address. This information will be used a few steps away to verify Tor has hidden our address. Open a web browser to http://whatismyip.com. Write down *Your IP*.

2. Open a web browser and go to *https://www.torproject.org*. Select the *Download Tor* button.

3. Select the *Download Tor Browser* button. The Tor installer will begin to download.

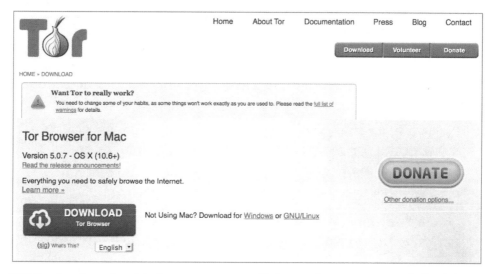

4. While the download is in progress, scroll down the page to read all of the other steps that one must take to ensure your privacy is maintained. These include:

   - **Use the Tor Browser.** If you are concerned about protecting your privacy and security, do not use other browsers.

- **Don't torrent over Tor.** If you wish to file-share via torrent, don't use Tor. It is painfully slow, it slows down others using the Tor network, and in many cases, torrent software bypasses all of the security and anonymity precautions built into Tor.

- **Don't enable or install browser plugins in Tor.** Tor is designed to protect your security and anonymity. Many innocuous-looking plugins break that security.

- **Use HTTPS versions of websites.** Tor has *HTTPS Everywhere* built in (more on HTTPS Everywhere later in this book.) It will force a secure connection if a website has an option for https. This will enable a point-to-point encryption between your computer and the web server.

- **Don't open documents downloaded through Tor while online.** Many documents–particularly .doc, .xls, .ppt, and .pdf–contain links or resources that will force a download when the document is opened. If they are opened while Tor is open, they will reveal your true IP address and you will loose your anonymity and security. If you are concerned about these issues, we strongly recommend that you instead:

  - **Open the documents on a computer fully disconnected from the Internet**. This prevents any malicious files from "phoning home" or infecting your computer.

  - **Install a Virtual Machine (VM) such as Parallels, Fusion, or VirtualBox, configured with no network connection, and open documents within the VM**. This is an alternate way to prevent malicious files from phoning home or infecting your computer.

  - **Or use Tor while within Tails**. This is an alternative way to prevent malicious files from phoning home or infecting your computer.

- **Use bridges and/or find company.** Tor cannot prevent someone from looking at your Internet traffic to discover you are using Tor. If this is a concern for you, reduce the risk by configuring Tor to use a *Tor Bridge relay* instead of a direct connection to the Tor network. Another option is to have many other users running Tor on the same network. In this way, your use of Tor is hidden.

5. Locate the Tor installer, and then double-click to open. It will mount and open a disk image onto the Desktop.

6. Drag the *TorBrowser.app* into your *Applications* folder.

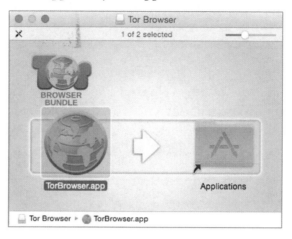

7. Locate the *TorBrowser* in your Applications folder, and then double-click to open it. The *Tor Network Settings* window appears. Select how you would like to connect to the Tor Network

   - *I would like to connect directly to the Tor network.* This will work in most situations. This option provides a faster Internet experience with no additional configuration. The possible downside is that a network administrator or your ISP is able to see that you are using the Tor Network.

   - *This computer's Internet connection is censored or proxied. I need to configure bridge or proxy settings.* This option provides a more secure and anonymous Internet experience as a network administrator or ISP is unable to see you using the Tor Network. The downside is a slower Internet experience, and some additional configuration.

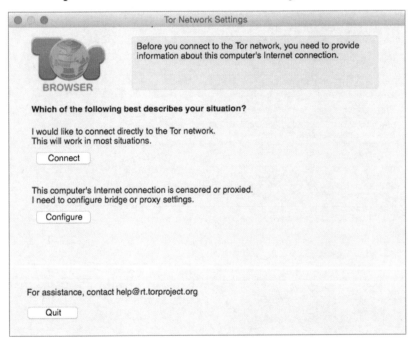

8. If you selected *This computer's Internet connection is censored or proxied. I need to configure bridge or proxy settings*, go to the next step. If you *selected I would like to connect directly to the Tor network*, skip to step 12.

9. If you elected to use a *Tor bridge relay*, the following window appears. If your network requires a proxy to access the Internet, go to the next step and select *Continue*. Otherwise, select *No,* select the *Continue* button, and skip to step 12.

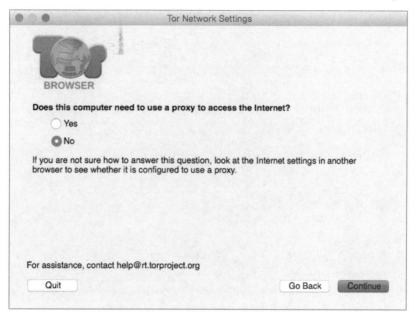

10. If you selected *Yes* to *Does this computer need to use a proxy to access the Internet* you will now see the Enter the Proxy settings window.

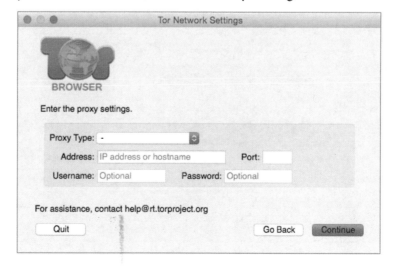

11. These will be the same settings your computer requires normally, and if used, will be found in *System Preferences > Network > Advanced > Proxies* tab. Copy your settings from this pane into the Tor window, and then select the *Continue* button. If your ISP blocks or otherwise censor's connections to the Tor network, go to the next step to create a Tor bridge relay. If they do not, skip to step 14 to start using Tor.

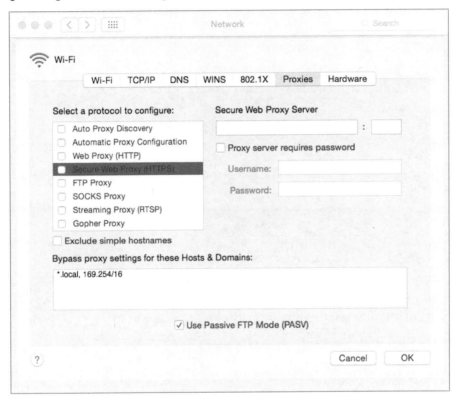

12. At the *Does your Internet Service Provider (ISP) block or otherwise censor connections to the Tor Network* window, for the overwhelming majority of users the answer is *No,* and then select the *Connect* button, and then skip to step 14. If your answer is *Yes,* select the *Yes* option, select the *Continue* button, and go to the next step.

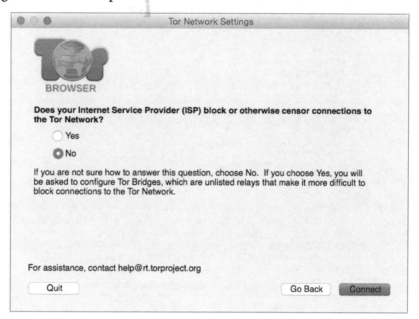

13. If you selected Yes to the *Does your ISP block or otherwise censor connections to the Tor* Network window, you now see the You may use the provided set of bridges or you may obtain and enter a customer set of bridges window. Select *Connect with provided bridges, Transport type obsf3 (recommended),* and then select the *Connect* button.

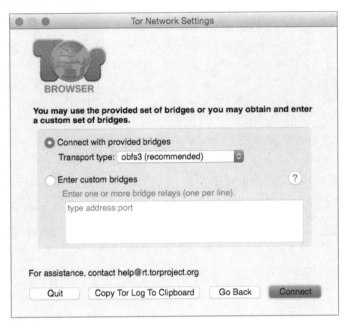

14. The Tor Browser updates often. If your copy is out of date, you will be welcomed by a message asking you to update. Follow the instructions, clicking on the *onion* icon > *Download Tor Browser Bundle Update…*to update. Once the download is complete, Quit TorBrowser, and then replace it with the new version. Otherwise, if you are up to date, skip to the next step.

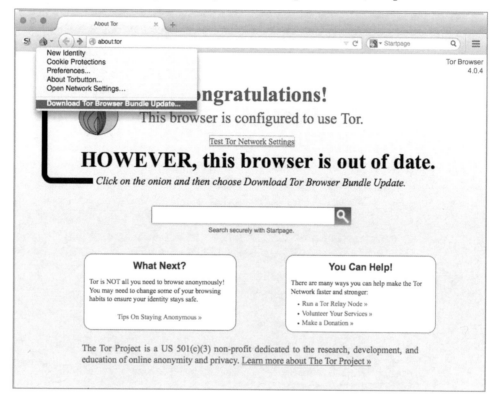

15. It is vital to test your connection to verify your IP address is hidden. While in Tor, go to *https://check.torproject.org.* You can also return to *https://whatismyip.com* as well.

Wahoo! You are now on Tor, completely anonymous and encrypted on the Internet. Next step is to configure Tor.

Assignment: Configure Tor Preferences

One of the first things one should do when launching an application for the first time is to configure its preferences. No different for Tor. In this assignment we will configure Tor preferences.

1. Open TorBrowser, and then select the *Tor Browser* menu > *Preferences* > *General* tab. This pane may be configured to taste.

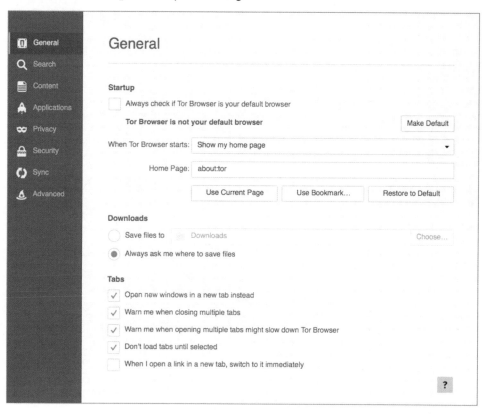

2. Select the *Search* tab.

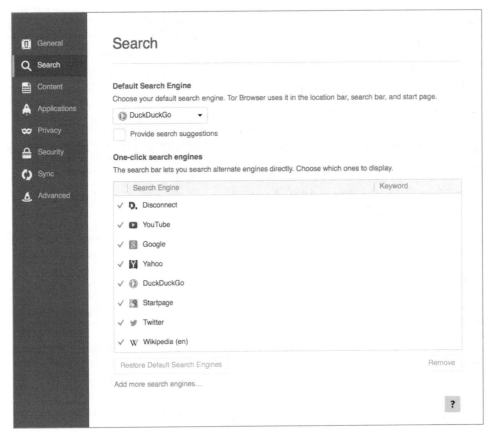

- For *Default Search Engine,* select *DuckDuckGo.*
- Other settings may be configured to your taste.

3. Select the *Content* tab. Configure to your taste.

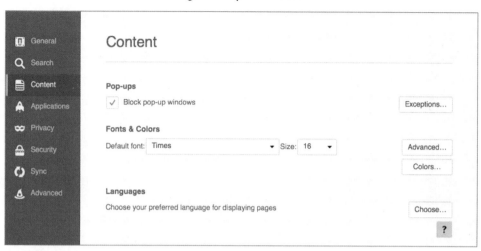

4. Select the *Applications* tab. Configure to your taste.

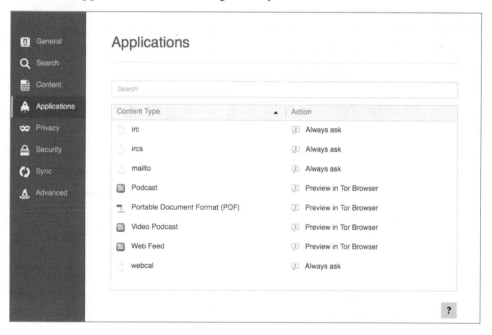

5. Select the *Privacy* tab.

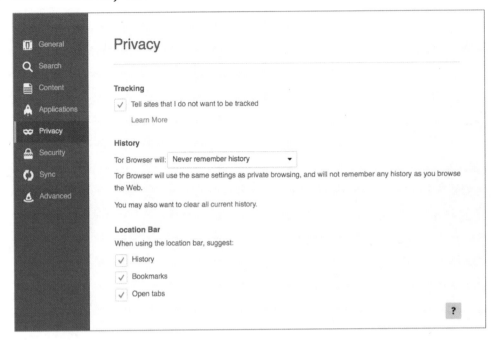

- Enable *Tell sites that I do not want to be tracked.*

- Configure other settings to your taste.

6. Select the *Security* tab.

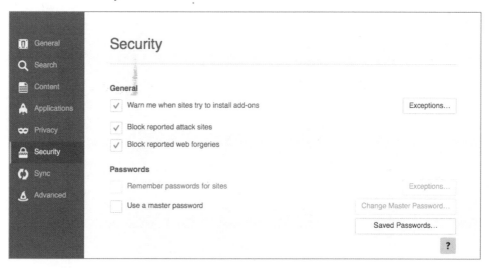

- Enable *Warn me when sites try to install add-ons.*

- Enable *Block reported attack sites.*

- Enable *Block reported web forgeries.*

- Configure other settings to your taste.

7. Select the *Sync* tab.

8. Select the *Security* tab. Configure as displayed below. Note that you will not be able to enable *Remember passwords for sites* or *Use a master password.*

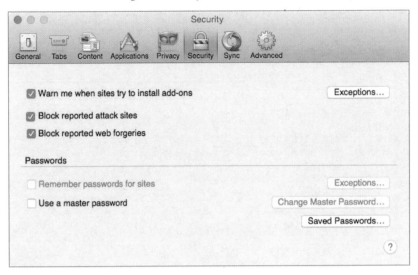

9. Select the *Sync* tab.

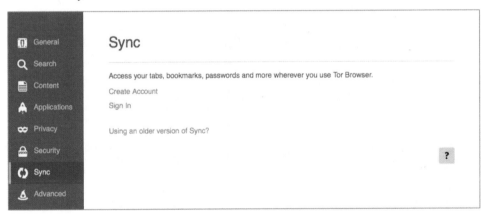

- Configure to your taste.

10. Select the *Advanced* tab, and then select the *General* tab.

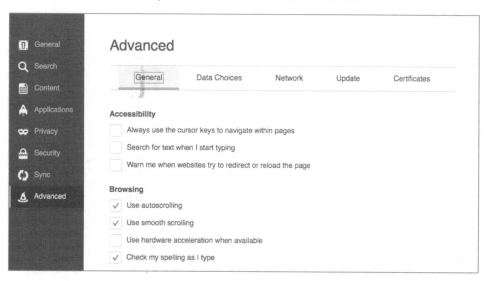

- Configure to your taste.

11. Select the *Data Choices* tab, and configure to your taste.

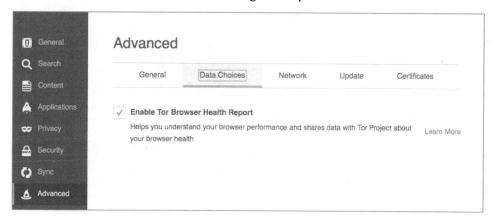

12. Select the *Network* tab.

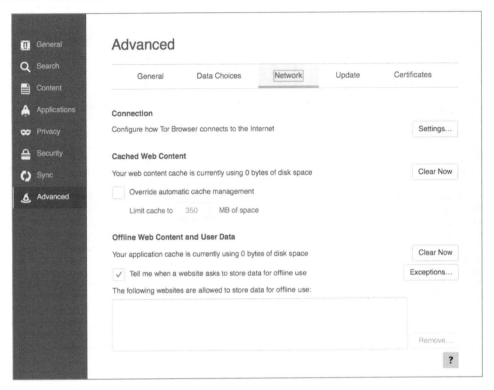

- Enable *Tell me when a website asks to store data for offline use.*
- Configure other settings to taste.

13. Select the *Update* tab.

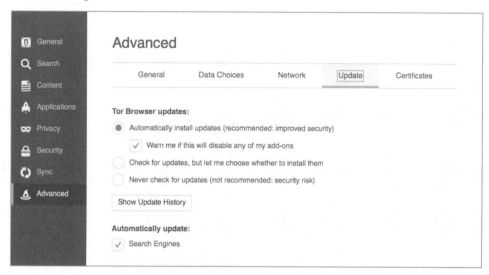

- Enable *Automatically install updates (recommended: improved security).*

- Enable *Warn me if this will disable any of my add-ons.*

- Enable *Automatically update: Search Engines.*

- Configure other settings to taste.

14. Select the *Certificates* tab.

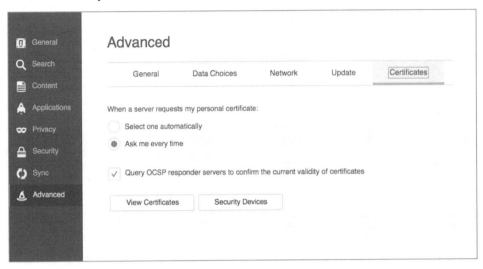

- Enable *Ask me every time.*

- Enable *Query OCSP responder servers to confirm the current validity of certificates.*

15. Close the preferences tab in Tor.

Great work! You are now ready to use Tor to securely and anonymously browse the Internet.

But remember, Tor is just one small part of *real* anonymity and security on the Internet. Many in the Internet Security field (including Edward Snowden) believe that to do this right, you will want a bootable Tails thumb drive. Learn all about it in our upcoming *Practical Paranoia: Tails Security Essentials* book. In the meantime, visit the Tails home page at *https://tails.boum.org.*

Onion Sites and the Deep Web

Tor not only allows you to have anonymous access to your regular web sites, it is also the only gateway to the *Deep web https://en.wikipedia.org/wiki/Deep_web_(search)*. The deep web is also known as the *Invisible Web*. It consists of web content deliberately not indexed with standard search engines, and only accessible by Tor. These sites are also called *Onion sites*, as they end with *.onion*.

Although the deep web is primarily thought of as a collection of sites to sell illegal products and services, it is also good and responsible uses for it. For example, in repressive countries such sites provide an avenue for freedom workers to work, for reporters to securely exchange information with sources (Ed Snowden did this), and there are sites to provide resources for whistleblowers.

As the deep web is not indexed by Google, Bing, or any other standard search engine, how do you go about discovering its resources? The list is in constant flux, but as of this writing, here are some good starting points:

- TorLinks *http://torlinkbgs6aabns.onion*
- Torch *http://xmh57jrzrnw6insl.onion/*

Review Questions

1. HTTPS uses the _____ encryption protocol.

2. To ensure your browser goes to https even if entering http, install the _____ plug-in.

3. To ensure your browser doesn't store browsing history, passwords, user names, list of downloads, cookies, or cached files, enable _____ mode.

4. By default, any two people will have the same results for a given Google search. (True or False)

5. By default, any two people will have the same results for a given DuckDuckGo search. (True or False)

6. TOR is based on the _____ browser.

7. It is OK to install browser plug-ins to TOR. (True or False)

14. Vulnerability: Email

Human beings the world over need freedom and security that they may be able to realize their full potential.

–Aung San Suu Kyi, Burmese opposition leader and chairperson of the National League for Democracy in Burma

The Killer App

It can be rightfully argued that email is the killer app that brought the Internet out of the geek world of university and military usage and into our homes (that is, if you can ignore the overwhelming impact of Internet pornography.) Most email users live in some foggy surreal world with the belief they have a God or constitutionally given right to privacy in their email communications.

No such right exists. Google, Yahoo!, Microsoft, Comcast, or whoever hosts your email service all are very likely to turn over all records of your email whenever a government agency asks for that data. In most cases, your email is sent and received in clear text so that anyone along the dozens of routers and servers between you and the other person can clearly read your messages. Add to this knowledge the recent revelations about PRISM *https://en.wikipedia.org/wiki/PRISM_(surveillance_program)*, where the government doesn't have to ask your provider for records, the government simply *has* your records.

If you find this as distasteful as I do, then let's put an end to it!

Phishing

The act of phishing is epidemic on the Internet. Phishing *https://en.wikipedia.org/wiki/Phishing* is the attempt to acquire your sensitive information by appearing as a trustworthy source. This is most often attempted via email.

The way the process often works is that you receive an email from what appears to be a trustworthy source, such as your bank. The email provides some motivator to contact the source, along with what appears to be a legitimate link to the source website.

When you click the link, you are taken to what appears to be the trustworthy source (perhaps the website of your bank), where you are prompted to enter your username and password.

At that point they have you. The site is a fraud, and you have just given the criminals your credentials to access your bank account. In a few moments your account may be emptied.

The key to preventing a successful phishing attack is to be aware of the *real* URL behind the link provided in the email.

The link that appears in an email may have nothing at all to do with where the link takes you. To see the *real* link, hover (don't click) your cursor over the link. After 3 seconds, the *real* link will pop-up.

Some of these scams are getting a bit more sophisticated in their choice of URL links, and attempt to make them appear more legitimate. For example, the email may say it is from *Bank of America*, and the link say *bankofamerica.com*, but the actual URL will be *bankofamerica.tv*, or *bankofamerica.xyz.com*.

If you have any doubts at all, it is best to contact your bank, stock broker, insurance agent, etc. directly by their known email or phone number.

Email Encryption Protocols

There are three common protocols that provide encryption of email between the sending or receiving computer and the SMTP (outgoing), IMAP (incoming), and POP (incoming) servers:

- **TLS** (Transport Layer Security)
  http://en.wikipedia.org/wiki/Secure_Sockets_Layer

- **SSL** (Secure Socket Layer), the TLS predecessor
  http://en.wikipedia.org/wiki/Secure_Sockets_Layer and

- **HTTPS** (Hypertext Transport Layer Secure) *http://en.wikipedia.org/wiki/Https*

Understand that these protocols only encrypt the message as it travels between your computer and your email server and back. Unless you are communicating with only yourself (sadly, as most programmers are prone), this does little good unless you know that the other end of the communication also is using encrypted email. If they aren't, then once your encrypted mail passes from your computer to your email server, it becomes clear text from your email server, through dozens of Internet routers, to the recipient email server, and finally onto the recipient's computer.

TLS and SSL

In order to use TLS or SSL, the following criteria must be met:

- Your email provider offers a TLS or SSL option. Many do not. If your provider does not offer this, *run*, don't walk, to another provider. If you are not sure which to select, I'm a fan of Google mail.

- You are using an email application as opposed to using a web browser to access your email.

- Your email application supports TLS or SSL.

- Your email provider has configured your email service to use TLS or SSL.

- You have configured your email application to use TLS or SSL

- Lastly, although not a requirement for TLS or SSL, a requirement to stall off breaking your password is that your email provider allows for strong passwords, and you have assigned a strong password to your email (many providers still are limited to a maximum of 8 character passwords.)

Assignment: Configure Email to Use TLS or SSL

If you use a web browser for email, you may skip this assignment and move on to the next where we configure your browser-based email to use https.

First we need to verify if your email currently uses TLS or SSL:

1. Open Mail.app, located in */Applications* and in your *Dock*.

2. Select the *Mail* menu > *Preferences*.

3. From the *Mail Preferences,* select the *Accounts* tab.

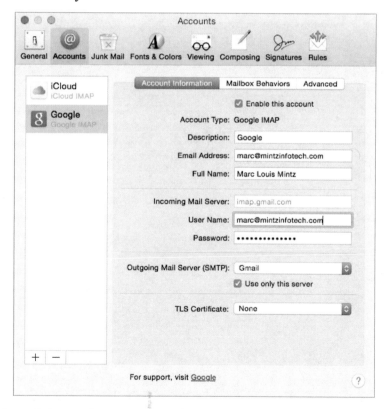

4. From the side bar, select your email account.

5. Select the *Account Information* tab.

6. From the *Outgoing Mail Server* (SMTP) pop-up menu, select *Edit SMTP Server List*.

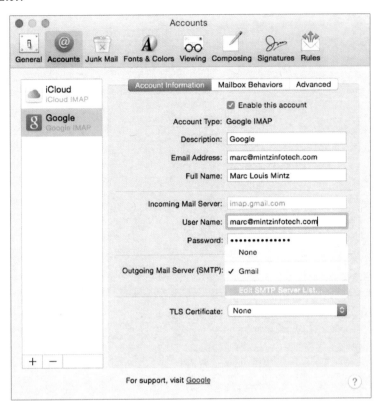

7. In the *Edit SMTP Server List* window, select the *Account Information* tab.

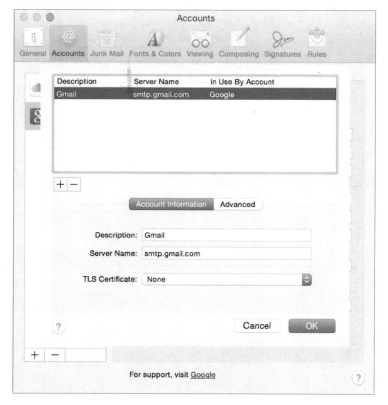

8. In the top field, select the server to be used by this email account.

9. In the *Description* field, enter the email address using this server.

10. In the *Server Name* field, enter the Fully Qualified Domain Name for this server. This information can be found by asking your email vendor.

11. Select the *Advanced* tab.

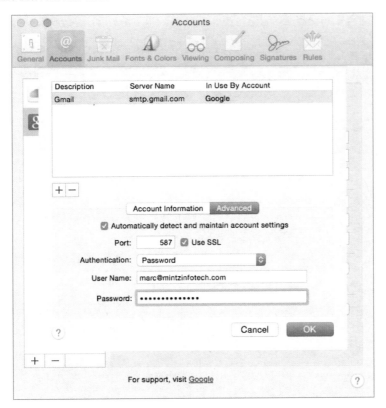

12. Verify that the Use Secure Sockets Layer (SSL) checkbox is enabled.

- Although OS X only provides a checkbox for SSL, this will enable TLS as well.

- If SSL is not enabled, contact your email provider and ask if they do work with TLS or SSL. If they don't, change providers NOW.

13. If they do support TLS or SSL, find out if there are any special settings that need to be changed in this window, and then make the changes.

14. Keep the provider on the line for the next steps.

15. Select the *OK* button, returning you to the *Accounts* window.

16. Select the *Advanced* tab in the *Accounts* window. About halfway down, verify that the *Use SSL* checkbox is enabled.

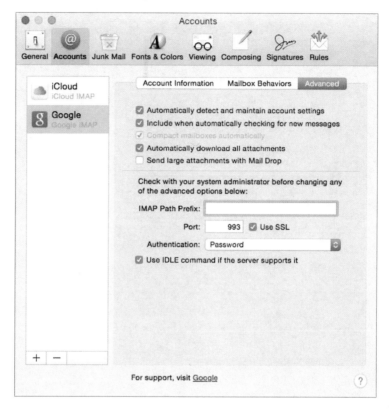

- Although OS X only provides a checkbox for *SSL*, this will enable TLS as well.

- If not, ask your email provider if there are any special settings that need to be changed in this window, and then make the changes.

17. If your password isn't strong (a minimum of 14 characters), now is the time to speak with your email vendor's technical support to have it changed. Once changed at that end, enter the new longer password in the *Mail Preferences > Account Information* tab.

18. Close the *Mail Preferences* window.

You now are sending and receiving encrypted email between your computer and your email server. Keep in mind you have no control over any encryption of your email between your server and the sender/recipient at the other end.

HTTPS

We discussed HTTPS in the previous chapter. It is an encryption protocol used with web pages. It also can be used to secure email that is accessed via a web browser. When using HTTPS your user name and password are fully encrypted, as are the contents of all email that you create or open.

When using a web browser to access email, it is vital that your email site use the HTTPS encryption protocol to help ensure data and personal security.

Assignment: Configure Browser Email to Use HTTPS

If you use a web browser to access your email, it is critical that your web connection use HTTPS. In this assignment we will verify that your browser-based email uses HTTPS:

1. Launch your web browser.

2. Go to your log in page for your email. In the example here we will be using Google Mail (Gmail).

3. As in the screen shot below, make sure that the URL field shows either the lock to the left of the URL, or *https://* and not *http://*. This indicates you are communicating over a secure, encrypted pathway.

4. If instead your browser shows the URL to be http://, try revisiting your email log in page, but this time manually enter https://.

5. If you get to the log in page, all is good. Just bookmark the https:// URL and use it instead of the previous non-secure URL.

6. If you cannot get to your log in page, change your email provider NOW!

End-To-End Secure Email With SendInc

Using TLS/SSL or HTTPS for email is a good start. Unfortunately, unless you are certain that the other end of the communication chain also is using *the same email system as yourself*, this is much like locking your front door when leaving for vacation, while leaving the back door open. The reason is that even if the other user has TLS/SSL or HTTPS, this only ensures security between their computer and their server. When the two of you exchange email, there is no guarantee that the email is not in plain text once it hits either server, or when being transmitted from sender to recipient servers.

If you are serious about email security, then you need to use an end-to-end secure email solution.

There are two ways to approach this:

- Use an email encryption utility. This works well as long as the other end of the communication also is using the same encryption utility. Our next chapter will cover this strategy using *GNU Privacy Guard* and *S/MIME*.

- Use a cloud-based option. This method makes it every bit as simple to send and receive email as the user is accustomed to. The downside is that instead of using an email client, a website is used to send and receive mail.

We will be discussing the email encryption later in this chapter. Here we will focus on the cloud-based option.

Our recommendation is to use *SendInc* <https://SendInc.com>. SendInc has several advantages for the typical user. These include:

- Both a free and pro service are offered.

- The pro service is only $5/month.

- Military-grade end-to-end encryption of username and password, email, and attachments are included.

- The free version automatically self-destructs the email after 7 days. The pro version allows the user to determine the destruction date and includes unlimited retention.

- The free version allows up to 20 recipients/day. The pro version allows 200.

- The pro version allows retraction of a sent email (if it has not yet been opened).

- The pro version allows for rich text email. The free version is text-only.

When sending from SendInc, you log into an HTTPS home page that also serves as your email composition page. Once the message is sent (fully encrypted), your recipient receives an email stating that a secure message is waiting. The recipient clicks the link, taking the recipient to an authentication page. Upon entering the password (which is automated if this is other than a first visit), the recipient then sees the message. The recipient can directly reply securely to the message, and you then receive an email informing you a secure message is waiting.

Although not quite as convenient as using your own email software, when security, convenience, and cost are taken into consideration against the impacts of violating HIPAA requirements, or the potential drama of confidential communications being intercepted, we find SendInc to be an easy choice.

Assignment: Create a SendInc Account

1. Using your web browser, visit SendInc *http://SendInc.com*. Select the *Sign Up* button.

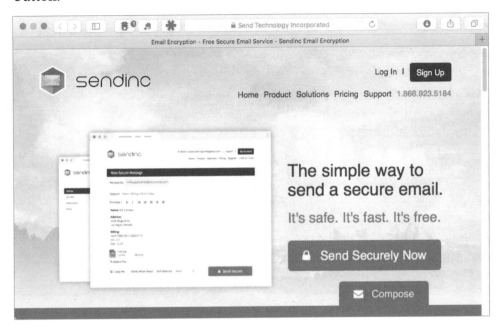

2. The *Sign Up* page opens. You can compare the *Pro* and *Corporate* options. Select the *Start Free Trial* button.

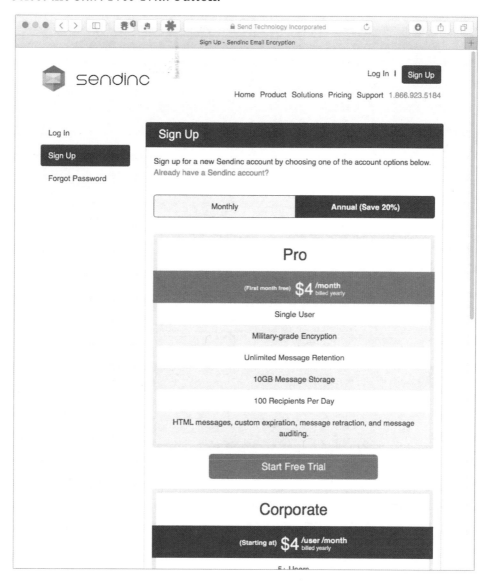

3. In the *Create Your Account* page, enter your *Email Address,* select your *Subscription Cycle*, and then select the *Continue* button.

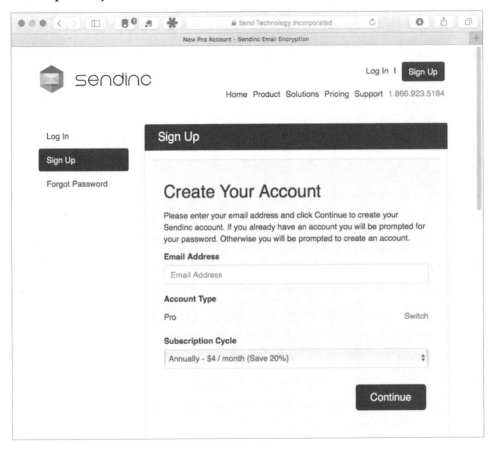

4. In the *Account Information* page, enter your *Name, Password, Activation Code* (check your email for this), enable the *I have read...* check box, and then select the *Create Account* button.

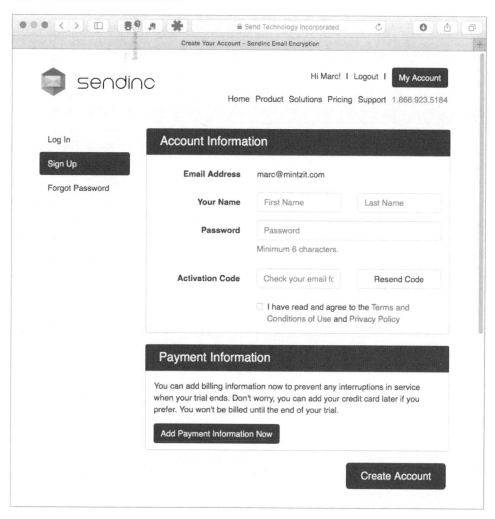

If all went well you will see the *New Secure Message* page. From here you can create your first encrypted email!

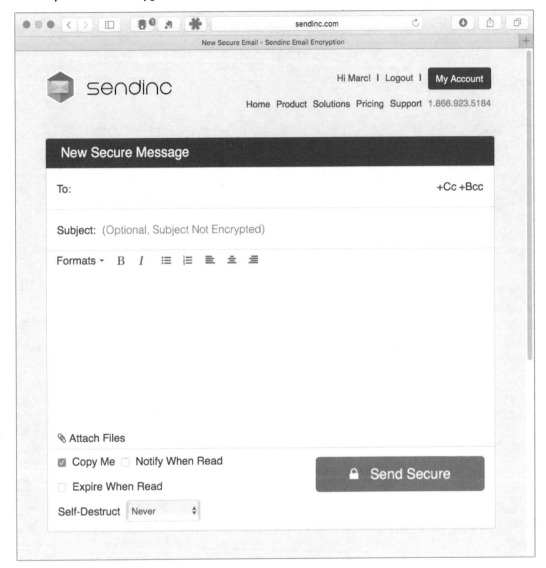

Assignment: Create and Send a SendInc Email

In this assignment, you will create and send a secure email using SendInc.

- Prerequisite: Completion of the previous assignment, or an existing SendInc account.

1. If you have just completed the previous assignment, the *Send a secure email now* window is open. If not, use your web browser to visit *SendInc* at *http://SendInc.com*, select the *Login* link, and then log in.

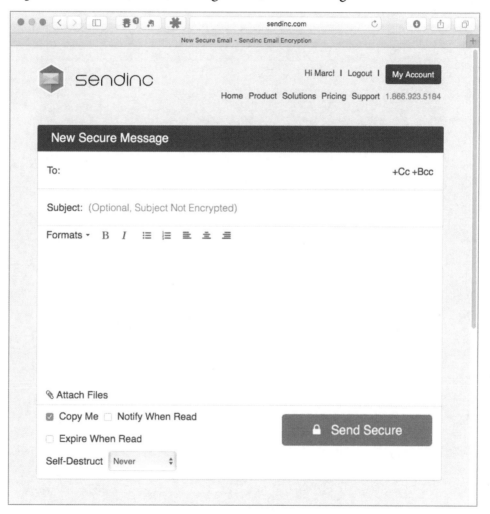

2. In the *To* field, enter the email address of the recipient.

3. In the *Subject* field, enter a subject message.

4. In the *Secure Message* field, enter the text of your message.

5. If you want to include an attachment, select the *Add Attachment* button, and select the file to attach.

6. From the *Self-Destruct* pop-up menu, select the lifetime of the message.

7. Select the Send Secure Message button.

Your email has been sent to the recipient.

Assignment: Receive and Respond to a SendInc Secure Email

In this assignment we reply to our first SendInc secure email. The previous two assignments must first be completed.

1. After you have sent an email from your SendInc account, the recipient gets the following email. To view the message, select the *View Secure Message* button within the email.

2. If this is the first time the recipient has visited SendInc, they will be prompted to create an account (as you did two exercises back.) If the recipient already has a SendInc account, go to step 3.

3. At the *Enter Password* window, the recipient will enter their account password.

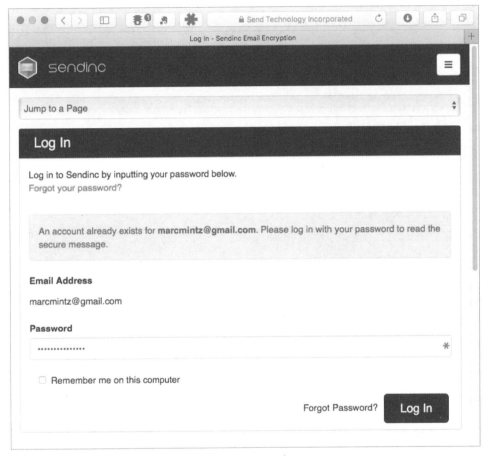

The email is decrypted and is fully viewable.

End-To-End Secure Email With GNU Privacy Guard

The gold standard for email security is to use an application to fully encrypt the message at the sender's computer in a format that only the intended recipient can decrypt. This tool also must be capable of alerting the recipient if the message has been tampered with in any way (i.e., a man-in-the-middle attack.) The leader in this arena is PGP (Pretty Good Privacy), now owned and maintained by Symantec. Fortunately, there is an open source utility that provides all of the core functionality and security of PGP, for free.

Setting up *GPG* (GNU Privacy Guard)–available for OS X, Windows, and Linux–takes a few more steps than our previous strategies in this section, and those with whom you wish to exchange secure email will need to also install GPG. But once both sender and recipient have their GPG in place, it is effortless to share fully encrypted messages.

Both PGP and GPG use the same strategy to securely encrypt email communications. Each user creates a *public key* and a *private key.* The Public Key typically is stored at a GPG server in the cloud, which can be found with a search for your name. The Private Key remains only on the user's computer. When sending an email to another person, your email application will automatically use the recipient's Public Key to encrypt the message. When the recipient receives the email, only the recipient' Private Key is able to decrypt and open the message.

If there are shortcomings to PGP and GPG, one is that there are only a few iOS apps that can use it–*oPenGP* and *SecuMail.* Also, GPG is designed to work within an email client application, not a web browser. Although there are plug-ins for FireFox to allow for GPG, you are best to stick with the built-in Mail.app. Another issue is that before one can exchange encrypted email with someone else, both need to manually retrieve each other's public key. This typically is just a two-click process, but still…

Cryptography can quickly become Ph.D.-level material. I will cover everything you are likely to need to fully enable encryption and digital signing using GPG. Should you wish to delve deeper, visit the GPGTools Support site at *http://support.gpgtools.org/kb.*

Assignment: Install GPG and Generate a Public Key

To encrypt your email, you will need to have GPG installed, and have your recipient's Public Key installed in your GPG keychain. In order for your intended recipient to decrypt and read your email, the recipient needs to have GPG installed (or Gpg4win <http://www.gpg4win.org> if using Windows, or GPA <http://www.gnupg.org/related_software/gpa/index.en.html> if using Linux.) The recipient will also need to have your Public Key stored in their computer.

In this first assignment, you will install GPG on your computer, and upload your Public Key to the *GPG Public Key Server*, making it available to anyone wishing to send encrypted email to you.

1. Use your browser to visit *GPGTools* <https://gpgtools.org>, and then select the *Download GPG Suite* button.

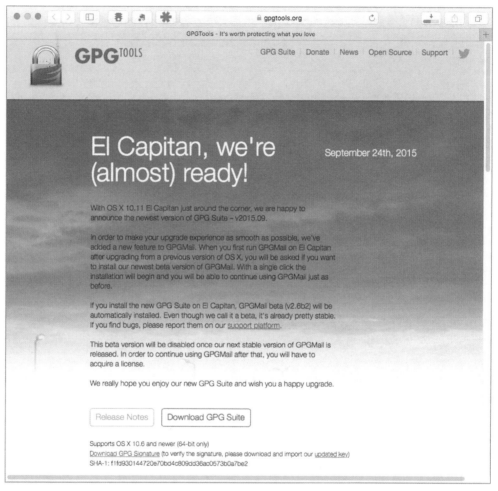

2. The software will begin to download to your computer.

3. Go to your Downloads folder, locate and then double-click on the *GPG Suite.dmg* file. This will mount the GPG disk image to your desktop, and then open the disk image to reveal the GPG Suite window.

4. Double-click the *Install.pkg* icon inside of the GPG Suite window to launch the *Install GPG Suite installer*.

5. Select the *Continue* button.

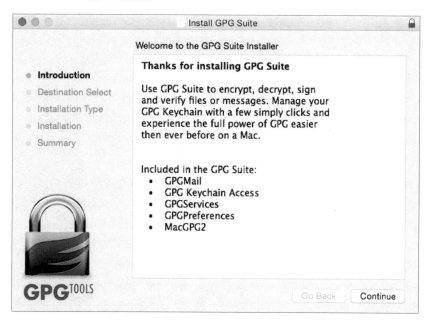

6. At the *Standard Install on "<Name of hard drive>"* window. Select the *Install* button.

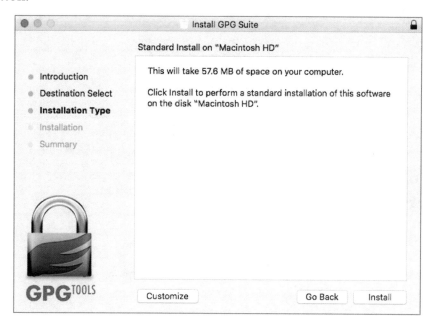

7. The authentication window will appear. Enter an administrator name and password, and then select the *Install Software* button.

8. *The installation was completed successfully* window appears. Just as nobody ever complained of bringing too much ammunition to a gunfight, you can never have too much information in your head. If time is of the essence, you can skip the tutorial as we will cover everything you need right here! Otherwise, take 10 minutes to read the *Quickstart Tutorial.*

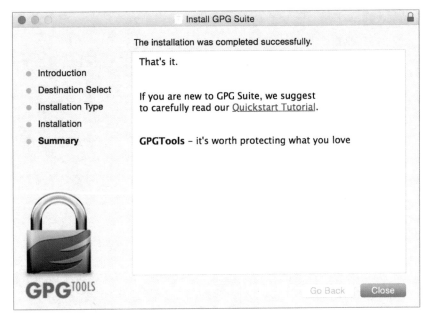

9. Launch the *GPG Keychain.app*, located in /Applications. The main window will open.

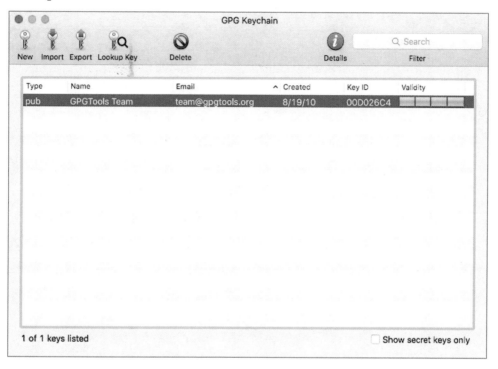

10. Select the *New* button in the tool bar. Configure as follows:

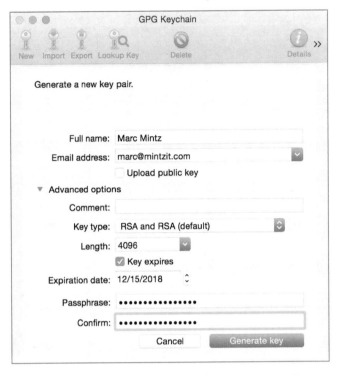

- *Full Name*: Enter your full name as used in your email.

- *Email* Address: Enter the email address for which GPG encryption is being configured.

- *Upload Public Key* after generation: Enable. Once you generate a key, this cannot be removed from the key server. Be certain that the name you are using is the one you want others to be able to find you by via a server search.

- Enable the *Advanced options* disclosure triangle.

- *Key type*: Select RSA and RSA (default).

- *Length*: Select 4096. The default is 2048. However, the larger the encryption bit depth, the more secure.

- *Key Expires*: I typically leave this disabled, allowing any of my encrypted email to be accessed (given the proper credentials) forever. However, if you prefer to set your key to self-expire, making any sent emails created with it unreadable after a certain date, then by all means enable this option.

- *Expiration Date*: If you have set your key to expire, this option will allow you to set the expiration date.

- *Passphrase*: This is a password to protect access to this record. As with all passwords, make it strong.

11. Select the *Generate key* button.

12. An authentication window will appear asking for you to create a password for your new GPG key. Enter a very long passphrase–a sentence that will be easy for you to remember. Record this in a secure location. I like to use the built-in Contacts or Address Book application.

13. The new key will start to generate. During this time, the random key generator uses activity on your computer to help create a random key. You should move your cursor, or type some characters in another application during this time.

14. When your Public Key generation completes, the *GPG Keychain Access* window will display your new key.

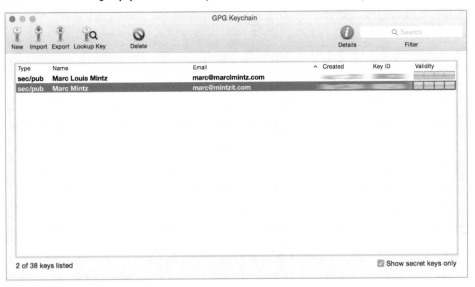

Congratulations! You have successfully installed GPG to help encrypt your email.

Assignment: Add Other Email Addresses to a Public Key

•   Prerequisite: GPGTools must be installed.

Many people have more than one email address. If you wish, you may create keys for each of your other addresses simply by repeating each of the steps in the previous assignment. However, you may find that both tedious and somewhat redundant.

An alternative is to bind all of your email addresses together under one key. In this assignment we will do just that.

1. Open *GPG Keychain*, located in your */Applications* folder, and then double-click on your entry from the previous assignment.

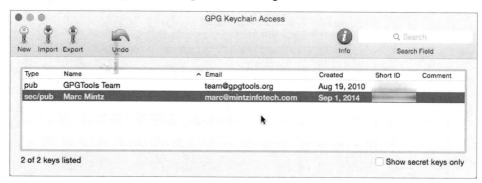

2. The *Key Inspector* window will open. Select the *User IDs* tab, select the account *Name,* and then select the + button.

3. In the window that opens, enter your *Full name,* along with the new *Email address* you want to be bound to your original email/key combination, and then select the *Generate user ID* button.

4. Repeat steps 2 and 3 for each of your email addresses.

5. When all of your email addresses have been added, select the one address you use most often, and then select the *Primary* button to set this as your primary account.

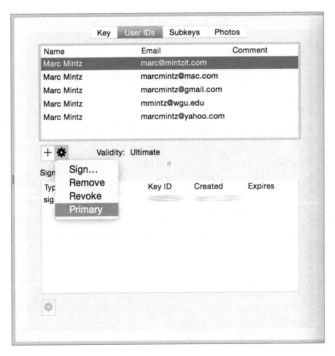

6. Though not required, let's add a photo to better identify you. Select the *Photos* tab.

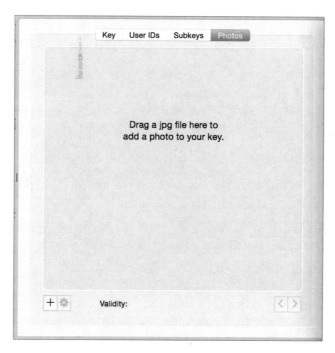

7. Select the + button, navigate your drive, and then select the desired ID picture. You are returned to the Photos window with the picture displayed.

8. You may have multiple ID pictures. After adding them, scroll through the Photos window to the one you want as your primary, and then select the Primary button.

9. Lastly, upload your changes to the Public Key Server. Select the *Key* menu > *Send Public Key to Server*.

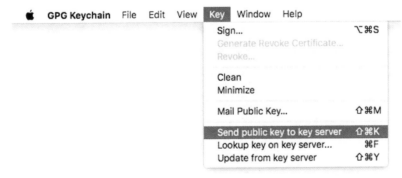

Congratulations! You have successfully added all of your email accounts to GPG, allowing encrypted communications with any account.

Assignment: Install a Friend's Public Key

- Prerequisite: GPGTools must be installed.

In order for you to send encrypted mail to someone else, it is necessary to have his or her *GPG Public Key*. In this exercise, you will find a friend's Public Key and add it to your GPG Keychain.

Option A: The No Sweat Strategy

The easiest way to add a friend's Public Key is to have them send you an email from their GPG-enabled account (signed, but not encrypted.) Once you have their email, you also have their Public Key. But you may be listening a long time to crickets before they send you an email.

Option B: DIY

1. Open the *GPG Keychain Access.app* located in your */Applications/ folder.

2. Select *Key* menu > *Lookup key on key server.*

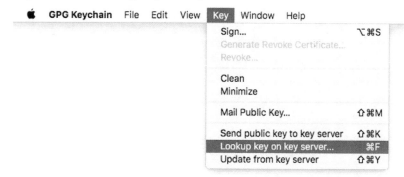

3. The *Search for key on keyserver* window opens.

4. Enter the full name of the person you wish to either send encrypted mail to, or receive from, and then select the *Search key* button. A list of possible matches appears. If you don't yet know anyone with a GPG key, feel free to use *Marc Louis Mintz*. Shown below are the search results for a *Marc Mintz*.

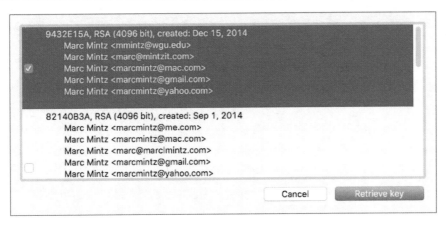

5. Once the *Search Key* has been selected, any public GPG keys that are stored will display. Select the target public key (if you aren't sure which is correct, select all of them), and then select the *Retrieve key* button.

6. The Public Key is now added to your GPG Keychain.

You are now ready to send encrypted email to your friends!

Assignment: Configure GPGMail Preferences

With GPG installed, the next step is to configure the *GPGMail Preferences* within your OS X Mail.app.

1. Open the *Mail.app*, open the *Mail* menu > *Preferences* > *GPG Mail*, and then click on the checkboxes to enable the following functions. Hover the cursor over an option for more information.

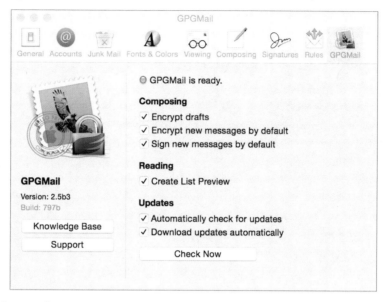

2. Close the *Preferences* window.

3. *Quit* Mail.app.

4. Open the *Apple* menu > *System Preferences* > *GPGPreferences,* select the *Settings* tab, and then configure as follows.

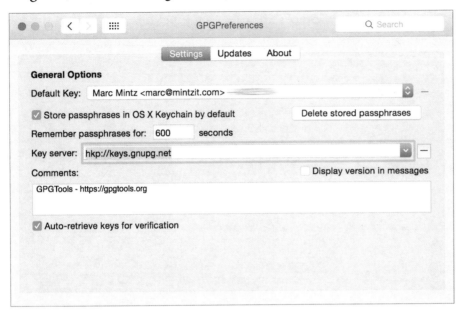

- *Default Key*: From the pop-up menu select your primary email account.

- *Store passphrases I OS X Keychain by default*: Enable checkbox.

- *Key server*: Unless your organization prefers using another server, stick with the default of *hkp://keys.gnupg.net.*

- *Auto-retrieve keys for verification*: Enable checkbox.

5. Select the *Updates* tab, and then configure as below:

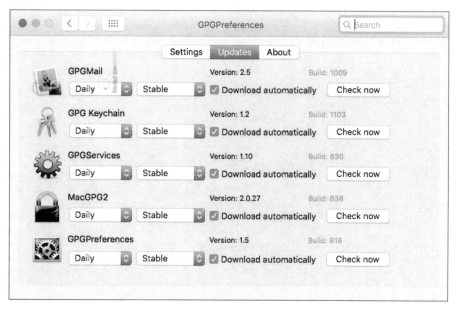

6. *Quit* System Preferences.

Your GPG is now fully installed, configured, and ready for use!

Assignment: Encrypt and Sign Files with GPGServices

GPGServices allows encryption, decryption, and signing of files–any type of file, cross-platform. After installing GPG (see previous exercises), verify all GPGServices have been activated:

1. Open *System Preferences > Keyboard > Shortcuts* tab > *Services* in sidebar.

2. From under the *Files and Folders* group, verify that all *OpenPGP* modules are enabled.

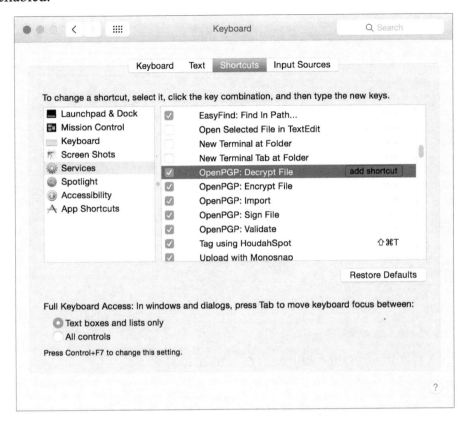

3. While still in the *System Preferences > Keyboard > Shortcuts* tab > *Services*, scroll down to the *Text* group, and then verify that all *OpenPGP* modules are enabled.

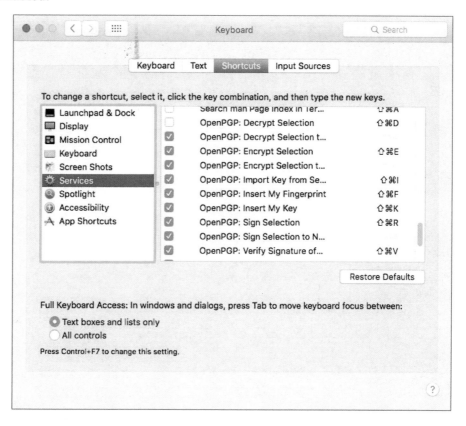

4. To sign or encrypt a file or folder, right-click on it. From the pop-up menu, select *Services > OpenPGP: Encrypt File.*

5. The *Choose Recipients – GPGServices* window appears. Configure as:

- Enable the checkbox for those you wish to allow to access this encrypted file or folder.

- Select which *Secret Key* will be used (which of your emails).

- Enable the *Sign* checkbox so the recipient can validate the file/folder came from you.

- You can further enhance security by enabling *Encrypt with password*.

6. Select the *OK* button.

7. At the *Pinentry Mac* window, enter the desired password in the *Passphrase* field, and then select the *OK* button.

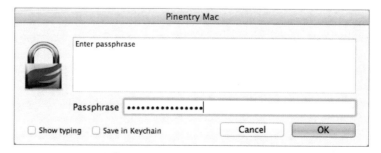

8. You will be prompted a second time to enter the passphrase, do so, and then select the *OK* button.

9. In a few seconds the *Encryption Finished* window appears. Select the *OK* button.

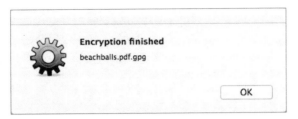

10. Your encrypted file will be found next to the original, with a *.gpg* file extension.

This encrypted file can now be attached to an email and securely sent to any recipient who also has GPG or PGP installed.

Assignment: Send a GPG-Encrypted and Signed Email

Once you have created your key and have the Public Key of the intended recipient from the previous assignments, you are ready to send your first encrypted and signed email.

1. Open your OS X *Mail.app*.

2. Create a new outgoing mail document. Notice that you have two new icons to the left of the *Subject* line.

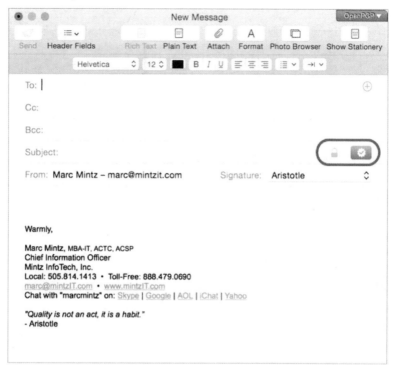

- *Lock* icon: Enables encryption for your document.

- *Signed* icon: Enables signed emails. A signed email will notify the recipient if the message has been altered in any way between the sender and recipient.

3. In the *To:* field, enter the email address of someone with GPG enabled on his or her computer (feel free to use my address of marc@mintzit.com for your test). Once you have entered an email address that is registered with GPG (as you have done in the previous assignment), the *Lock* icon will turn black, allowing selection/enabling.

4. Click the *Lock* icon to encrypt the message.

5. Select the *Send* button, and your email is on its way to the recipient, fully secure because only the designated recipient will be able to read the email.

Wahoo! You have sent your first securely encrypted email.

Assignment: Receive a GPG-Encrypted and Signed Email

1. When the email arrives at the recipient, it automatically is decrypted (assuming the recipient also has followed the steps detailed in the *Get Your Friend's Public Key* assignment). The message will have an indicator if it is encrypted or signed.

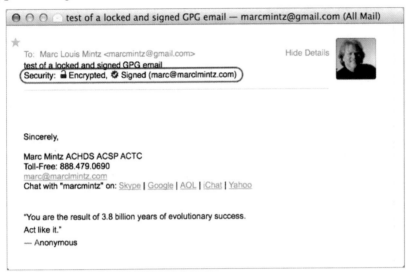

2. Should the recipient have any doubts as to the authenticity of the email, click on the *Signed* icon. The certificate will display. Note the Short ID to the right of the sender's email address.

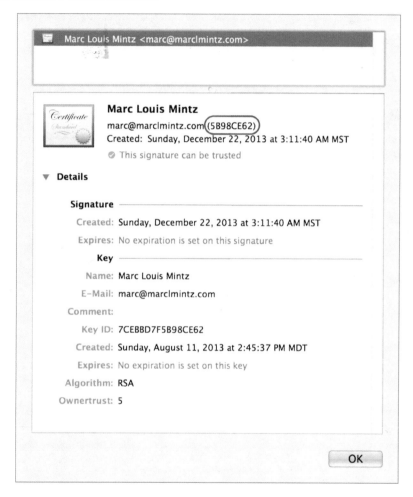

3. This Short ID can be verified. The recipient can open *GPG Keychain Access* to view the sender's Short ID.

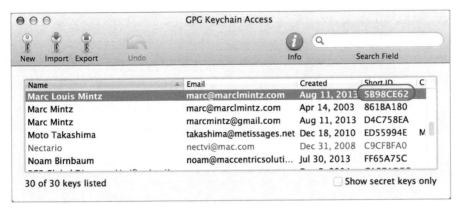

End-To-End Secure Email With S/MIME

S/MIME (Secure/Multipurpose Internet Mail Extensions) *http://en.wikipedia.org/wiki/S/MIME*, uses the same fundamental strategy of employing both Public and Private Keys to secure email as do PGP and GPG. Each person has a Private Key to decrypt a received email, and a Public Key that others may use to encrypt email to send out. An advantage of S/MIME over GPG is that there is no need to manually retrieve the other person's Public Key. Simply by signing an email and sending it to the other person, that person now has your Public Key. When the other person has done the same for you, the two of you may exchange encrypted email. Another benefit is that S/MIME is built right into both the OS X Mail.app and the iOS Mail.app. No need to install another application.

Unlike GPG, you will need to acquire an *email certificate* from a *Certificate Authority (CA)*. There are many Certificate Authorities available. Your Internet Provider or Web Host may be able to do this for you. Free certificates for personal use, which are valid for one year, are available. However, using these can become tedious, as you will need to repeat all the steps below every year. Purchasing a commercial certificate will set you back $10 to $100 per year, but you will only have to go through the process once.

S/MIME offers three certificate classes:

- **Class 1**: This level of certificate is acquired without any background check or verification that the person requesting it has anything to do with the email address it will be assigned to. In fact, it is even possible to roll your own certificate! That said, it will verify that the email address in the *From* field is actually the address that sent the email, and do the job of encrypting email so that only the intended recipient can decrypt and read it.

- **Class 2**: This level takes it a step further, validating that not only is the email address in the *From* field the one that actually sent the email, but that the name in the *From* field is tied to that email address.

- **Class 3**: This is the highest-level validation, with a background check performed to verify not only the name of the individual or company, but physical address as well. **This is the only class suitable for healthcare (HIPAA), legal, and business use.**

Assignment: Acquire a Free Class 1 S/MIME Certificate

In this assignment you will sign-up for a free 1-year free S/MIME certificate for personal use from a leading Certificate Authority, Comodo. This can be converted into a long-term commercial certificate.

1. Open your web browser and surf to Comodo at *http://comodo.com*.

2. From the navigation bar, select the *Personal* tab > *Free Personal Email Certificate*.

3. This takes you to the *Email Security & Messaging* page. Select the *Free Email Certificate > Free Download* button:

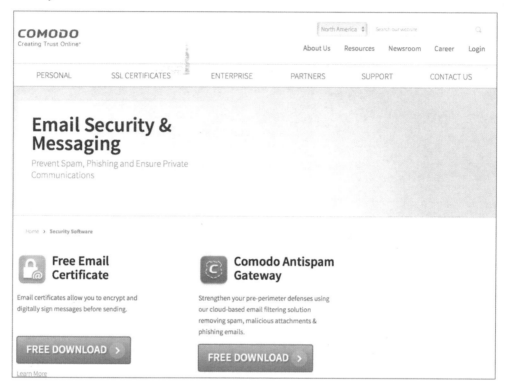

4. The *Application for Secure Email Certificate* page opens. Complete the form, specifying *2048 (High Grade)* for your *Key Size*, and then select the *Next* button.

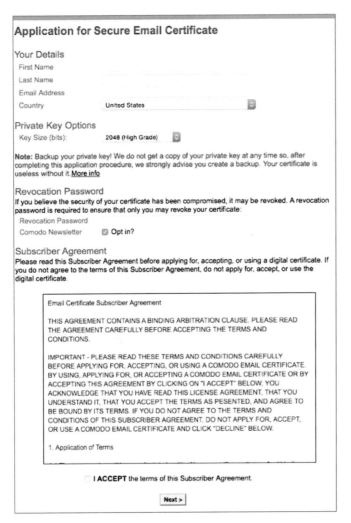

5. If all was completed correctly, you will see the *Application is Successful* page!

Application for Secure Email Certificate

Application is successful!

Details on how to collect your free Secure Email Certificate will be sent to **marcmintz@icloud.com**.

Congratulations on choosing Secure Email Certificates to keep your email confidential.

6.   The certificate will be sent to the email address you specified.

7.   Open your Mail.app to find the email, and then select the *Click & Install Comodo Email Certificate* button.

8.   Although the button says *Click & Install Comodo Email Certificate*, all it really does is download the certificate. You will need to manually install the certificate.

9.   Once downloaded, the certificate will be found in your *Downloads* folder, named something like *CollectCCC.p7s*. Navigate in the Finder to your *Downloads* folder to find this certificate file.

10. Double-click the *CollectCCC.p7s* certificate. An *Add Certificates* window will open asking if you want to add the certificate to your Keychain. From the *Keychain* pop-up menu, select *Login*. This will add the certificate to your own default Keychain database, and then select the *Add* button.

11. Quit the Keychain Access application.

12. Repeat steps 1-10 for each of your email addresses for which you need secure communications.

Wahoo! The hard part is over. You now are the proud owner (at least for a year) of email certificates for each of your email accounts. Next step is to start using your new powers!

Assignment: Acquire a Class 3 S/MIME Certificate for Business Use

Getting a Class 3 certificate is significantly more involved than that of a Class 1. This is due to the need for identity verification, but also to the need for an infrastructure to help with managing potentially thousands of email addresses within an organization.

To set up a Class 3 certificate account with Comodo:

1. Using your web browser, visit *Comodo.com*

2. From the Navigation bar, select *Enterprise > Secure Email Certificate.*

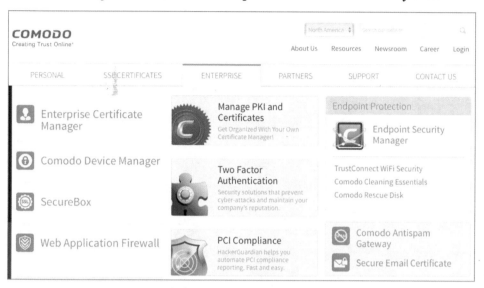

3. In the *Secure Email Certificates* page, select the *Buy Now button.*

4. In the *Purchase Corporate Secure Email Digital Certificate* page, enter your desired *Term* and *Quantity*. And then select the *Next* button.

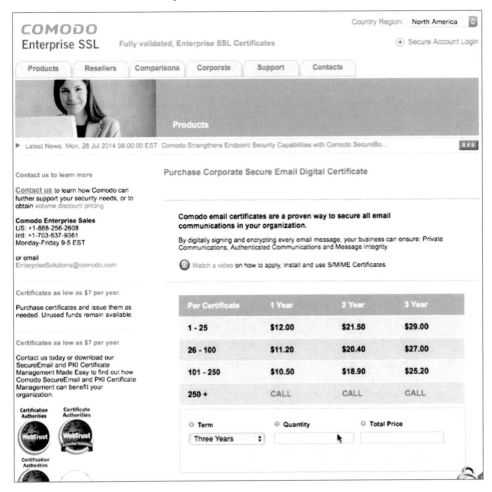

5. In the *Open an Enterprise S/MIME Enterprise PKI Manager (E-PKI) Account* window. Enter a domain name for your certificates, and then select the *Next* button.

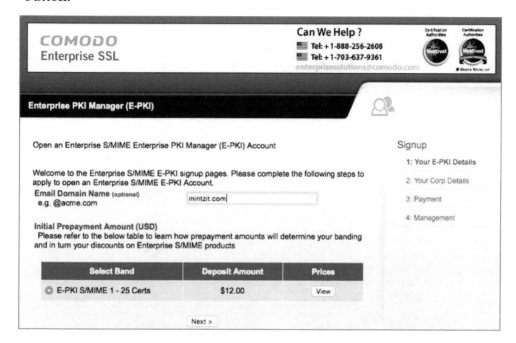

6. In the *Step 2: Your Corporate Details* page, enter all requested information, and then select the *Next* button.

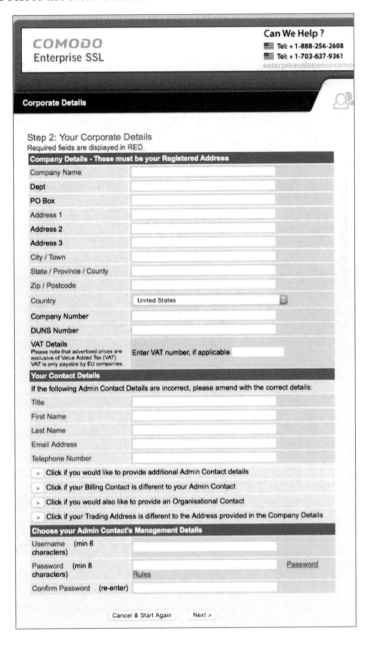

7. At the *Agreement* page, select the *I ACCEPT* button.

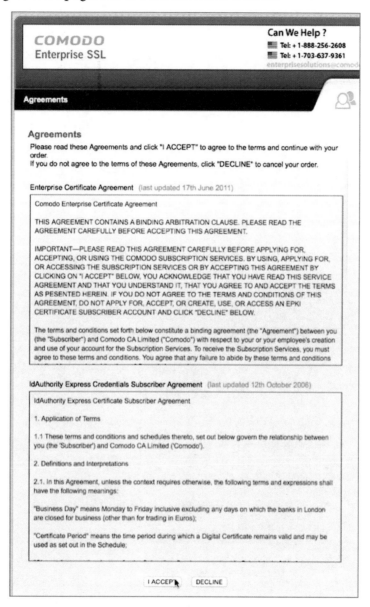

8. In the *Secure Payment Page,* enter your credit card information, and then select the *Make Payment* button.

9. You will receive an email from Comodo informing you of receipt of your order, and stating that you will soon be receiving another email requesting documents to validate your identity.

10. Soon you will receive an email requesting the validation documents. Submit the requested documents and information.

COMODO Validation Team 📎

To: Marc Louis Mintz

Information Required Order

CV

Thank you for your recent order.

We have begun validating your information so that we can issue your order. The following is the account information you submitted:

Company: Mintz InfoTech, Inc.
Domain Name: mintzit.com
Address 1: 7000 Phoenix Ave NE
Address 2: 310
Address 3:
City: Albuquerque
State: NM
Postal Code:87110
Country: United States of America

Although we have begun processing your order, we have been unable to complete validation for the following reasons:

In order to verify the existence of your organization we must be able to find it listed either in an official government database or a third party database such as Dunn & Bradstreet (www.dnb.com)

If the address on your account does not match the database record we may use one of the following documents for verification of the address. Please provide us with one of the following documents so we may complete your validation:

A. Articles of Incorporation (with address)
B. Government Issued Business License (with address)
C. Copy of a recent company bank statement (you may blacken out the Account Number)
D. Copy of a recent company phone bill
E. Copy of a recent major utility bill of the company (i.e. power bill, water bill, etc.) or current lease agreement for the company

*Note:Recent=dated within the last 6 months

Please fax any validation documentation to 1-866-831-5837(U.S. and Canada) or +1 801-303-9291 (Worldwide). When faxing documents, please include the attached coversheet. You may also respond by going to https://support.comodo.com, registering, and opening a ticket and attaching the documents. Please be sure to include your name, order number, domain name, e-mail address, and phone number in either your fax or support ticket.

If you need assistance, or wish to speak to a Customer Service Representative, please contact us toll-free at anytime at 1-888-266-6361 (U.S.) and +1-206-203-6361 (Worldwide).

Regards,
COMODO Validation Team

---

11. You will receive an email informing you that your account has been created, with a link to their *Getting Started Guide*. Although the steps outlined in this book will take you through the process, it is not a bad idea to download and read the Guide as well. Download the *Getting Started Guide*.

12. Register for Comodo technical support by clicking the link provided in the email, and then follow the on-screen instructions. This will save you significant time and headache in the event that you ever need technical support from Comodo.

Assignment: Purchase a Class 3 S/MIME Certificate for Business Use

Once you have set up your Class 3 business account with Comodo, you are able to order S/MIME certificates for you and your staff at any time. In this exercise, you will purchase your first certificate.

1. From your web browser, go to the Comodo home page at *http://comodo.com*.

2. Select the *Login* link, and then login. This opens the *SSL CA Providers Comodo Account Management* page.

3. In the *Comodo Certificate Authority* area, enter your *Username* and *Password* used to start your account with Comodo, and then select the *Log on* button.

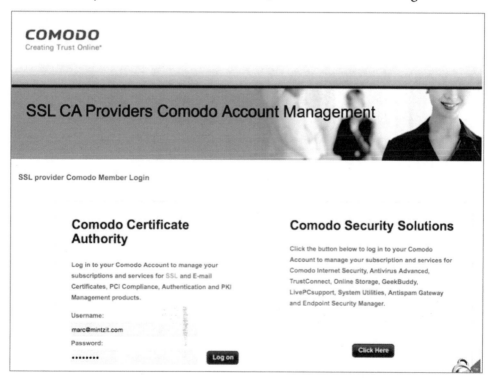

4. The *Account Options: Management* window opens. Select the *E-PKI Manager* link.

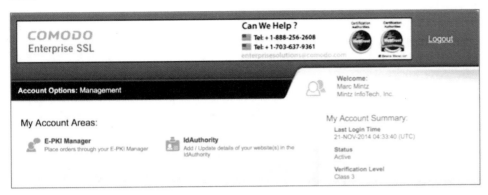

5. This will take you to the *E-PKI Manager: Account Options: Management* page. With Comodo, you pay for certificates not directly, but by pulling from monies on deposit with Comodo. If there are inadequate funds on deposit, you will need to deposit money now. To do so, select the *Deposit additional funds* link.

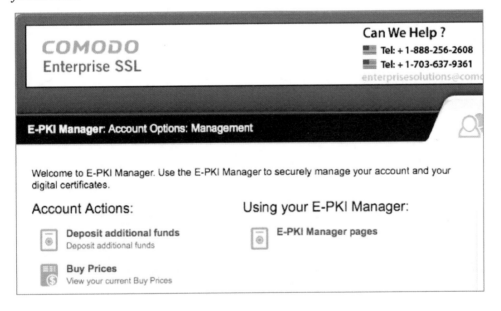

6. In the *Deposit Funds: Account Options: Management* page, enter at least the amount needed to purchase your S/MIME certificates. Rates per certificate as of this writing are.

Per Certificate	1 Year	2 Year	3 Year
1 - 25	$12.00	$21.50	$29.00
26 - 100	$11.20	$20.40	$27.00
101 - 250	$10.50	$18.90	$25.20
250 +	CALL	CALL	CALL

7. In the *Secure Payment* page enter your credit card information, and then select the *Make Payment* button.

8. Return to the *Account Options: Management* page, and then select the *E-PKI Manager* link.

9. In the *E-PKI Manager: Account Options: Management* page, select the *User Management* link.

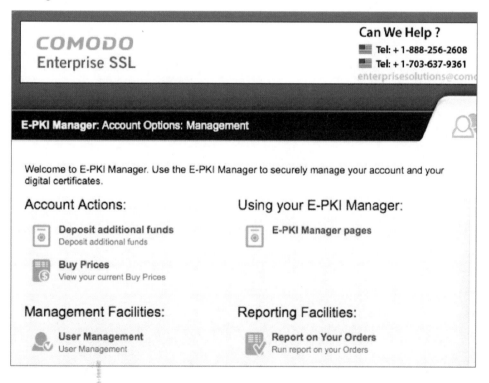

10. In the *User Management: Account Options: Management* page, select the *New User* button.

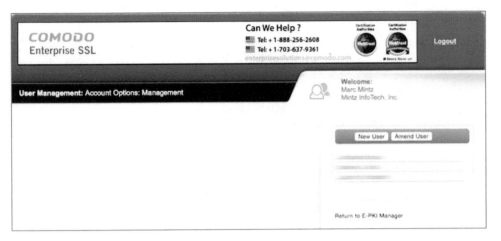

11. In the *New User* window, enter all information for your new user, and then select the *Save Changes* button.

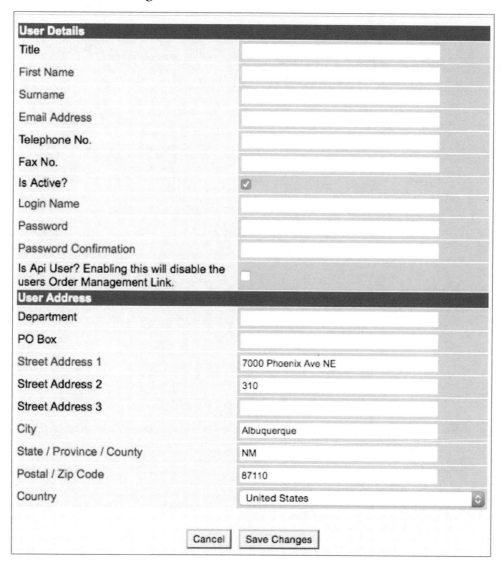

12. Repeat steps 7-10 to enable each user/email account to have an S/MIME certificate.

13. When all certificates have been requested, return to the *User Management: Account Options: Management* window, and then select the *Return to E-PKI Manager* button.

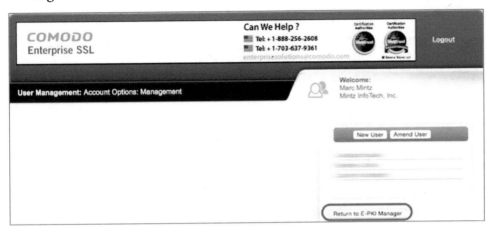

14. In the E-*PKI Manager: Account Options: Management* page, scroll to the bottom, and then select the *Corporate Secure Email Certificate Buy* button.

15. In the *Corporate Secure Email Certificate: E-PKI Manager: Management* page, complete the information for the user/email address you wish to assign an S/MIME certificate, and then select the *Submit* button.

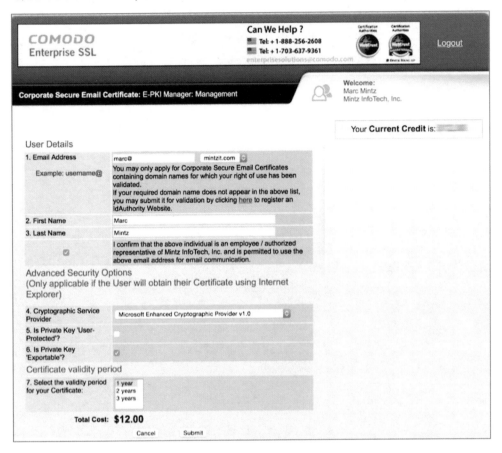

16. At the *Order Confirmation: E-PKI Manager: Management* page, print your receipt, and then select the *Management Area...* button.

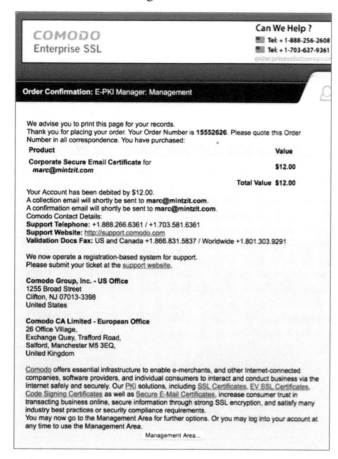

17. Repeat steps 13-15 for each user/email account to be assigned an S/MIME certificate.

Assignment: Download and Install a Business S/MIME Certificate

Once you have completed the steps above to provide a user/email account, that email address will receive notification of S/MIME certificate availability.

1. At the user's computer, check email for a message from Comodo, select and
   copy the *Your Certificate Password*, and then select the *Begin Corporate Secure
   Email Certificate Application* button.

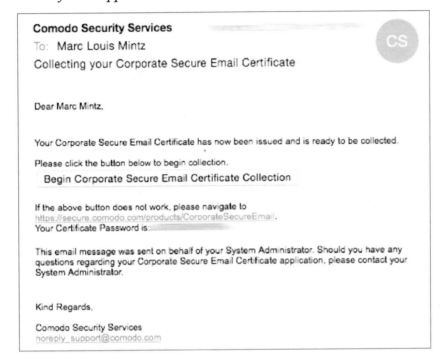

Comodo Security Services

To: Marc Louis Mintz

Collecting your Corporate Secure Email Certificate

Dear Marc Mintz,

Your Corporate Secure Email Certificate has now been issued and is ready to be collected.

Please click the button below to begin collection.

Begin Corporate Secure Email Certificate Collection

If the above button does not work, please navigate to
https://secure.comodo.com/products/CorporateSecureEmail.
Your Certificate Password is:

This email message was sent on behalf of your System Administrator. Should you have any
questions regarding your Corporate Secure Email Certificate application, please contact your
System Administrator.

Kind Regards,

Comodo Security Services
noreply_support@comodo.com

2. In the *Corporate Secure Email Certificate Center*:

- Enter the **exact same email address** as used during the certificate creation.

- Paste in the *Certificate Password* that was included in the Comodo email sent to the email address.

- Enable the *I Accept* checkbox.

- Select the *Submit & Continue* button.

Corporate Secure Email Certificate Center

User Details:

Please enter the following details:

Email Address   marc@mintzit.com

Certificate   ·····················
Password

Subscriber Agreement

Please read this Subscriber Agreement before applying for your certificate.
If you do not agree to the terms of this Subscriber Agreement, do not click the "I ACCEPT" tickbox.

Email Certificate Subscriber Agreement

THIS AGREEMENT CONTAINS A BINDING ARBITRATION CLAUSE. PLEASE READ THE AGREEMENT CAREFULLY BEFORE ACCEPTING THE TERMS AND CONDITIONS.

IMPORTANT - PLEASE READ THESE TERMS AND CONDITIONS CAREFULLY BEFORE APPLYING FOR, ACCEPTING, OR USING A COMODO EMAIL CERTIFICATE. BY USING, APPLYING FOR, OR ACCEPTING A COMODO EMAIL CERTIFICATE OR BY ACCEPTING THIS AGREEMENT BY CLICKING ON "I ACCEPT" BELOW, YOU ACKNOWLEDGE THAT YOU HAVE READ THIS LICENSE AGREEMENT, THAT YOU UNDERSTAND IT, THAT YOU ACCEPT THE TERMS AS PESENTED, AND AGREE TO BE BOUND BY ITS TERMS. IF YOU DO NOT AGREE TO THE TERMS AND CONDITIONS OF THIS SUBSCRIBER AGREEMENT, DO NOT APPLY FOR, ACCEPT, OR USE A COMODO EMAIL CERTIFICATE AND CLICK "DECLINE" BELOW.

1. Application of Terms

☐ **I ACCEPT** the terms of this Subscriber Agreement.

Submit & Continue

---

3. The *Corporate Secure Email Certificate: Collection* page will open, your certificate will be generated and begin to download.

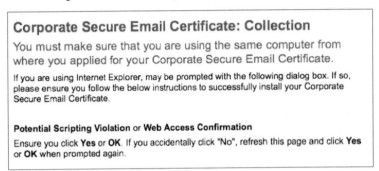

4. When the certificate has been generated, it will start downloading. When downloaded, you will find it in your *Downloads* folder named something like *CollectCCC.p7s*.

5. Open your *Downloads* folder and locate the *CollectCCC.p7s* file.

6. To install your S/MIME certificate into the *Keychain Access.app*, double-click on the *CollectCCC.p7s* file.

7. The *Add Certificates* window opens. Select *Keychain: login*, and then select the *Add* button.

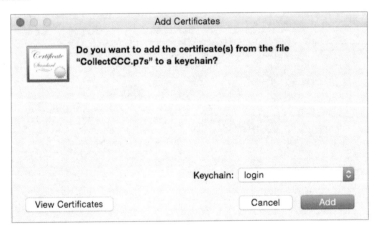

8. *Quit* Keychain Access.

9. Quit the Mail.app.

10. *Open* the *Mail.app*. This forces the Mail application to search for new certificates.

11. If you use multiple computers, place a copy of your *CollectCCC.p7s* file on each of your computers, and repeat steps 6-10.

Your S/MIME certificate, which includes both your *Public Key* (used by others to encrypt email to you) and *Private Key* (used by you to decrypt email received by you) is now installed.

Assignment: Exchange Public Keys with Others

Before you are able to send or receive encrypted email with others, you need to exchange Public Keys with each other. This is as simple as sending a signed email to each other. To start, you will send a signed email to a friend. This will give this recipient your Public Key, as well as instructions for the recipient to set up S/MIME on their own system.

1. From a computer that now has your newly acquired email certificates, *Open* the *Mail.app*. This process forces *Mail.app* to look for new certificates.

2. Select the *File* menu > *New Message*.

3. From the *From:* pop-up menu, select the email account with the new certificates. (If you have only one email account, the *From* field typically does not appear.)

4. At the bottom right of the header area, note the two new icons–an encryption lock and signed check. If you have performed the earlier GPG assignments, these are the same and are shared between the two systems. The lock becomes available when you have the Public Key of the recipient, allowing for encryption. The check is available for anyone once you have your certificate. It will verify that the sender (you) are who you say you are.

5. If you have performed the earlier GPG assignments, the drop-down menu at the top right corner allows you to select either GPG or S/MIME as your encryption protocol. If you have not performed the earlier GPG assignments, this menu is absent.

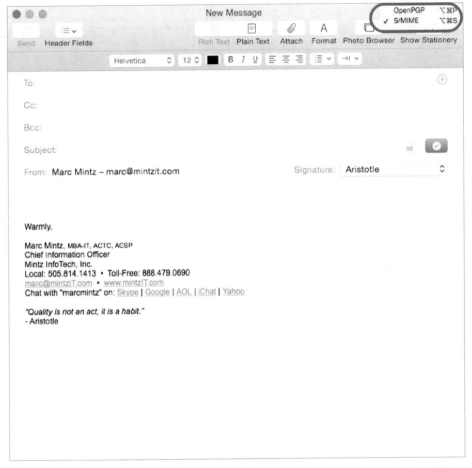

6. Address your email to an associate with whom you would like to be able to exchange encrypted email. Feel free to address the email to me at *marc@mintzit.com.*

7. If you have installed both PGP and S/MIME, ensure the *S/MIME* is the selected protocol, and that the *S/MIME signed check* is enabled (it should be by default.) This will ensure your Public Key is sent to your designated recipient.

8. In the Subject line, be clear about the intent of the email by noting something like: *S/MIME Public Key Attached.*

9. In the body area you may want to include instructions for how to acquire an email certificate–or better yet–point to this book at its website *http://thepracticalparanoid.com*:

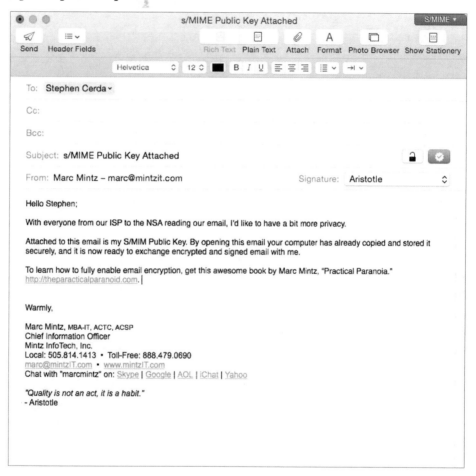

10. When the recipient receives and opens the email, that recipient now has your Public Key and can determine that the email truly did come from you due to your signing the email with your certificate.

Marc Louis Mintz

To: Marc Louis Mintz

S/MIME Public Key Attached

Security: ⬤ Signed (Marc Mintz)

Hello;

With everyone from my ISP to the NSA reading our email, I'd like to have a bit more privacy.

Attached to this email is my S/MIME Public Key. By opening this email your computer has already copied and stored it securely, and is now ready to exchange encrypted and signed email with me.

To learn how to fully enable email encryption, get this awesome book by Marc Mintz, "Practical Paranoia." http://thepracticalparanoid.com.

Warmly,

Marc Mintz, MBA-IT, ACTC, ACSP
Chief Information Officer
Mintz InfoTech, Inc.
Local: 505.814.1413 • Toll-Free: 888.479.0690
marc@mintzIT.com • www.mintzIT.com
Chat with "marcmintz" on: Skype | Google | AOL | iChat | Yahoo

"Quality is not an act, it is a habit."
- Aristotle

11. The recipient then needs to repeat the steps in this and the previous assignments to acquire an email certificate, and then send a signed email to you. Once this is done, the two of you may exchange encrypted email.

Assignment: Send S/MIME Encrypted Email

To exchange encrypted email using S/MIME, the previous assignments must be completed by yourself and at least one other person with whom you wish to have secure communication. Once done, each has an email certificate, a private key, and a public key that is embedded in the other's computer.

1. Open your *Mail.app*.

2. Create a new message, addressed to someone with whom you share public keys.

3. If you have also installed GPG, set the *GPG-S/MIME* menu in the top right corner of the message to *S/MIME*.

4. Enable the *encrypted* lock icon in the bottom right area of the message header.

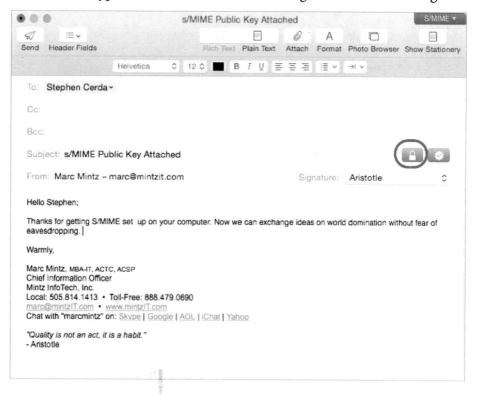

5. Send the message. When received by the recipient, the message is instantly and automatically decrypted, and the recipient gets a notice that the message is encrypted as well as signed.

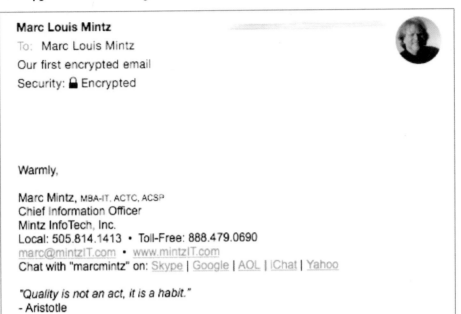

Congratulations! You are now able to send and receive securely encrypted email using the S/MIME protocol.

Closing Comments on Encryption and the NSA

Using PGP, GPG, S/MIME, or secure email hosts will give 100% protection against your communications being intercepted or eavesdropped by pranksters, criminals, master criminals, and virtually all government personnel (my apology for being redundant.) The bad news is that the NSA may have the ability to bypass virtually any security system should the NSA take a strong enough interest. The question then becomes: *Am I someone of such strong interest to the NSA that they will focus their full legal (and illegal) powers upon me?* If so, you may want to consider a change of career or lifestyle.

Review Questions

1. The attempt to acquire your personal or sensitive information by appearing as a trustworthy source is called _____ .

2. Three common protocols to encrypt email between email server and user are _____, _____, and _____ .

3. OS X 10.11 Mail.app has separate settings for SSL and TLS. (True or False)

4. The encryption protocol used for web-based email is _____ .

5. Email encrypted with either PGP or GPG can be decrypted with either. (True or False)

6. S/MIME Class 1 certificate is designed for business use. (True or False)

15. Vulnerability: Apple ID and iCloud

Even in the common affairs of life, in love, friendship, and marriage, how little security we have when we trust our happiness in the hands of others!

–William Hazlitt, English writer and philosopher

Apple ID and iCloud

In 2012 a well-known journalist had his Apple ID hacked, allowing the hacker full access to the victim's Apple ID, and through that, his iCloud account, including calendar, contacts, and email. This was accomplished not by traditional black hat hacking, but with a bit of social engineering. All the hacker needed was to discover the victim's birthdate and email address associated with his Apple ID. With a quick email to Apple saying something like, *I've forgotten my Apple ID password and would like to reset it. Here is my birthdate and my email address,* the hacker was able to reset the Apple ID password. With this, he could access the victim's iCloud website as if he were the victim himself.

Over the past 6 months I have had 3 clients whose iTunes accounts have been compromised in a similar fashion, one to the tune of $1,400 in music purchases.

As of March 21, 2013, Apple has implemented an optional Two-Step Verification (also referred to as a 2-Factor Authentication) process to harden your Apple ID security. Adding this security layer makes it extremely difficult for anyone to hijack your Apple ID and make fraudulent purchases. I consider this a mandatory step for all iCloud users.

Remember that every password can be broken. Your defense is to make it so difficult and time consuming to break that the hacker moves on to an easier target. The vast majority of security questions can be accurately guessed or broken through social engineering (*What is your birthday? In what city did your parents marry? What is the name of your first pet?* etc.) Both of these types of security are based on what you know. And if there is something that you know, someone else can know it as well. Unfortunately, even those you love and trust may occasionally use this information against you.

Apple has implemented Two-Step Verification for Apple ID so that whenever you sign in to your Apple ID on the web to manage your account, purchase something from iTunes, App Store, or iBookstore from a new (unknown) device, or attempt to get Apple ID-related support from Apple, a code is sent to your previously verified i-device. You are prompted to provide this code before the purchase or support can be made.

In the event that your iOS device has been stolen or lost, you can log in to *https://appleid.apple.com* to remove that device from the verified list, so that no code will be sent to that device.

Assignment: Create an Apple ID

If you already have an Apple ID, skip this exercise. If you do not already have an Apple ID, no better time than the present to create one!

1.   Open *Apple* menu > *System Preferences* > *iCloud.*

2. In the *iCloud* pane, select the *Create Apple ID...* link.

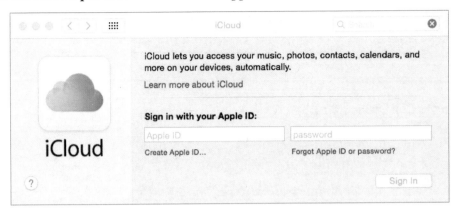

3. In the *Create an Apple ID* pane, enter accurate information, and then select the *Next* button.

- Note that it is almost always a bad idea to enter accurate information in security question areas. However, in this instance you *must* enter the real deal. Reason is that should you ever need to prove your identity to Apple via drivers license, birth certificate, etc., the records from your Apple ID had better match.

4. In the *Create an Apple ID* pane, complete the required fields, and then select the *Continue* button

5. In the *Create an Apple ID: Security Questions* pane, set up your security challenge questions. As the truthful answers are easy to discover by someone looking to hack your account, it is strongly recommend providing false answers. Do make sure to record the questions and answers (I do so in my Contacts.app.).

6. At the *Accept the iCloud Terms and Conditions to use iCloud* pane, gather round your team of attorneys, review the document, enable the checkbox, and then select the *Continue* button.

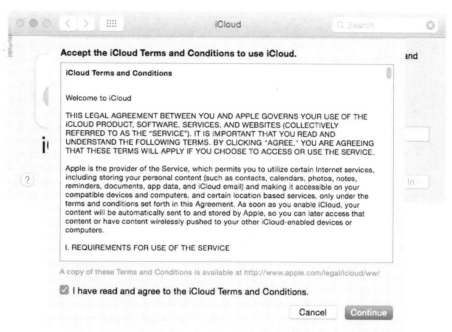

7. At the *iCloud Terms and Conditions* window, select the *Agree* button.

8. At the *A verification email has been sent to <your email address>*, select the *Next* button.

9. Check your mail app for the verification email, and then click the *Verify Now* link.

10. A browser will open to the *My Apple ID* page. Enter the email address and password used above to create the account, and then click the *Verify Address* button.

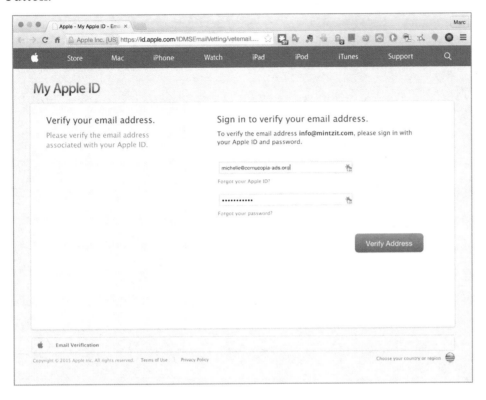

11. The *My Apple ID – Email address verified* page will appear. You may close your browser and open *System Preferences > iCloud.*

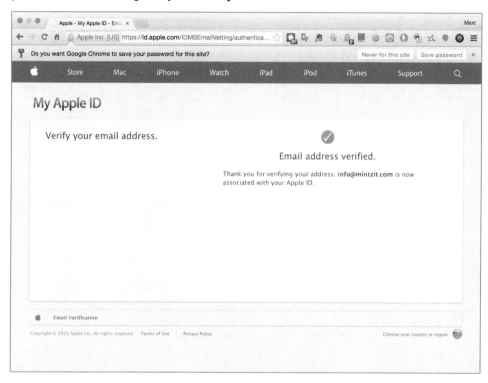

12. In the *iCloud* pane, click the *Enter Password* button.

13. In the *iCloud* pane, enable the desired features.

14. Mavericks introduced the ability to synchronize your Keychain with iCloud, sharing it with all of your devices. If you would like to do this, enter your *Apple ID password,* and then select the *OK* button.

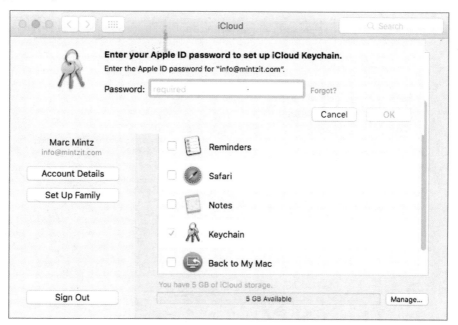

15. At the *Create an iCloud Security Code*, enter a 6-character code to allow setting up iCloud on this device, and then click the *Next* button. This will be the same code used to synchronize Keychain on your other devices.

16. The same window will reappear as a verification stage. Reenter your 6-digit code, and then click the *Next* button.

17. At the *Enter a phone number that can receive SMS messages* dialog, enter a phone number that you will always have access to in order to verify your identity. This is part of setting up 2-factor authentication. Then click the *Done* button.

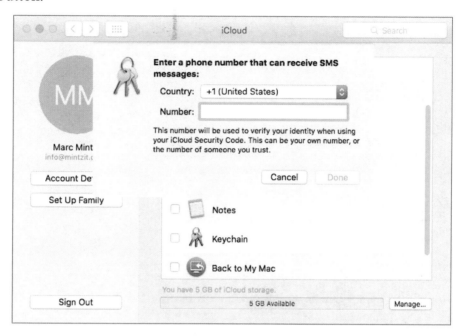

18. Allow *Find My Mac to use the location of this Mac* may help you locate and retrieve your computer in the event it is stolen. As I can't imagine any negative consequence of activating this feature, select the Allow button.

19. Once brought back to the *iCloud* pane, verify that all of your desired features are enabled, and then *Quit* System Preferences.

Congratulations! You have successfully created a new Apple ID, and have secured your identity with Two-Step Verification.

Assignment: Implement Apple ID Two-Step Verification

Two-step verification, also called two-step authentication, helps to prevent someone else from pretending to be you to reset your Apple ID settings. Anytime significant settings are modified, you will receive an alert on your mobile phone. If you made the changes, ignore the alert. If you did not make the changes, the alert will provide a link to take security actions.

1. Open a browser to *https://appleid.apple.com*. Select the *Manage your Apple ID* button.

2. The *Sign In* page opens. Enter your Apple ID and password, and then select the *Sign in* button.

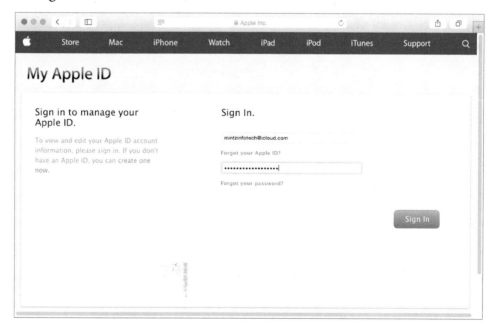

3. The *Security Questions* page opens. If you know your proper answers to the Security questions, do so. Then select the *Continue* button.

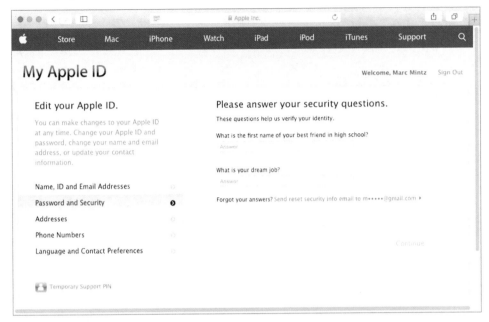

a. If you don't remember your answers, select the *Forgot your answers? Send reset security info email to* •••••••• link.

b. You will immediately receive an email from Apple with a link to reset your questions.

c. Go to your email inbox and open the Apple email.

d. Click the link to reset your security questions.

4. The *Manage your security settings* page opens. Complete the security questions, and then click the *Save* button.

5. You are taken to the beginning of the two-step verification process. Read the instructions and then select the *Continue* button.

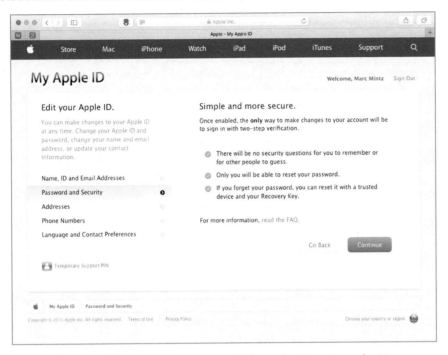

6. The second page of instructions opens. Select the *Continue* button.

7. The third page opens. Select the *Get Started* button.

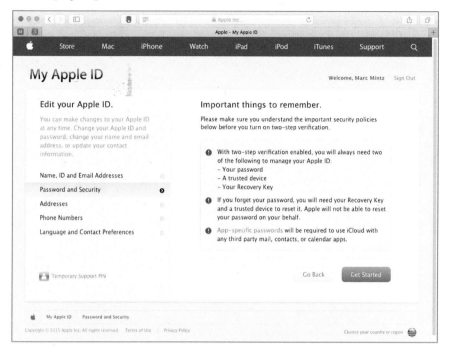

8. At *Step 1 of 4: Set up your trusted device* page, enter a phone number that can receive SMS messages, and then click *Continue*.

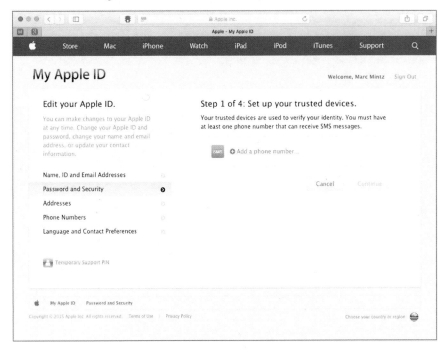

9. A 4-digit code will be sent to your iPhone, iPad, or SMS telephone number on record with your Apple ID. Check your device, enter the code on the following screen, and then select the *Verify Device* button.

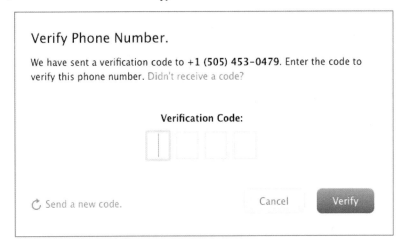

10. As an extra precaution, you may enter the phone number of a second mobile phone so that you can receive verification codes even if you lose your i-device. Enter your mobile phone number, and then select the *Next* button.

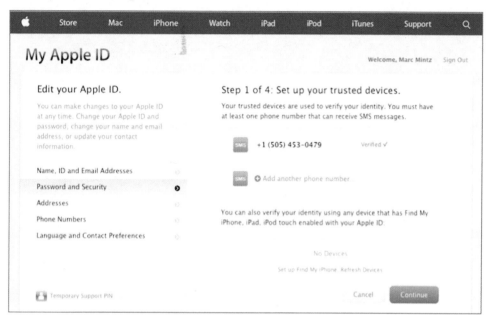

11. If you have added as second SMS device, a verification code will be sent via SMS to the mobile phone number just entered. Check your phone for the code, enter it in the next screen, and then select the *Verify* button.

12. The *Step 2 of 4* page will present your Apple ID Recovery Key. If you forget your Apple ID password or do not have access to one of your i-devices, you will have to have access to your recovery key. Without this, you will have no option but to create a new Apple ID, and lose access to any purchases you have made with your existing Apple ID. Record this recovery key in a secure location, then select either the *Print Key* or *Continue* button.

13. The importance of having a record of the recovery key is emphasized in the *Step 3 of 4* screen, where you manually reenter your recovery key, and then select the *Confirm* button.

14. In the *Step 4 of 4* screen, read the warnings, enable the check box, and then select the *Enable Two-Step Verification* button.

15. The verification process has been completed! All that is left for you to do is select the *Done* button.

16. Exit from this page.

You have now made it virtually impossible for anyone to impersonate you to Apple, thereby preventing anyone from gaining access to your Apple ID and iCloud information!

Review Questions

1. In the event that your iOS device is stolen or lost, you should log in to _____ to remove that device from the verified list, so that no 2-step verification code will be sent to it.

2. You must have a current email address in order to create an Apple ID. (True or False)

3. The services that can be synchronized using iCloud are: _____ .

4. A mobile phone number that is capable of receiving texts is a requirement for iCloud 2-step verification. (True or False)

16. Vulnerability: Documents

Tradition becomes our security, and when the mind is secure it is in decay.
–Jiddu Krishnamurti, Philosophy and spiritual writer and speaker

Document Security

If your documents never leave your computer, and you have encrypted your storage devices using FileVault 2, there is no need to go the extra step to encrypt your documents. But should you ever need to email your sensitive data to someone else, or pass a sensitive document via any storage device, encrypting the document goes a long way to a good night of sleep.

There are several options to document encryption, each with its own benefits and drawbacks. We will discuss each here.

Password Protect a Document Within Its Application

A few applications are designed with document security in mind, and offer their own encryption scheme. Microsoft Office, Adobe Acrobat Pro, and Apple Preview are common examples.

Microsoft Office products make it an easy process to password protect your documents. Office 2008 (for OS X) and earlier used an easily breakable encryption scheme, making it unsuitable for security. As of Office 2007 (Windows) and Office 2011 (OS X) and higher, AES 128-bit is used for Office document encryption. This is the same as used by government, and is considered secure.

Assignment: Encrypt an MS Word Document

In this assignment we will encrypt a Microsoft Word file (although the process is nearly identical for an Excel file) from within the application.

1. Open the target document in Microsoft Word 2016.

2. Select *Review* tab > *Protect* > *Protect Document*.

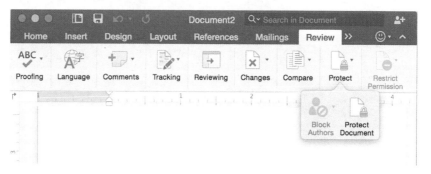

3. The *Password Protect* dialog opens. You may set a separate password to *Open*, and to *Modify* this document. Enter a password for the desired function.

    *   Note: Passwords for Microsoft Office products are limited to 15 characters.

4. Re-enter the password, and then click *OK*.

5. Click the *OK* button at the bottom right of the *Password Protect* dialog, closing it.

Your document is now protected.

Encrypt a PDF Document

As there are only a few applications that can encrypt their own documents, chances are you will be working with a file whose application cannot perform the encryption. OS X comes with the application Preview. Preview is able to password protect pdf files. OS X can "print" any document to pdf format.

Adobe Acrobat 9 and higher use AES 256-bit encryption. This is considered secure, as long as strong passwords are used.

Assignment: Convert a Document to PDF for Password Protection

1. Open any printable document currently on your computer.
2. Select *File* menu > *Print*.

3. From the *Print* window, select the *PDF* button > *Save as PDF*.

4. In the window that opens, in the *Save As* field, name the pdf version of the document, and then select the *Security Options...* button.

5. In the *PDF Security Options* window, enable the *Require password to open document* check box, enter a desired password in the *Password* and *Verify* fields, and then select the *OK* button.

6. Quit the current document and application.

The pdf version of the document is now encrypted. If the original document is no longer needed, it may be trashed.

Encrypt a Folder for Only OS X Use

Perhaps you need to securely send an entire folder of files. An easy way to accomplish this is to use a utility to archive (compress to a single file) the files or folder, and have that same utility protect the archive with a password.

OS X has a built-in utility to do this for you–*Disk Utility*. The only downside is that the archives created with Disk Utility are only readable on another OS X computer–they are not cross-platform compatible. However, if your documents will be passed along only to others using OS X, it is an excellent tool.

Assignment: Create an Encrypted Disk image

In this assignment you will create an encrypted disk image to may store some or all of your most sensitive data.

1. Open Disk Utility, located in */Applications/Utilities.*

2. Select *Disk Utility File* menu > *New Image* > *Blank Image…*

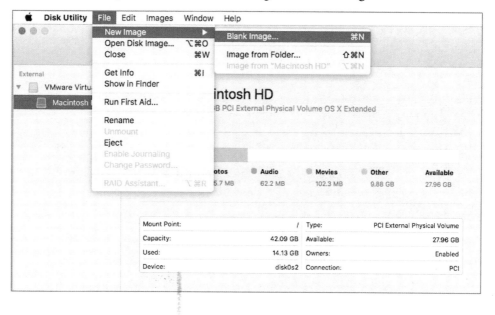

3. Configure the *New Image* screen as below.

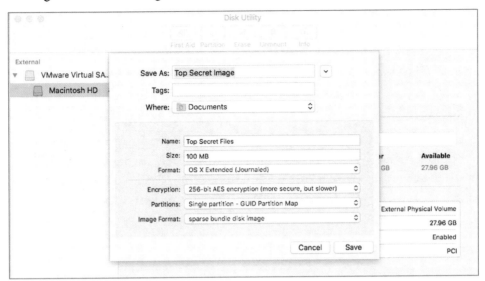

- *Save As:* The desired name for the archive that will hold all of your files to be password protected.

- *Where:* Navigate to where you want the archive to be saved.

- *Name:* Enter the name of the mounted disk image. To avoid confusion, this is normally named the same as the *Save As* field. For demonstration purposes, we are naming them differently in this example.

- *Size:* This should be somewhat larger than the total size of files the archive will hold. It can be much larger, as the archive will compress out all unused space.

- *Format: Mac OS Extended (Journaled).* This is the OS X standard format.

- *Encryption:* 128-bit takes less time to encrypt and decrypt than 256-bit, but is also less secure. When selecting this option, you will be prompted to provide a password. Enter your desired password, and then click *OK*.

- *Partitions:* Single Partition, GUID Partition Map. This is the OS X standard.

- *Image Format: Sparse Bundle Disk Image.* This is the format that will compress out all unused space.

4. Select the *Save* button.

5. The archive is saved, and the Disk Image (the opened format of the archive) is displayed in the Finder Window Sidebar, and depending on your *Finder Preferences* menu > *General* > *Hard Disks,* may display as mounted on the Desktop. You now have an encrypted, password protected archive, but it's empty. Time to fill it.

6. Locate the mounted disk image on the Desktop. In our example, it will be called *Top Secret Files.*

7. Drag the various files and folder that you have targeted for password protection into the mounted image.

8. Eject/unmount the mounted image. It will close, remove itself from the Desktop, leaving just the password protected archive in the location you specified in step 3 above (Desktop).

This archive can be securely passed to OS X users by any method. If they know the password, double-clicking the archive will mount the disk image to their Desktop, and they will have full read and write access to the documents inside.

Encrypt a Folder for Cross Platform Use with VeraCrypt

If you need to exchange a file or files with others and they do not use OS X, we can use the same strategy as we did with Disk Utility, but this time we need to password protect our archive in a format that is readable by any OS. Although there are over a dozen cross-platform compression formats, *zip* has become the most common standard.

OS X has the built-in ability to create zip archives, but it has left out the encryption option from the user interface. In order to encrypt our zip archives, we will need to get under the hood and use the command line. No need to go running for the hills. I promise this won't hurt at all.

Once you have created an encrypted archive of your file or files, the archive can be uploaded to a file server, shared by email, or passed along via drive, disc, or thumb drive. As long as the other party knows the (strong) password, your data is safe from spying eyes.

By many in the IT and security fields, the ultimate in document encryption comes with *VeraCrypt* at *http://veracrypt.codeplex.com*. VeraCrypt is free encryption software developed by *IDRIX https://www.idrix.fr*, who specialize in security solutions. It is based on *TrueCrypt http://en.wikipedia.org/wiki/TrueCrypt* that ceased development in 2014.

Although Linux, OS X, and Windows versions are available, no Android or iOS support is offered. Android users may create and decrypt, as well as read and write to TrueCrypt files using *EDS* (Encrypted Data Store), available from Google Play. iOS users may use *Disk Decipher,* available from the App Store, to create and decrypt, as well as read and write to TrueCrypt files.

VeraCrypt is actually a disk encryption utility, as opposed to file encryption. It creates an encrypted virtual disk, or as it is referred to by VeraCrypt, a container.

VeraCrypt presents a slightly higher level of complexity to the end-user, with a resultant very high level of security. Given the speed of current systems and a strong password, data stored in a container may be considered immune from brute-force attacks.

As VeraCrypt creates a container, you are able to place anything within the container for secure storage. The container may reside only on the local drive, or be placed on a server for network access, or within a cloud storage solution (such as DropBox, Google Drive, etc.) to provide Internet access to files and folders, without the cloud provider (or hacker, malware, or government) being able to view the contents.

Assignment: Install FUSE for OS X

VeraCrypt makes use of the *FUSE for OS X* utility, and it must be installed prior to installing VeraCrypt. FUSE for OS X enables your computer to create and work with non-native file systems, such as the *container* system created with VeraCrypt.

1. Open your browser and go to the *OSXFuse* github repository at *http://osxfuse.github.io.* From the right-hand *Stable Releases* sidebar, select the version appropriate for your computer. The installer will begin downloading.

2. Locate the installer in your Downloads folder, and double-click to open. It will mount and open a disk image. Double-click to launch the installer.

3. The *Install FUSE for OS X* installer welcome screen will appear. Select the *Continue* buttons until you see the *Custom Install on <hard drive>*. Enable both *OSXFUSE Preference Pane* and *MacFUSE Compatibility Layer* check boxes, and then select the *Continue* button.

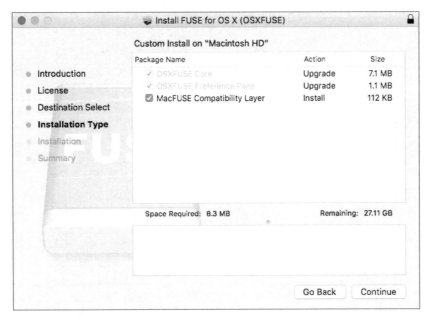

4. Continue selecting the appropriate buttons to complete the installation.

5. Verify FUSE for OS X has installed by opening *System Preferences,* and seeing its icon

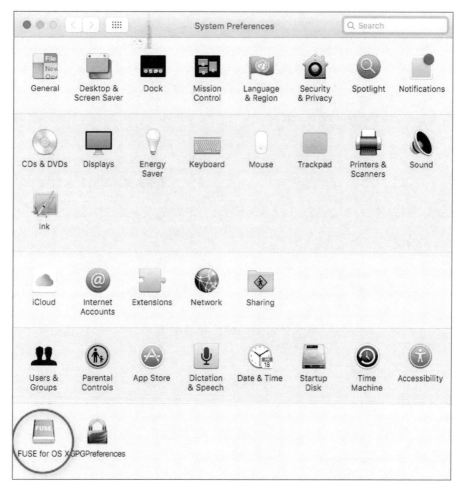

6. Close System Preferences.

The *really* easy part is done. Now on to the easy part–installing VeraCrypt.

Assignment: Download VeraCrypt

1. Open your browser and go to the VeraCrypt home page at
   http://veracrypt.codeplex.com, and then select the *Downloads* tab.

2. From the *Downloads* page, select the version appropriate for your OS. The installer will start to download.

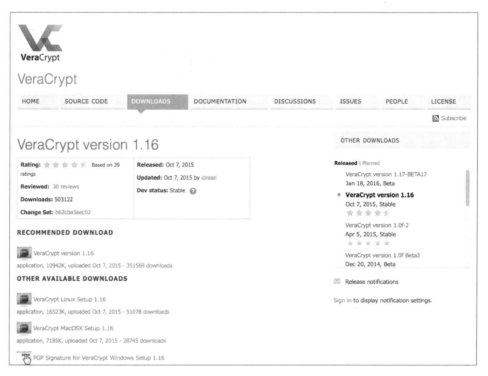

3. Locate VeraCrypt in your Downloads folder, and then double-click to mount the installer disk image.

4. Open the disk image, and double-click the VeraCrypt installer. Complete the VeraCrypt installation.

Assignment: Configure VeraCrypt

As with most applications, it helps to view and configure VeraCrypt preferences before using it. In this assignment, we will examine VeraCrypt preferences.

1. Open VeraCrypt.

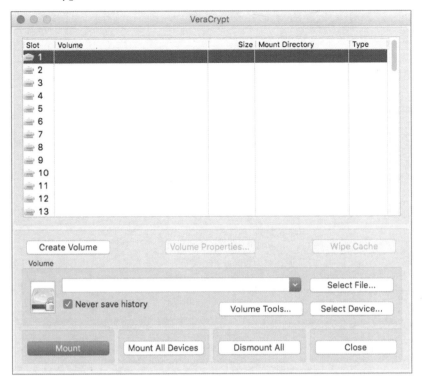

2. Select the *VeraCrypt* menu > *Preferences.*

3. Select the *Security* tab. Most of the options may be configured to taste. The exception is *Preserve modification timestamp of file containers*, which should be *disabled* if the containers will be used with cloud-based file storage service (DropBox, Google Drive, SugarSync, etc.) as it will conflict with the service's ability to update the timestamp. When complete, select the *OK* button.

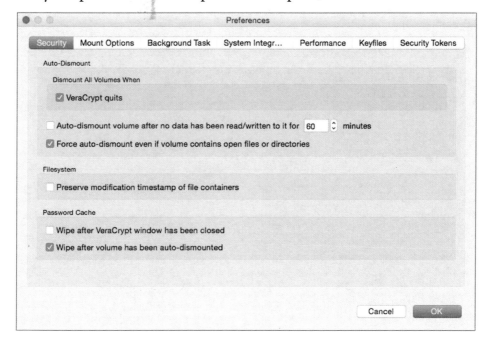

4. Select the *Mount Options* tab.

- *Mount volumes as read-only* will prevent accidental editing or deletion of the container contents if left deselected.

- *Cache passwords in memory* will provide higher security against hackers gaining access to container passwords if left deselected.

- *TrueCrypt Mode* option should be left deselected unless you will be using software that can only work with the older TrueCrypt mode. When complete, select the *OK* button.

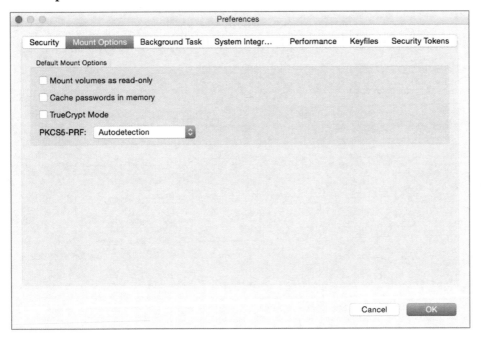

5. Select the *Background Task* tab. All options may be configured to taste. Listed below are my settings. When complete, select the *OK* button.

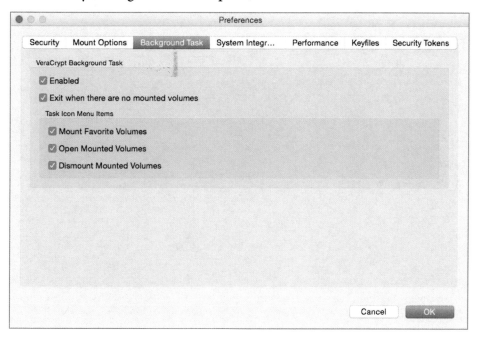

6. Select the *System Integration* tab. You may configure to taste. Listed below is my setting. When complete, select the *OK* button.

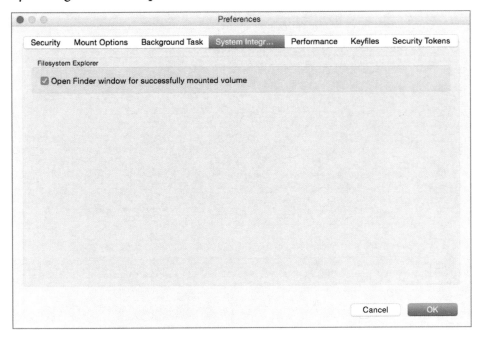

7. Select the *Performance* tab. If your computer supports hardware acceleration of AES encryption protocols, you will probably want to leave the checkbox disabled. Doing so will improve encryption and decryption up to 4 fold. When complete, select the *OK* button.

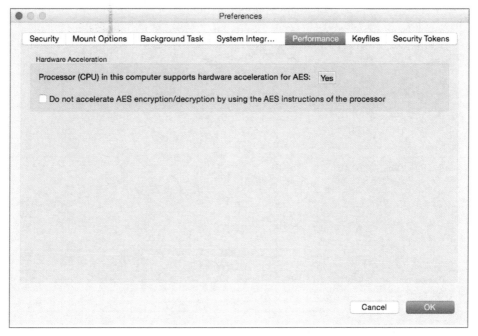

8. The Keyfiles tab is an advanced option. Please see the VeraCrypt online documentation *https://veracrypt.codeplex.com/documentation* for additional information.

9. The *Security Tokens* tap is an advanced option. Please see the VeraCrypt online documentation *https://veracrypt.codeplex.com/documentation* for additional information.

10. Close the VeraCrypt Preferences window.

We are now ready to create our first encrypted VeraCrypt container!

Assignment: Create a VeraCrypt Container

Complete VeraCrypt documentation may be found at
https://veracrypt.codeplex.com/documentation. Although we will cover the basics
of using VeraCrypt, you may find it useful to dive deeper into the topic.

1. *Open* the *VeraCrypt* application, located in the /Applications folder. Then
   select the *Create Volume* button.

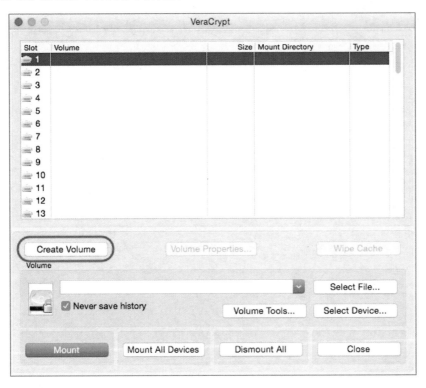

2. To create an encrypted container, at the *VeraCrypt Volume Creation Wizard*, select the *Create an encrypted file container* radio button, and then select the *Next>* button.

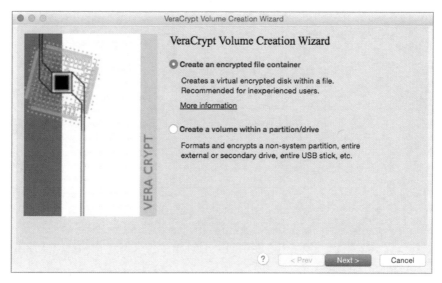

3. At the *Volume Type* window, select the *Standard VeraCrypt volume* radio button, and then select the *Next>* button.

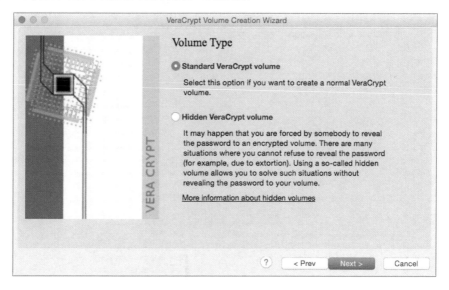

4. At the *Volume Location* window, select the *Select File…*button.

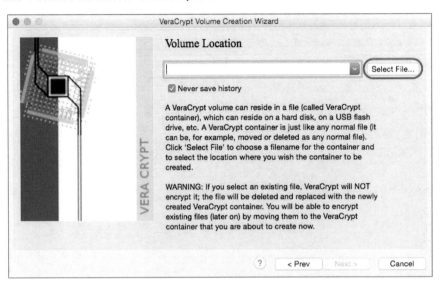

5. When the *Save* window appears, select the *Disclosure arrow* to the right of the *Save As* field. This will expand the window, making it easier to select where to save the container. In the *Save As* field, enter a name for your container, navigate to where you wish to save your container, and then select the *Save* button.

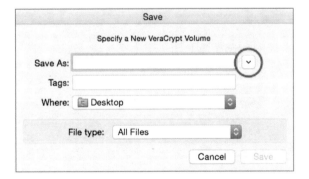

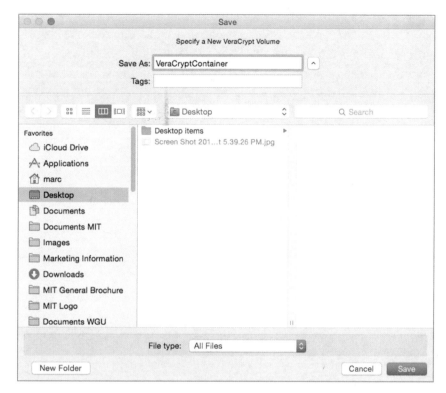

6. When returned to the *Volume Location* window, select the *Next>* button.

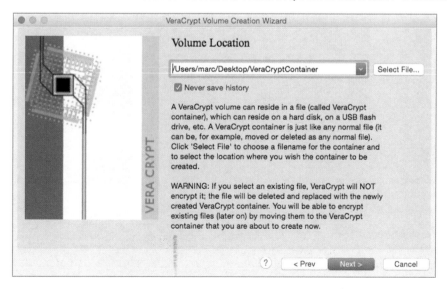

7. At the *Encryption Options* window, from the *Encryption Algorithm* pop-up menu, select your desired option. *AES* is the industry standard, however, as the NSA and NIST were involved with its acceptance, some experts recommend selecting another option. Then, from the *Hash Algorithm* pop-up menu, select the desired option. *SHA* was developed by the NSA, so some experts recommend selecting *Whirlpool*. For our example, we will use the industry standards–*AES* and *SHA-512*, and then select the *Next>* button.

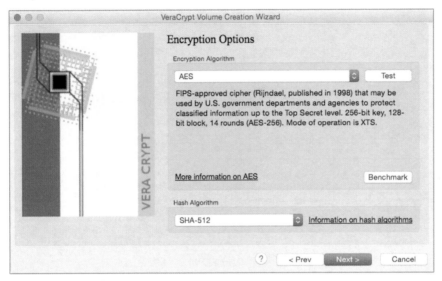

8. In the *Volume Size* window, set the size of your container. If intending on emailing, or copying the container to a thumb drive, keep in mind that each email provider has hard limits on the maximum file size that may be sent or received, and a storage device needs to keep approximately 20% free space for the directory and housekeeping needs. Then select the *Next>* button.

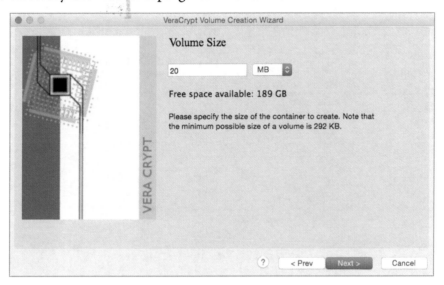

9. At the *Volume Password* window, in the *Password* and *Confirm Password* fields, enter a strong password for the container, and then select the *Next>* button.

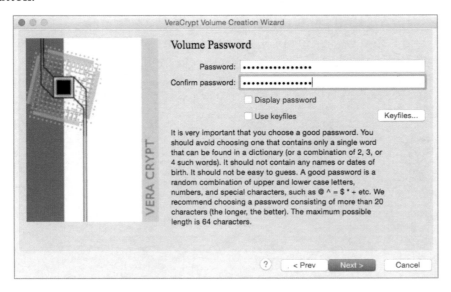

10. At the *Format Options* window, from the *Filesystem type* pop-up menu, select the desired option, and then select the *Next>* button.

   • *FAT* offers full compatibility for Linux and Windows use. OS X can read and write to FAT, but one should not hold OS X applications here.

   • *Mac OS Extended* offers full compatibility for OS X. Linux and Windows users are unable to read this format without the assistance of 3rd-party system add-ons.

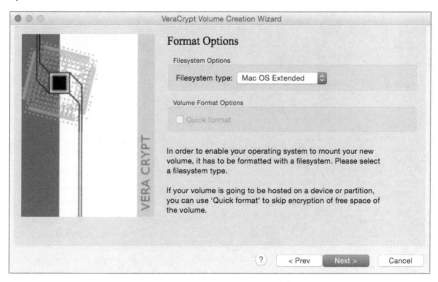

11. At the *Cross-Platform Support* window, select either the *I will mount the volume on other platforms*, or the *I will mount the volume only on Mac OS X* radio buttons, and then select the *Next>* button.

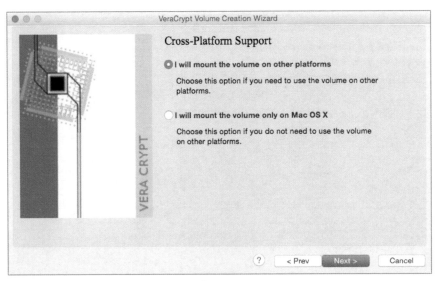

12. At the *Volume Format* window, move your cursor as randomly as possible within the window for at least 30 seconds, and then select the *Format* button.

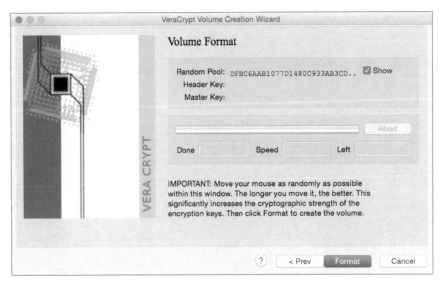

13. Once the container encryption has completed, the *Success* alert appears. Select the *OK* button.

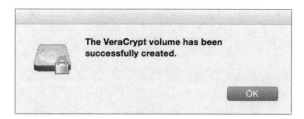

14. At the *Volume Created* window, select the *Next>* button.

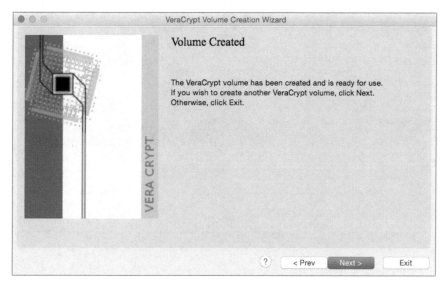

15. You will find yourself back at the start of the process, with VeraCrypt assuming that you wish to create another container. You may select the *Cancel* button to exit the process.

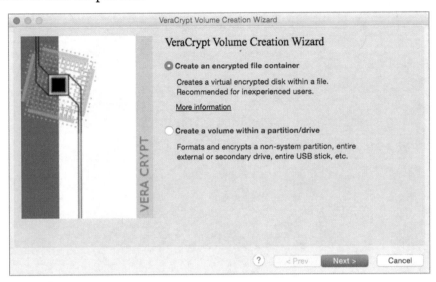

16. You will now find, at the location you specified earlier, the encrypted container.

Congratulations, you have created your first truly spy-class encryption!

Assignment: Mount an Encrypted VeraCrypt Container

Once you have a VeraCrypt container, you will eventually need to open it to read the contents, add to the container, or make edits to the files. In this assignment, we will mount the VeraCrypt container, which gives you access to all of its data.

1. Open *VeraCrypt,* and then select one of the *Slot* numbers along the left side
    bar. This will become the temporary number of the VeraCrypt container to be
    mounted. Select the *Select File...* button.

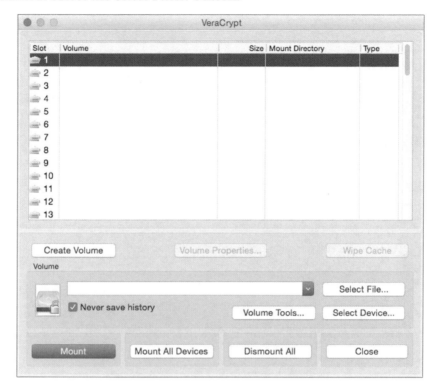

2. Select the *Select File...* button. The standard *Open* window appears. Navigate to the folder holding the target container. Select the container, and then select the *Open* button.

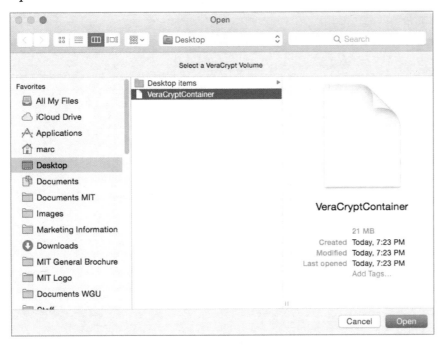

3.   In the VeraCrypt window, select the *Mount* button.

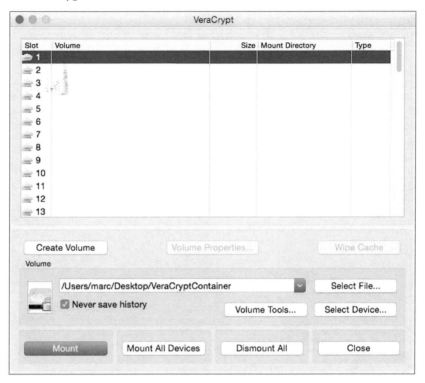

4.   The *Enter password* window appears. Enter the password assigned to the container, and then select the *OK* button.

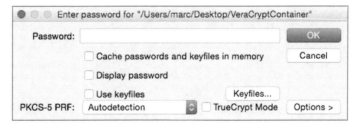

5.   On your Desktop you will see the mounted volume, named *Untitled*. Double-click to open the volume.

6. You may rename the mounted volume as you would any other item.

7. You may drag and drop or save files and folder into the container.

8. To unmount, return to the VeraCrypt window, and then select the *Dismount* button. The mounted volume will disappear from the Desktop.

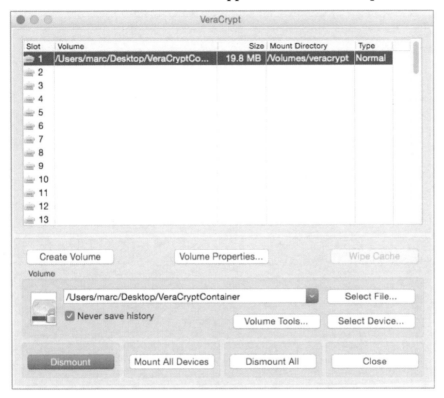

OMG… You *really* are doing high-end security work now! This container may be copied to a thumb drive, optical disc, DropBox, Google Drive, or other Cloud-based storage, and remain secure.

Review Questions

1. Microsoft Office for Mac version _____ and higher use strong AES encryption.

2. Microsoft Office for Mac is limited to a maximum of _____ characters for the encryption password.

3. Adobe Acrobat 9 and higher use _____ encryption.

4. Disk Utility can create encrypted disk images readable by both OS X and Windows. (True or False)

5. VeraCrypt can create encrypted containers readable by both OS X and Windows. (True or False)

17. Vulnerability: Instant Messaging

The ignorance of one voter in a democracy impairs the security of all.

–John F. Kennedy

Instant Messaging

In 2009 the CTIA reported that on average, US cellphone subscribers send an average of 534 text messages a month. AT&T reported in 2012 that their subscribers under 25 years old averaged 5 times this number!

And if the raw number of texts isn't mind-numbing enough, the topics of discussion most certainly are. With almost nobody giving any thought to the facts that:

- The cellular provider likely archives your text messages for years.

- The government has full access to all of your messages and also archives them.

- The encryption scheme used by cellular providers was broken years ago, and any kid can listen in on your messaging.

- If you are in business, it is possible the competition listens in on your messaging.

- If you are involved with healthcare and text *any* patient information–even to the patient–you are probably in violation of HIPAA compliance and may be subject up to a $50,000 fine.

Unless you are texting innocuous comments, such as: *I love you* (assuming this is a relationship in the open), *remember to bring home milk*, or *I'll be home by 6pm*, your texting should be secure by way of encryption.

The texting app that is included with iOS and OS X–*Messages*–has been verified by the *Electronic Frontier Foundation (EFF)* as secure, but only when both sender and recipient are using *Messages*. When texting between different text apps or different smartphone OS's, *Messages* no longer can encrypt the data stream.

There are a few texting apps that meet military and HIPAA requirements for security and encryption. One of our favorites is *Wickr*. That it works well, allows for the sender to set a time of auto-destruct, and is free helps to put it at the top of the list.

If there is a downside to Wickr, it is that you can only communicate securely with others who are also using Wickr. But this is the nature of the security beast.

Assignment: Install and Configure Wickr

In this assignment we will be installing and configuring Wickr on your OS X computer in order to create secure, encrypted text communications with other users of *Wickr* on their Android, iOS, Linux, OS X, or Windows device also running *Wickr*.

1. On your OS X computer, open a browser to *Wickr* at *http://www.wickr.com*.

2. Select the *Download Wickr* button.

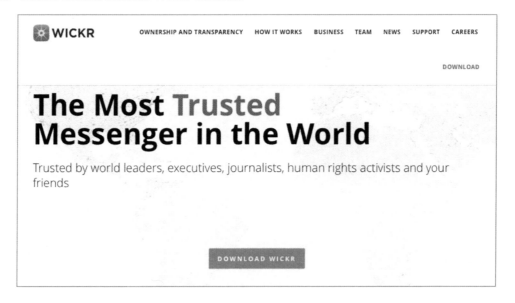

3. At the *Downloads* page, select the *OS X Download* button. The *Wickr Top Secret Messenger Installer* will download.

4. Once downloaded, double-click the *Wickr TopSecret Messenger.dmg* file. This will mount and open a virtual disk on your Desktop.

5. In the *Mac App Store Preview* window, select the *View In Mac App Store* button.

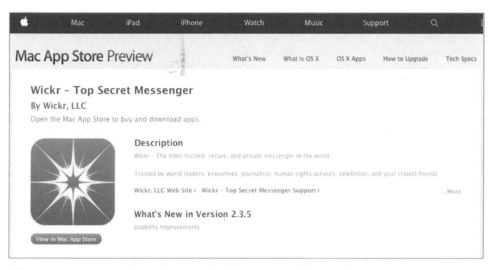

6. The *App Store* app launches and takes you to the *Wickr–Top Secret Messenger* page. Select the *Get* button, and then the *Install* button to download and install Wickr.

7. At the authentication window, enter your *Apple ID* and *Password* to permit installation.

8. Open *Wickr* (located in */Applications)*.Double-click the *Wickr.app* in your *Applications* folder. The *Sign up* window will open.

- If you don't yet have an account, select the *Sign Up* button.

- If you have an existing account, select the *Log In* button, and then enter your account credentials.

9. At the *Notice, Don't forget. There are no password resets!* alert, select the *OK* button.

10. At the *Create a new account* window, enter your desired credentials, and then select the *Sign Up* button.

11. The *Friend Finder* window appears. Configure to taste.

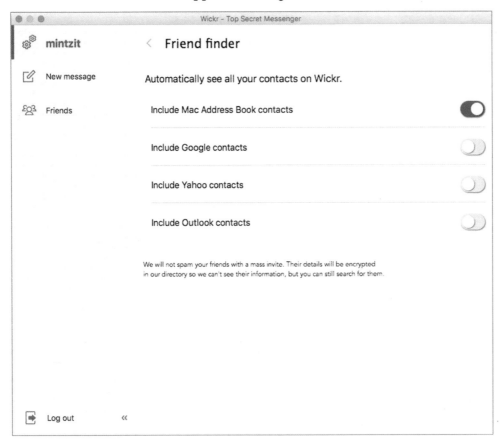

As with most applications, before jumping on in, it's best to configure the preferences.

12. Select your Wickr ID at the top left of the window to open the Wickr Settings. The *Settings* window opens.

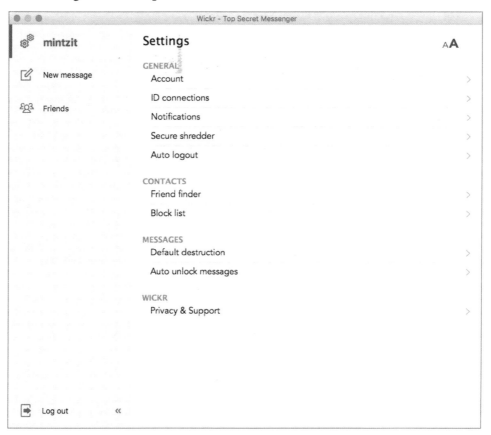

13. Select *ID Connections*. The *ID Connections* window opens. Add your mobile phone and email to make it easier for friends to find you on Wickr.

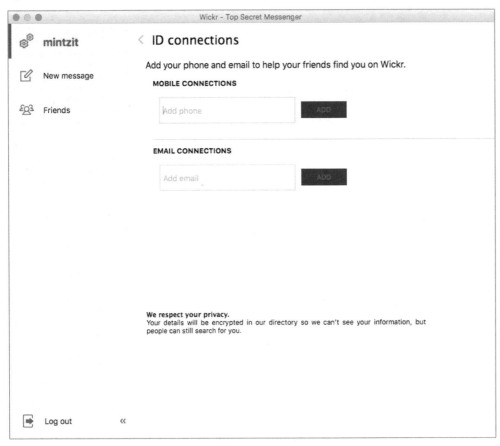

14. Select the back icon (<) to the left of *ID Connections* to return to *Settings*.

15. Select *Notifications*. The *Notifications* window opens. Configure to your taste, and then select the back button to return to *Settings*.

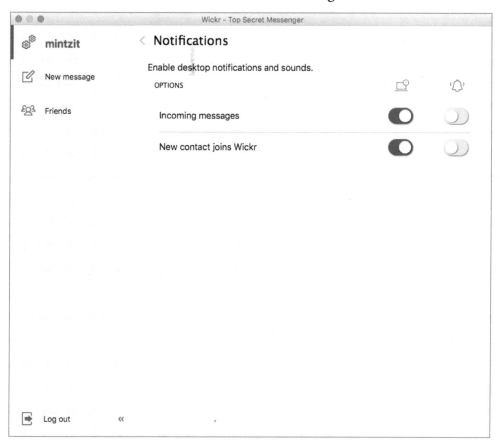

16. Select *Secure Shredder.* The *Secure Shredder* window opens. Configure to your taste, and then select the back button.

    • Note: As of this writing there is no documentation on the specific timing of each setting.

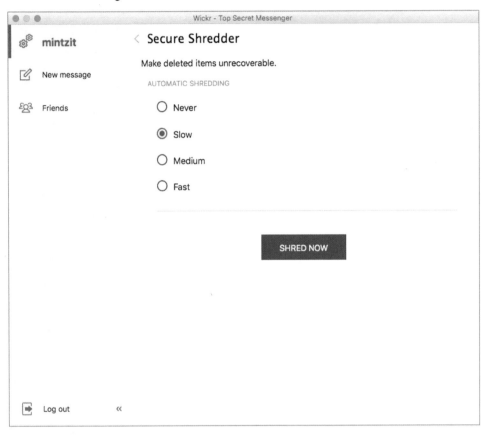

17. Select *Auto Logout*, configure to your taste, and then select the back button.

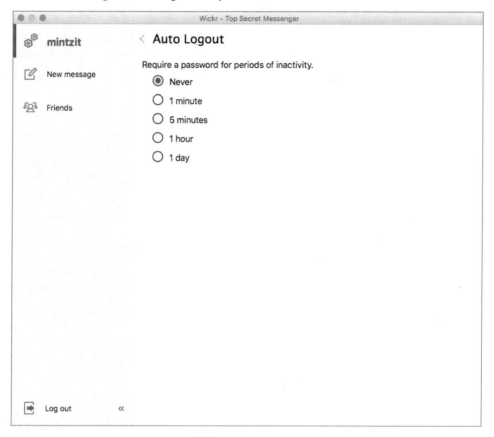

18. Select *Default Destruction,* configure to your taste, and then select the back button.

19. Select Auto unlock messages, configure to taste, and then select the back button.

   • Note: Although my default is set to *On,* this may well be considered insecure in some environments.

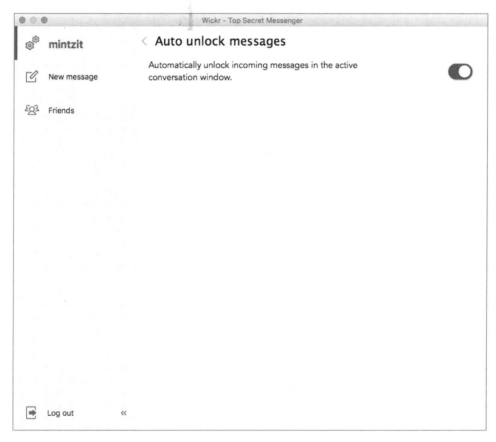

Wickr is now ready to send and receive military-grade encrypted text messages with other *Wickr* users.

Assignment: Invite Friends to Wickr

Once you have Wickr configured, it's time to take it out for a test drive. You will need to have at least one other friend with a Wickr account with whom to text.

In this assignment you will invite a friend to join Wickr so that the two of you may communicate securely.

1. Open *Wickr,* and then select *Friends* from the sidebar.

2. Scroll through your contacts (pulled from either or both your *Address Book* and *Google Contacts.*)

3. Select a friend with whom you would like to communicate securely, and then select the *Add Friend* icon to their far right.

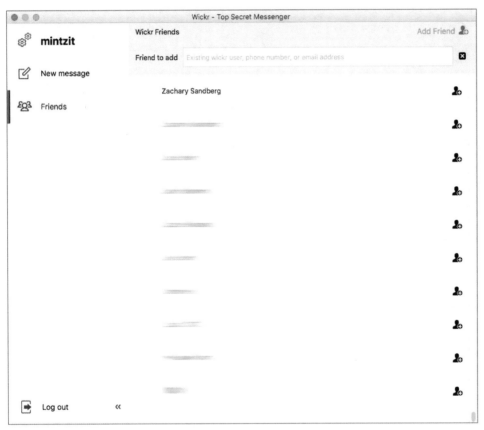

4. Your email application will open, a new email will be created inviting your friend to download *Wickr*, and will include your *Wickr* ID. Send this email.

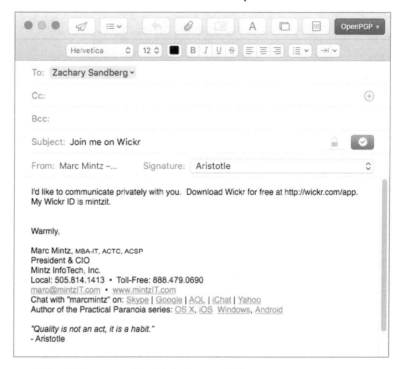

5. Once your friend has installed *Wickr,* and then sent you a message, you will have their ID and it will be stored in the *Wickr* contacts. How to do that in the next assignment.

Assignment: Add Friends to Wickr

Once you know the Wickr ID of someone, you can add their ID to Wickr for faster messaging.

In this assignment you will add a Wickr ID to your Wickr app.

1. I'm one of your friends, and I just informed you of my Wickr ID, which is *mintzit*. To add it to Wickr, start by opening the Wickr app, and then select *Friends* in the sidebar.

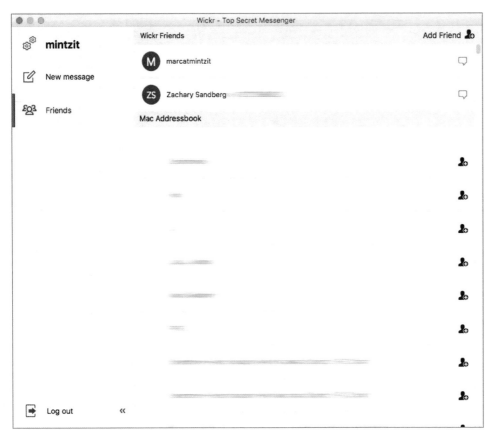

2. Select the *Add Friend* icon in the top right corner. The *Friend to add* text field will appear.

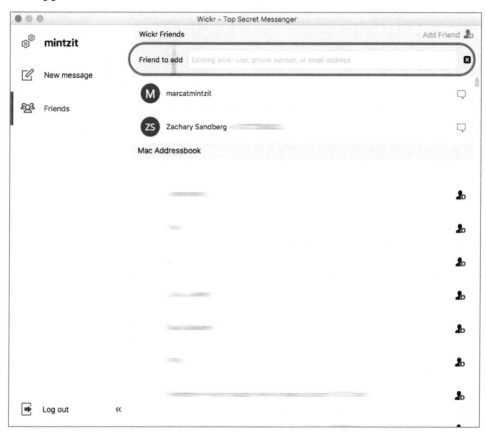

3. In the *Friend to add* field, enter the *Wickr ID, phone number, or email address* of this person. If you are using me, enter *mintzit*. When done, press the *Return* or *Enter* key.

4. The *Edit Friend* window opens. In this window you may *Add Photo* of this contact, *Star* them as a *Favorite, Start a conversation, Block them from messaging you,* or *Delete* the ID.

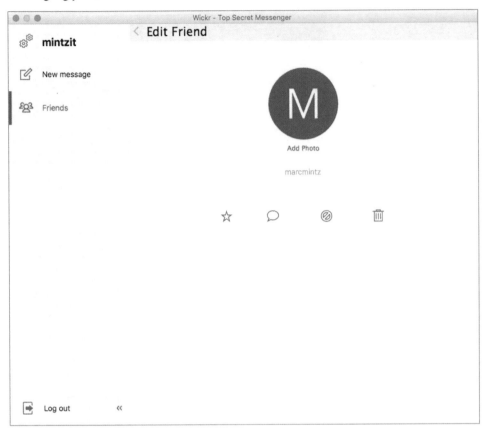

5. Repeat steps 2–4for each of your contacts to be added to Wickr.

Assignment: Send a Wickr Message

In this assignment you will send a secure message via Wickr to a contact. Feel free to use my *mintzit* address.

1. Open Wickr.

2. Select *New message* from the sidebar.To start a mew message with a friend, start by selecting New Message from the Wickr sidebar. Your Wickr contacts will appear.

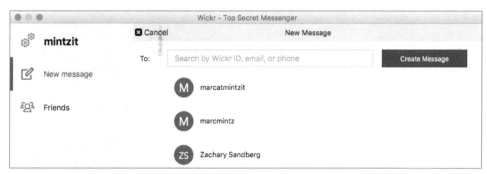

3. Select the friend or friends to be included in the message. You will see their ID's added in the *To* field.

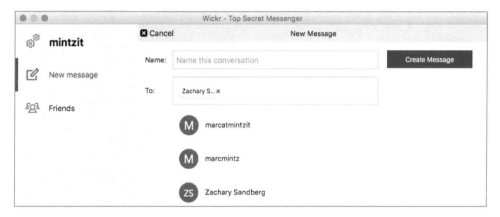

6. Select the *Create Message* button. The *Message* window will appear, addressed to your friend(s).

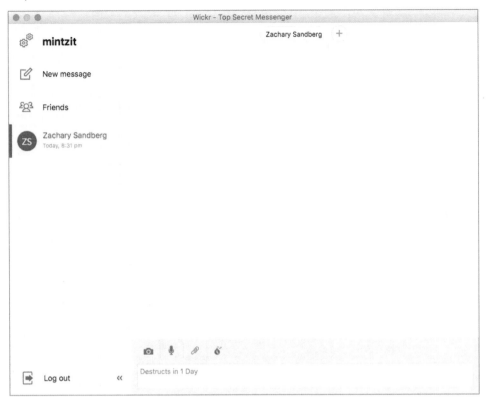

7. Enter your text in the bottom field that lists the self-destruct time for the message.

   • Note: The icons directly above your text you are able to take and attach a picture, attach a voice message, attach a file, and configure self-destruct time.

8. Tap the *Return* or *Enter* key to send the message.

Congratulations! You and your friends are now able to communicate, secure in the knowledge that your communications are not intercepted.

Review Questions

1. Instant messages sent via *Messages* between iOS and OS X are securely encrypted. (True or False)

2. There are currently no cross platform secure instant messaging applications available. (True or False)

18. Vulnerability: Voice and Video Communications

Surveillance technologies now available–including the monitoring of virtually all digital information–have advanced to the point where much of the essential apparatus of a police state is already in place.

- Al Gore

Voice and Video Communications

Every time you send or receive a text message, phone call, or videoconference on your computer or mobile device, the conversations and metadata are stored by third parties. The carriers (Verizon, AT&T, etc.) for each party have the ability to intercept any traffic that crosses their networks, which may also extend to any third parties that work with your carrier, such as contractors, or subsidiaries.

Aside from the telecom companies themselves, your local and federal government have the ability to monitor in dragnet style snooping.

Online voice & video services such as Facebook messenger and Google Hangouts may be more secure in transit between your computer or device and their servers, but because your conversations are stored on their hardware without end-to-end encryption, there is no guarantee of privacy.

So how can you communicate easily and securely using your computer and mobile device? The common options are:

- *FaceTime*: If you are to videoconference between another iPhone, iPad, or OS X user, you can use the built-in FaceTime app. FaceTime is fully encrypted, Apple does not have a back door, so neither does a criminal or government.

  The only downside to FaceTime is that it only works with other Apple devices or computers.

- *Skype*: Skype is Microsoft's premier video conferencing solution that offers voice, video chat and desktop sharing for up to 25 people in a group. Recently setting a record for over 35 million people online simultaneously, Skype is one of Microsoft's core technologies, and is bundled into Windows, XBOX, and Windows mobile.

  It is well known that Skype allows Microsoft and several major governments to listen in on conversations as well as the potential to gain access to files and metadata on the user's computer. As a result, Skype should be treated as a completely insecure service that any number of organizations and governments have access to.

- *Google Hangouts*: In the past several years, other proprietary alternatives to Skype have surfaced, most notably is Google Hangouts. Hangouts tightly integrates Google's social network, Google+, along with Chat, Screen Sharing, and integration with other Google services into a plugin based application. Hangouts is free, and supports up to 10 users simultaneously with any free Google account. Google Business accounts support up to 15 users.

  Like Skype, Hangouts has many privacy implications. Google Hangouts doesn't have end-to-end encryption, and in a recent online interview with Google's director for law enforcement and information security, it was revealed that Governments, law enforcement and Google itself have access to your chats, and calls.

Secure Alternatives

If you are interested in cross-platform, end-to-end encrypted, voice and video conferencing solutions, there are several alternative services that provide encrypted calls and work with many existing open source clients.

OStel *https://ostel.co* is our choice for end-to-end encrypted voice and video communication. Ostel provides encrypted communication to OS X clients using a program called Jitsi. Jitsi is open source communication software that in addition to OStel's SIP protocol, will also handle other popular 3rd party protocols such as Facebook chat, Gchat, XMPP and more.

The only downside to OStel is that it is currently in beta.

Assignment: Sign up for an OStel account

In this assignment we will start the process of creating an OStel account. Getting an OStel account is probably the most painless experience you will ever have. An email address and a password are the only two things you will need to get started.

1. Open a browser, and then go to *https://ostel.co.* The OStel home page opens. Click the orange *Sign Me Up!* button.

2. In the box provided, type your email address and click *Sign up.*

3. On the next screen pick your code name and a password. When finished, click *Create my account.*

4. The confirmation page will display a message at the top telling that your account has been successfully created.

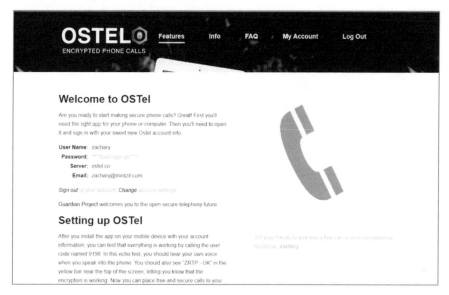

Congratulations. You have successfully created your OStel account, and are now ready to install the software to start making encrypted mobile communications.

Assignment: Install the OStel App

Now that the Ostel account set up, we need to download and install the appropriate client app that will allow us to use the Ostel network to securely call others.

1. Scroll down the Ostel page you were left on in the previous assignment, to *Download the App* section.

2. Within the section for your target OS and device, click the link to download the appropriate app. In this assignment, this will be the section for *Mac,* with a link for *Jitsi app.*

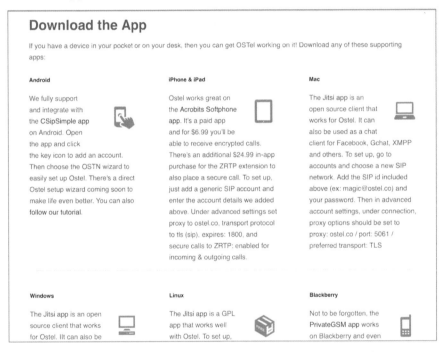

Download the App

If you have a device in your pocket or on your desk, then you can get OSTel working on it! Download any of these supporting apps:

Android

We fully support and integrate with the **CSipSimple app** on Android. Open the app and click the key icon to add an account. Then choose the OSTN wizard to easily set up Ostel. There's a direct Ostel setup wizard coming soon to make life even better. You can also follow our tutorial.

iPhone & iPad

Ostel works great on the **Acrobits Softphone** app. It's a paid app and for $6.99 you'll be able to receive encrypted calls. There's an additional $24.99 in-app purchase for the ZRTP extension to also place a secure call. To set up, just add a generic SIP account and enter the account details we added above. Under advanced settings set proxy to ostel.co, transport protocol to tls (sip), expires: 1800, and secure calls to ZRTP: enabled for incoming & outgoing calls.

Mac

The Jitsi app is an open source client that works for Ostel. It can also be used as a chat client for Facebook, Gchat, XMPP and others. To set up, go to accounts and choose a new SIP network. Add the SIP id included above (ex: magic@ostel.co) and your password. Then in advanced account settings, under connection, proxy options should be set to proxy: ostel.co / port: 5061 / preferred transport: TLS

Windows

The Jitsi app is an open source client that works for Ostel. IIt can also be

Linux

The Jitsi app is a GPL app that works well with Ostel. To set up,

Blackberry

Not to be forgotten, the PrivateGSM app works on Blackberry and even

3. At the jitsi.org webpage, click the *Stable Builds* button.

4. At the *Jitsi Stable Build Line* page, click on the *Mac OS X packages*. The software will begin to download.

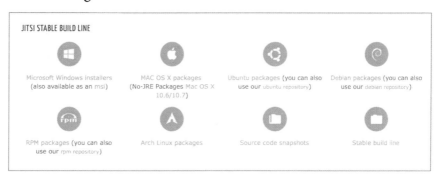

5. Locate the *jitsi-latest.dmg* file in your Downloads folder, and then double-click to open it.

6. When the file opens, drag the *Jitsi.app* into the *Applications* folder

7. Locate the *Jitsi.app*, and then double-click to open it.

8. Select the *Accounts* button, and then click the *Add* button.

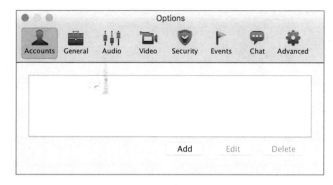

9. In the *Add new account* window, configure as follows. When complete, click the *Add* button.

- *Network*: SIP

- *SIP ID*: Your username created your OStel account appended by *@ostel.co*

- *Password*: Your password used when creating your OStel account.

10. Once the account is set up, the status in Jitsi will be displayed as *Online*.

11. You can look up another member by typing their username in the search box. Jitsi will then search your system's shared contacts for a match. In this example below, I have located my friend Anthony's username. To initiate a call with Anthony, I simply click the phone icon under his name.

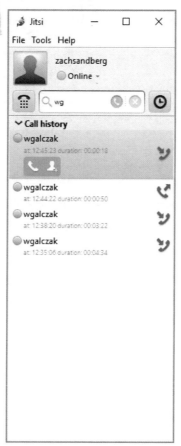

12. Once the voice call initiates, each participant can share webcam video if desired. Clicking the video icon on the bottom row will start the sharing.

13. Another feature of Jitsi (similar to Skype) is desktop sharing. To activate, click the desktop icon on the bottom row. Once initiated, you will be prompted to either allow the other chat member to take control of your computer or to simply view your screen.

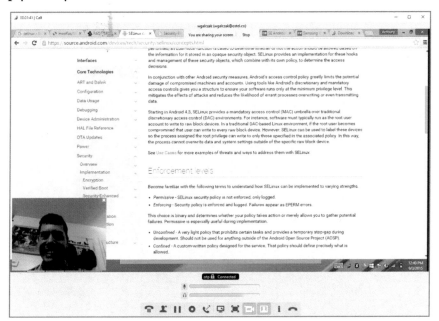

Review Questions

1. When using Facetime between iOS and OS X computers, the communications are fully secure. (True or False)

2. Skype is fully secure between any devices. (True or False)

3. Google Hangouts has end-to-end encryption. (True or False)

19. Vulnerability: Internet Activity

If you have built castles in the air, your work need not be lost; that is where they should be. Now put the foundations under them.

–Henry David Thoreau, *Walden*

VPN–Virtual Private Network

In case you have been sleep reading through this book, let me repeat my wake-up call: *They are watching you on the Internet. They* may be the automated governmental watchdogs (of your own or another country), government officials (again, of your own or another country), bored staff at an Internet Service Provider or broadband provider, a jealous (and slightly whackadoodle) ex, high school kids driving by your home or office or sitting on a hill several miles away, or criminals.

Regardless, your computer and data are at risk.

Perhaps one of the most important steps that can be taken to protect you is to encrypt the entire Internet experience all the way from your computer, through your broadband provider, to a point where your surfing, chat, webcam, email, etc. cannot be tracked or understood. This is accomplished using a technology called *VPN–Virtual Private Network.*

Gateway VPN

There are two fundamental flavors of VPN *http://en.wikipedia.org/wiki/Virtual_private_network*. The most common is called a *gateway VPN* (mesh VPN is discussed later.) Historically, gateway VPN involved the use of a VPN box resident at an organization. Telecommuting staff is able to use the gateway so the Internet acts like a very long Ethernet cable connecting their computer to the office network. In addition, all data traveling between the users computer and the gateway is military-grade encrypted. The downside to this strategy is that these boxes are relatively expensive (from $600 to several thousand dollars), and they require significant technical experience to configure correctly.

In greater detail the concept works like this:

1. Your computer has VPN software installed and configured to connect to a VPN server at the office. This server is connected to your office network. OS X comes with VPN software built into the Network System Preferences that works with many of the commercially available VPN servers, including the most popular–Cisco. Other VPN servers require their own proprietary client software to be installed.

2. On your computer you open the VPN software and instruct it to connect to the VPN server. This typically requires entering your authentication credentials of user name and password, along with a long key.

3. The VPN server authenticates you as an allowed account and begins the connection between itself and your computer.

4. As you send data from your computer to the network connected to the VPN server (typically the regular business network), all of it is military-grade encrypted. When the data is received at the VPN server or at your computer, the VPN software decrypts it.

5. Once your data reaches the VPN server, it is then forwarded to the appropriate service on your organizations network (file server, printer, mail server, etc.)

Although this may sound a bit complex, all a user must do is enter a name, password, and key. Everything else is invisible. The only indicator that anything is different is that speed slower than normal. This is due to the overhead of encryption/decryption process.

We can use this same strategy so that instead of securely exchanging data with our office server, we can securely surf the Internet. The workflow is just slightly different:

1. Your computer has VPN software configured to connect to a VPN server that is not associated with your office, but is just another server "on the Internet."

2. On your computer you open the VPN software and instruct it to connect to the VPN server. If you are using our recommended software, it is pre-configured with all the settings necessary–nothing much more to do but launch.

3. The VPN server authenticates you as an allowed account and begins the connection between itself and your computer.

4. As you surf the web, all data is military-grade encrypted. When the data is received at the VPN server or your computer, the VPN software decrypts it.

5. Once your data reaches the VPN server, it is then forwarded to the appropriate service on the Internet.

Using this strategy (a VPN Internet server), all of your Internet traffic is military-grade encrypted between your computer and the VPN server. It is not possible to decipher any of your traffic (user names, passwords, data) or even the type of data coming and going.

One downside is that once the data exits the VPN server, it is readable. However, your data is intermingled with thousands of other users data, making the process of tweezing out your data a task that perhaps only the NSA can accomplish.

Another concern is that some VPN providers maintain user activity logs. This is law in most countries, so that government agencies are able to review who is doing what through the VPN. Ideally, you want to work only with a VPN provider operating in a country doesn't require logs, and in fact, do not keep logs.

There are thousands of VPN Internet Servers available. Most of them are free. I don't recommend using the free services for two reasons:

1. You get what you pay for (typically here today, gone tomorrow, unstable, etc.)

2. You don't know who is listening at the server side of things. Remember, your data is fully encrypted up to the server. But once the data reaches the server on the way to the Internet, it is readable. There needs to be a high degree of trust for the administration of the VPN server. I see no reason to have such trust with free services.

When determining the best VPN provider for your use, there are some key variables to look for:

- **Speed**. How fast is your Internet experience. Using VPN introduces a speed penalty due to the encryption/decryption process, as well as the need to process all incoming and outgoing packets through a server instead of point-to-point. VPN providers can reduce this penalty in a number of ways, including; faster servers, reducing the clients:server ratio, better algorithms, filtering content to remove advertisements and cookies, and faster server internet connections.

- **Logs**. Are logs kept on client activities. In many countries it is required by law that all Internet providers maintain logs of client activities. If so, although the logs may not record *what* you were doing, they keep a record of *where* you traveled. It is ideal to have a VPN provider that keeps no logs whatsoever.

- **Support**. VPN adds a layer of complexity to your Internet activities. Should something not work correctly, you don't want to be the one troubleshooting. Ideally, your VPN provider has 24/7/365 chat support. Even better if they offer telephone support.

- **Cross-Platform Support**. Most of us have more than one device. Perhaps a Windows and OS X computer, an Android phone, and an Apple iPad. It would be madness to have to use a different VPN product for each of these. Look for a provider that supports all of your current and potential devices.

- **Multi-Device Support**. Most, but not all, providers now offer from 3-5 concurrent device licensing. This allows your VPN service to be operational on all of your devices at the same time. Providers that offer only single-device licensing may be quite costly should you have multiple devices.

- **DNS-Leak Protection**. Although VPN encrypts all data that comes and goes from your device, before you can reach out to the Internet to connect to your email, a website, or text, your device must connect to a DNS server for guidance on where to find the mail, web, or text server. If you are using your default DNS server (typically one by your Internet broadband provider, data between your system and the DNS server is not encrypted *and* is recorded. It is ideal if your VPN provider offered their own DNS servers. Using this strategy, then the data between your device and the DNS server is now either encrypted, or is not logged.

VPNArea

One of our favorite VPN providers is *VPNArea.net*. Although they do not offer a free or trial option, their yearly rate is a reasonable $59. With this you get servers in almost every country you can name, use on 5 devices, unlimited bandwidth, humans on the other end of the tech support call, and highly responsive bandwidth.

The dominant feature of VPNArea is it is registered in Bulgaria, with servers located in Switzerland. Switzerland national data protection laws are among the strictest in terms of protecting private data, and permitting a VPN provider to not keep logs of client traffic. Other differentiating features include the option to use OpenVPN, L2TP, or PPTP (OpenVPN would be our only choice), 7-day money back guarantee, and their list of over 10,000 alternate DNS servers so that you do not need to use those provided by your organization or Internet provider. This last option is important, as if you are using your ISP, Google, or other common DNS servers, your web travels are logged (called a *DNS Leak*). They also offer the upgrade to your own dedicated VPN server. This provides a significant speed boost as your server isn't timesharing with dozens or hundreds of other users.

Assignment: Create a VPNArea Account

In this assignment, we will create a paid account (with a 7-day cancellation policy) with *VPNArea.net*, and then configure VPN services.

- NOTE: VPNArea has extended a special discount to *Practical Paranoia* students and readers. When registering, enter *pparanoia* in the coupon field to get your discount.

- NOTE: As of this writing, the default VPNArea application, Chameleon, only works when logged in with an administrative account, not standard accounts. If you do not want to log in with an administrative account, contact VPNArea for a customized version of the 3rd-party VPN application, *Viscosity*. Viscosity is also available directly from the developer at <https://www.sparklabs.com/viscosity/> for $9. The assignment for Viscosity is found later in this chapter.

1. Open a browser, visit VPNArea at *http://vpnarea.com,* and then select the *Get Started–Prices* button.

2. After reviewing the available plans, click the *Buy Now* button for the desired plan.

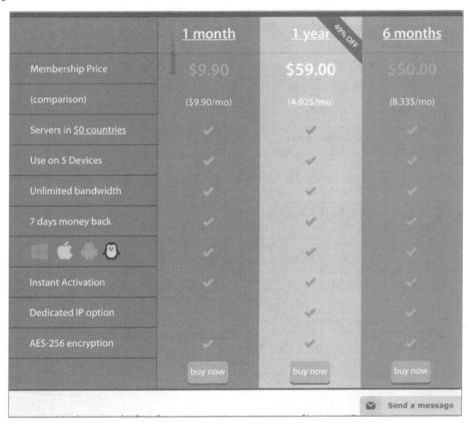

	1 month	1 year 49% OFF	6 months
Membership Price	$9.90	**$59.00**	$50.00
(comparison)	($9.90/mo)	(4.92$/mo)	(8.33$/mo)
Servers in <u>50 countries</u>	✓	✓	✓
Use on 5 Devices	✓	✓	✓
Unlimited bandwidth	✓	✓	✓
7 days money back	✓	✓	✓
	✓	✓	✓
Instant Activation	✓	✓	✓
Dedicated IP option		✓	✓
AES-256 encryption	✓	✓	✓
	buy now	buy now	buy now

✉ Send a message

3. Scroll down the page to the *Sign up in seconds* area. Enter all the requested information, remember to record your *Username* and *password,*

4. In the *Coupon Code* field, enter *pparanoia* to receive your *Practical Paranoia* student and reader discount, and then click the *Buy Now* button.

Assignment: Install VPNArea Chameleon

VPNArea has their own utility to interface with OpenVPN, named *Chameleon*. It is a powerful, yet very easy to configure utility. If there is a downside to it, it is that Chameleon requires that the user account be an administrator account. If you need or wish to log in as an administrator, use this assignment to install and configure Chameleon.

If you need or wish to log in with a non-administrator account, VPNArea uses the 3rd-party utility *Viscosity http://www.sparklabs.com/viscosity/*. The assignment to install and configure Viscosity follows this one.

1. After your payment is processed, you are taken to the *Thank You* page. Select the *Go to Members Area* button.

2. In the *Members Area* page, select the *Mac Yosemite / Lion / Mavericks* button.

In this page will be complete setup instructions. They are repeated here.

3. For OS X, it is necessary to download the VPNArea VPN utility *Chameleon*. Select the *Setup File* button to download the file.

4. Once the *Chameleon* dmg file has downloaded, double-click to open it. Inside the virtual disk now mounted on your desktop will be the *VPNAreaChameleon.app*. Drag it into your *Applications* folder. This is important, as it will not function properly if located anywhere else.

5. Double-click to launch *VPNAreaChameleon.app* in your *Applications* folder.

6. If prompted to allow opening, select the *Open* button.

7. *VPNAreaChameleon.app* will open. Enter your *Username* and *Password* as created when you created your account, from the *Select a server* pop-up menu select a server, and then select the *Connect* button.

8. At the prompt for a password, enter your OS X user account password, not your VPNArea password, and then select the *OK* button.

9. When connected you will see the *Connection Status* change to *Connected.* Also, the *Chameleon* menu item will change to green.

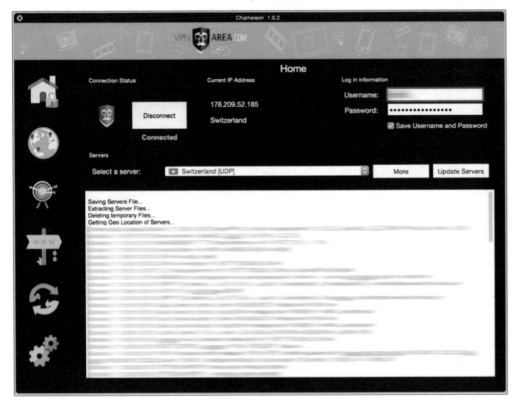

10. To add extra assurance that you will only ever use VPN when connecting to the Internet, from the *Chameleon* sidebar, select the *Kill Switch* icon, and then enable the *Enabled* checkbox.

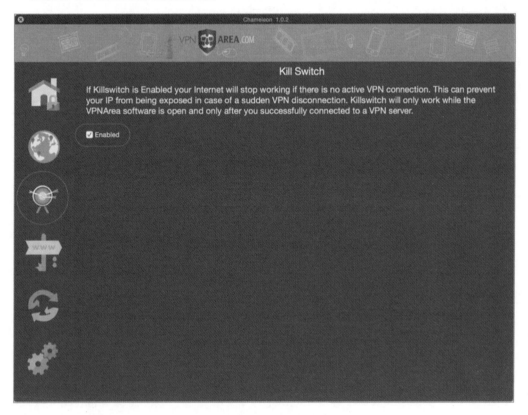

11. To reduce the possibility that your DNS activity is tracked or recorded (called a *DNS Leak*) by your organization or Internet provider, you will want to change your DNS Servers when connecting to VPN. With most other VPN providers, this must be done in the *System Preferences > Network > Advanced > DNS* pane. However, VPNArea makes this automatic! To find your desired DNS servers, open a browser and go to *http://vpnarea.com/front/member/dns.* You can get here manually from logging in to vpnarea.net, selecting *Members Area,* and then select *Change DNS.*

12. Scroll through the list to find a DNS server in the country of choice, and then copy the *IPv4* address from the left column.

13. Select the *www Anti DNS Leak* icon from the *Chameleon.app* sidebar, click in the *Primary* field, and then *Paste*.

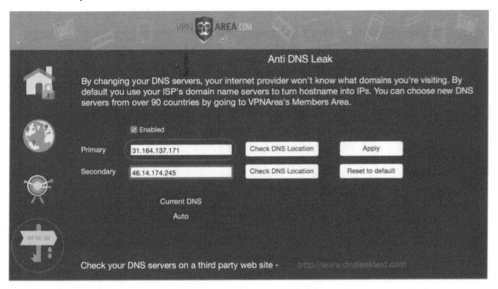

14. Repeat for another DNS server in your desired country, and then *Paste* in the *Secondary* field.

15. Click the *Check DNS Location* for each DNS server to verify it is working properly. When verified, click the *OK* button.

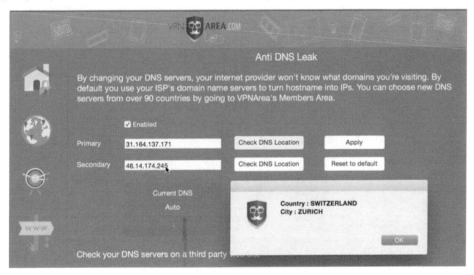

16. Enable the *Enabled* checkbox, and then click the *Apply* button. Your computer is now using VPN with *Anti-DNS Leak* enabled.

17. If at any time you wish to change your VPN server or country, click on the *VPNArea* menu item, scroll through the list of servers, and then select the desired server.

18. The last piece of configuration is found by selecting the *Settings* icon in the *Chameleon* sidebar. Configure to taste. Shown below are my recommendations:

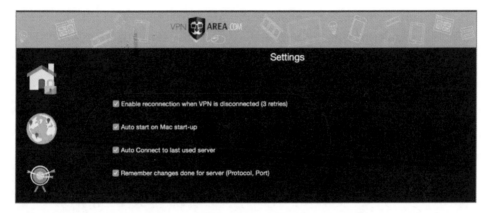

19. To turn VPN and Anti-DNS Leak off, click on the *VPNArea* menu item, and then select the *Exit* button.

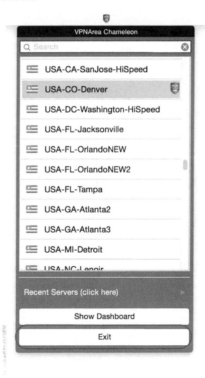

20. When you wish to reactivate VPN, open *VPNArea Chameleon.app*. You can see that VPN is active when the *VPNArea* menu icon changes to green.

Congratulations! You have configured VPN so that any time you need complete privacy with your Internet communications, it is ready for you.

Assignment: Install Viscosity for VPNArea

VPNArea uses the 3rd-party utility *Viscosity* as the front-end interface for OpenVPN for users who need or want to log in with a non-administrator accounts. If you need or want to log in as an administrator, VPNArea uses their own *Chameleon* utility to work with OpenVPN. If you will be logging in as an administrator, you may skip this assignment, and complete the previous one for Chameleon.

1. After completing registration for a VPNArea account, send an email to *viscosity@vpnarea.com*, requesting a copy of *Viscosity*. Include your email address and VPNArea account information.

2. Within 3 hours you will receive an email with a link to your customized version of Viscosity.

3. Click the link to download Viscosity.

4. The Viscosity download will be named *Viscosity Bundle*, containing two items: the Viscosity.app, and the VPP folder.

5. Drag the Viscosity Bundle folder into your */Applications* folder.

6. Double-click the Viscosity.app, located in */Applications/Viscosity Bundle*.

7. The *Viscosity Helper Tool Installation* window opens. Select *Install.*

8. The *Welcome to Viscosity* window appears. You may close it as Viscosity is up and running without it.

Assignment: Create a Viscosity VPN Internet Connection

In this assignment, we will use the 3rd-party OpenVPN application *Viscosity* to create a secure VPN Internet connection through VPNArea.

- Prerequisites: The previous assignments must have been completed to have an active VPNArea account, and Viscosity.app is installed on your computer.

1. Open Viscosity.app, located in */Applications*.

2. From the menu bar, select the Viscosity menu icon 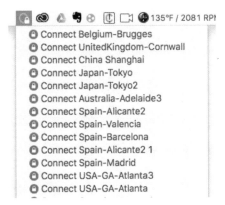 . The drop-down menu will display all available VPNArea servers. Select your desired server. As a general rule, the closer the server to your location, the faster your Internet service will be.

3. At the Viscosity authentication window, enter an administrator username and password, and then click OK.

   • NOTE: You may be logged in with either an Administrator or Standard user account, but you must enter Administrator credentials in this window.

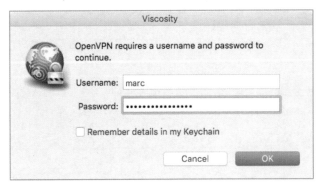

4. Within a few seconds a notification alert will appear briefly announcing that your connection is complete.

5. To verify your VPN is working properly, open a browser to *https://whatismyip.com*. It will show your Internet IP address, as well as your geographical location, which is based on IP address. If all is working well, you will not have your normal public IP address, and your reported location will be somewhere else.

Assignment: Disconnect your Viscosity VPN Internet Connection

When you wish to have a native connection to the Internet instead of VPN, you will need to disconnect from your VPN provider. In this assignment we will disconnect from VPNArea while using Viscosity.app.

1. Click the Viscosity menu icon, and then from the drop-down menu, go to and select the server to which you are currently connected.

2. In a few seconds you will be disconnected.

Assignment: Configure Viscosity OpenVPN Utility

Viscosity is one of the few applications that is well configured by default, and you may not wish to change any setting. In this assignment, we will review the settings that we use at Mintz InfoTech, Inc.

1. If Viscosity is not already running (it's icon cannot be seen in the menu bar), launch Viscosity, located in */Applications.*

2. From the Viscosity menu icon drop-down menu, scroll to the bottom and then select *Preferences.* The Preferences window opens.

3. Select the *General* tab, and then configure as below:

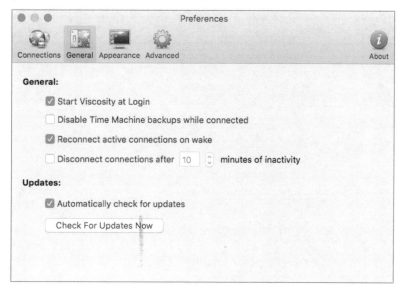

4. Select the *Appearance* tab, and then configure as below:

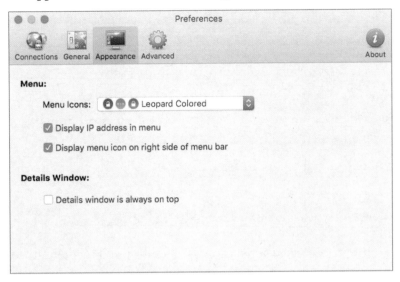

5. Select the *Advanced* tab, and then configure as below:

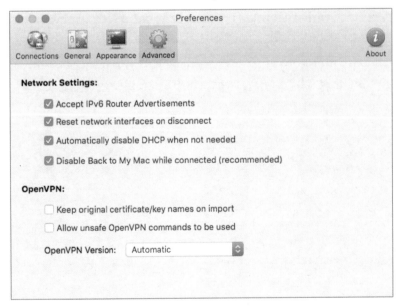

6. Close the Viscosity Preferences window.

Done!

Mesh VPN

Another way in which VPN can be configured is a *mesh VPN*. This strategy places multiple computers within the same virtual network regardless of where they are geographically located on the Internet. All the computers operate as if they are on the same physical network, and all traffic between each of the computers is military-grade encrypted. Mesh VPN is ideal for groups of people to exchange files, screen share, and access databases from each other, while maintaining full privacy from the outside world.

We now have software that enables mesh networks for a trivial cost. Keep in mind that VPN is only as secure as the provider, and the vendor of choice is a US company, subject to US federal laws and National Security Letters giving the NSA full access to logs and data crossing the vendor servers.

LogMeIn Hamachi

LogMeIn *http://logmein.com* is a US-based company with a line of top-grade cloud services. They are best known for their *LogMeIn* remote support software, allowing technical support staff both attended and unattended access to client and server computers.

One of their lesser-known, but game-changing products is *Hamachi* at *https://secure.logmein.com/products/hamachi/*. Hamachi is a cloud-based VPN, completely eliminating the need for expensive VPN boxes. As if that weren't enough, it also allows for three different types of VPN configurations: Gateway, mesh, and hub & spoke. We will restrict discussion here to the mesh option.

As of this writing, Hamachi is free for use with 5 or fewer nodes (computers). Up to 32 nodes on one network is available for $29/year. Up to 256 nodes on a network is available for $119/year.

Assignment: Create a LogMeIn Hamachi Account

In this assignment, we will create a LogMeIn Hamachi account, so that we can deploy a free Hamachi network for up to 5 computers. Should you eventually need more computers on the network, your account can easily be upgraded at any time.

1. Open a browser, and go to the Hamachi home page at *https://secure.logmein.com/products/hamachi/default.aspx*. The Hamachi home page opens.

2. Select the *Try it Free* button. In the *Sign Up* field, enter all requested information, and then select the *Create Account* button.

3. In the *Complete Your Registration* page, enter all requested information, and then select the *Register* button.

4. At the *Get LogMeIn* page, select the *Download and Install Software* button to install the software on this computer. If you don't need the software on this computer, but want to install on other computers, skip to step 12.

5. The software will begin to download, and the guide page will appear. Do not select the *Continue* button quite yet.

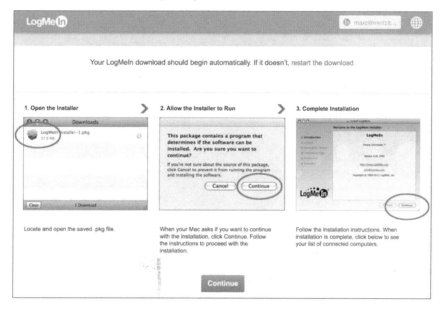

6. Go to your Downloads folder, and open the *LogMeIn Installer.app*. Enable the *I have read and agree...* checkbox, and then select the *Install* button.

7. At the authentication prompt, enter an administrator username and password, and then select the *Install* button.

8. At the prompt, enter a name for your computer, and then select the *Continue* button.

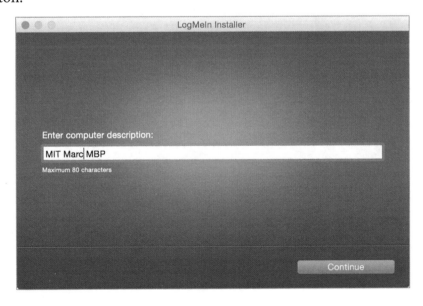

9. At The *Installation Was Successful* pane, select the *Finish* button.

10. The *LogMeIn Client Log In* window appears. Enter the same email and password used to create the account, and then select the *Log In* button.

11. The *LogMeIn Client* window will now display all users who are members of this network (currently, just yourself.) To add additional users, skip to step 13.

12. If you have jumped to here from step 4, select the *Add a different computer* link.

13. Open your email to check for a verification message from LogMeIn. Click the reply link.

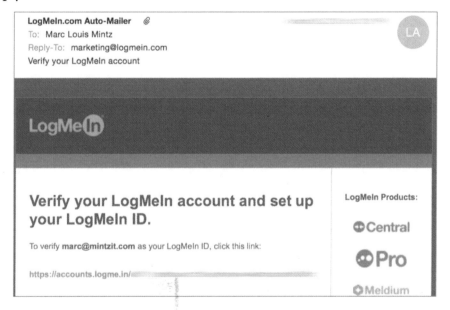

14. Returning to your browser, in the *Deployment* screen, select *Networks > My Networks*, and then select *Create Networks*.

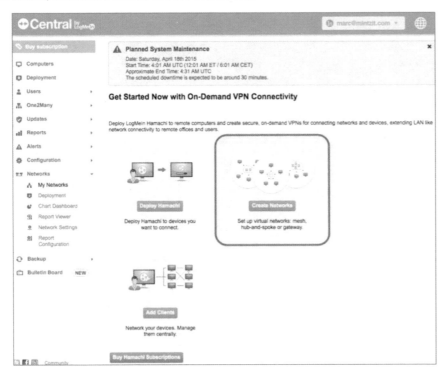

15. In the *Add Network* page, in the *Network Name* field, give your network a human-readable name, select the *Network Type* (in this example, we are creating a *Mesh* network), and then select the *Continue* button.

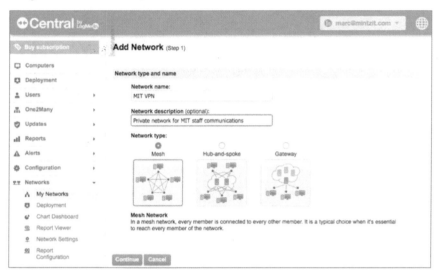

16. In *Add Network (Step 2)*, in *Join Requests*:

- In *Join Requests,* specify how users will be able to join the VPN network. If security is a concern we recommend *Must be approved* in order to keep strangers out.

- In *Network password,* configure if a password is required to join the network. Assuming all user computers have strong passwords, and full-disk encryption, it would be extremely unlikely anyone other than the authorized user would be attempting network connection. However, if security is a concern, enable the password requirement, and then set a strong password.

- In *Subscription,* specify what subscription level is requested. For the purposes of this assignment, select *Multi-network via Control (up to 5 members, any number of networks.)*

17. Select the *Continue* button.

18. The *Add Network (Step 3)* appears. Select the *Finish* button.

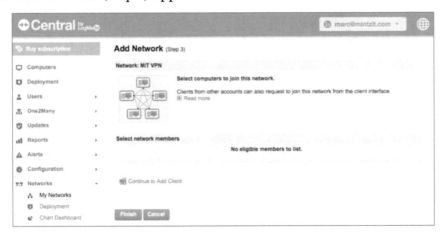

19. In the *Edit Network* page, make note of your network *ID,* as this will be used when joining the network. Select the *Save* button.

Congratulations, your account is created and you are ready to add users to your mesh VPN network.

Assignment: Add Users to a Hamachi VPN Network

In this assignment we will add users to the Hamachi VPN network created in the previous assignment.

- Prerequisite: Completion of the previous assignment.

1. Open a browser and go to *https://secure.logmein.com*, and then login with your username and password. The *LogMeIn Central* page appears.

2. Select the *Networks > Deployment* link, and then select the *Add New Link* button.

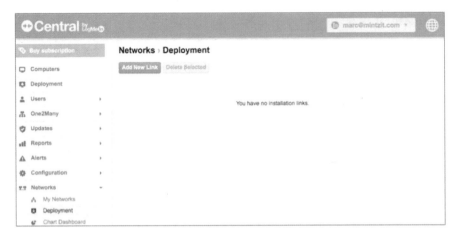

3. In the *Add Client* page, you will create a link that can be used to allow a custom installation of Hamachi.

- In the *Description* field, enter information for your own reference.

- In the *Maximum number of remote installations* field, enter, well, the maximum number of installations permitted (with a free account, this is 5.)

- In the *Expiration* pop-up, specify when the link expires.

- In *Networks,* enable the checkbox for the network this link will be used.

4. Select the *Continue* button.

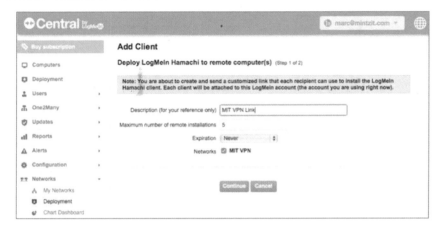

5. The *Add Client* link page appears. You have the option to *Copy* or *Send* the link. For our assignment, select *Send*.

The default email client will open, with the link pre-entered in the body area, awaiting entry of recipient(s) and a message.

6. Enter recipient address(es).

7. Enter a subject.

8. Enter additional information in the body area explaining what to do next. Something like: *Listed below is a link to download LogMeIn Hamachi. This software will allow all of us to create a private encrypted network within which we may continue our plans for world domination.*

9. Send the email.

10. When the recipient clicks the link, they are taken to the *Hamachi Installer* page. Enable the *I have received this link from a trusted source* check box, and then select the *Continue* button.

11. At the *Download* page, select the *Download Now* button.

12. The *LogMeIn Hamachi Installer* will download. Once complete, launch the installer, enable the *I have read...* check box, and then select the *Install* button.

13. The *Attach client to LogMeIn account* screen appears. Select the *Next* button.

14. When the installation completes, select the *Finish* button.

15. Open *LogMeIn Hamachi.app,* located in */Applications/LogMeIn Hamachi.* In my case, there are networks that I currently belong to listed, one of which I am connected (the green button), and one I am not connect with (white button). Neither of which is the MIT VPN network (yet).

   • If your target network appears in the *LogMeIn Hamachi* window with a green button, all is done!

   • If your target network doesn't appear in the *LogMeIn Hamachi* window, we have a few more steps to complete.

16. In LogMeIn Hamachi select *Network* menu > *Join an existing network…*

17. Enter the *Network ID* as displayed in step 18 of the previous exercise, and then select the *Join* button.

18. At the dialog box asking *Would you like to submit a request for membership?* Select the *Yes* button.

19. Back at your computer, or the computer used to administer this network, in the *LogMeIn Central* page > *Networks* > *My Networks* will be found all of the users who have received and responded to their links from the previous steps. Select the *Edit* link.

20. In the *Edit Network* page, select *Join Requests*. If the pending join request is from someone who should join the network, select the *Accept* radio button. If they are someone who should not join the network, select the *Reject* radio button, and then select the *Save* button.

21. In the *LogMeIn Central* page > *Networks* > *My Networks* > *Members* you will see that this user is now part of the group.

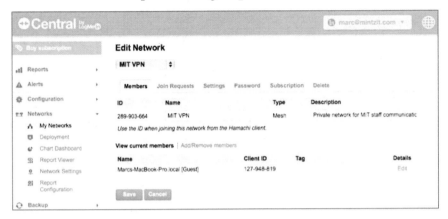

22. Returning to the user who has just been accepted into the group, their Hamachi window will now reflect they are part of the network (the network appears in the window) and that they are actively joined to the network (green button next to the network name.)

Awesome! You have your first member of the VPN network. Of course you can't do anything with just one person. The value of VPN comes with additional members. Repeat the steps in this assignment to have at least one more computer part of your network, and then move on to the next assignment.

Assignment: File Sharing Within a Hamachi VPN Network

In this assignment we will file share within a Hamachi VPN network. Completing the previous assignment is a prerequisite.

In the typical OS X network environment, one Mac can see another Mac over the network using an automatic discovery protocol, *Bonjour*. This protocol isn't in effect over a VPN connection, so we will need a different method of accessing other computers for file sharing and other network activities.

Before we begin, please make sure the other computer has *System Preferences > Sharing > File Sharing* enabled, that SMB file sharing is enabled, and that you know a username/password allowed to file share.

1. Launch *Hamachi*, and verify the target computer is showing as *Online*. In this example, the other computer is named *MIT-Spare-MBA.local*.

2. On your OS X computer, in the *Finder,* select the *Go* menu > *Connect to Server.* Enter *afp://<name of computer>* (to create an *Apple Filing Protocol* connection), or *smb://<name of computer>* (to create a *Server Message Block* connection) and then select the *Connect* button.

    •   AFP is the legacy standard of communication between Apple computers. As of OS X 10.10, Apple is moving away from it in favor of SMB, the long-time Windows standard. You will likely have faster network throughput using SMB.

3. When the *Authentication* window appears, select *Registered User,* and then enter your authorized *Name* and *Password,* and then select the *Connect* button.

4. The available volumes (sharepoints) will appear. Select the desired volume, and then select the *OK* button.

5. The volume will mount to your desktop. Double-click to open and navigate it just as if it were located on your physical network.

6. To file share, all you need do is drag and drop between your computer drives and the mounted volume.

7. When you are ready to disconnect from the remote computer, drag the mounted volume into the *Eject* Dock icon.

Assignment: Screen Share Within Hamachi VPN

In this assignment we will screen share within the Hamachi VPN environment. If you have followed the previous assignment, then screen sharing is almost identical to file sharing.

Before we begin, please make sure the other computer has *System Preferences > Sharing > Screen Sharing* enabled, and that you know a username/password allowed to screen share.

1. Launch *Hamachi,* and verify the target computer is showing as *Online.* In this example, the other computer is named *MIT-Spare-MBA.local.*

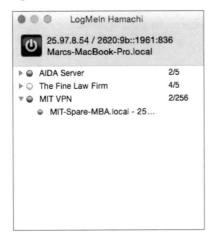

2. On your OS X computer, in the *Finder,* select the *Go* menu > *Connect to Server.* Enter *vnc://<name of computer>* (to create a *Virtual Network Control* connection), and then select the *Connect* button.

3. At the authentication prompt, enter the authorized *Name* and *Password*, and then select the *Connect* button.

4. The screen of the remote computer will appear. You will be able to control it with your mouse and keyboard.

5. To exit out of screen sharing, close the *screen sharing* window.

Assignment: Exit the Hamachi VPN Network

In this assignment we will stop VPN so that we are no longer connected to the VPN network.

1. On your computer, in the Hamachi window, right-click on the connected network name, and then select *Go Offline* menu. The network button will turn from green to white, indicating you are no longer connected.

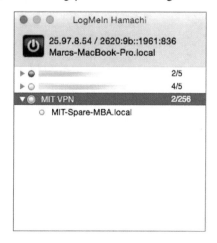

2.   You may now *Quit* LogMeIn Hamachi.

Great work! You can now create a military-grade, encrypted network, on the fly, so that your friends or business associates can share files, screen share, etc. without fear of data or activities being spied upon.

Resolving Email Conflicts with VPN

Some email servers will send up a red flag and then block user access to email when the user switches to a VPN connection. This is a good thing as it indicates the email provider is highly sensitive to any possible security breach. In all cases there is a resolution available, although the steps to take will vary with each provider.

As an example I have outlined below what occurs when using VPN with a Gmail account, and how to gain access to your email after the blockage.

1. The user starts a VPN program to encrypt all data between the user's computer and the Internet.

2. The user attempts to receive Gmail using the Apple Mail.app program.

3. Google sees attempted access from an unknown machine (the Proxy Server), and blocks access to the account.

4. Both an email and a text from Google are sent notifying the user of suspicious activity. Select the link in either message.

5. The first support file opens. Select the link.

6. In the authentication window, enter your email and password, and then select the Sign In button.

7. Another support window opens, explaining the next steps to take. Select the Continue button.

8. The final support window opens. Following the instructions, return to your email application and access your Gmail within 10 minutes. This will provide Google with the authentication to release your account.

Review Questions

1. VPN will encrypt all incoming and outgoing Internet traffic from the device it is installed on. (True or False)

2. VPN will hide or change your public IP address. (True or False)

3. Viscosity.app requires being logged in with an Administrator account. (True or False)

4. Chameleon.app requires being logged in with an Administrator account. (True or False)

5. The software that can link multiple devices together into a VPN is named _____ .

The Final Word

If you have followed each of the steps outlined in this book, your computer now is secured to a level higher than even the NSA requires for its own staff. Although this won't prevent one of the bad guys from stealing your computer, it will prevent them from accessing your data. And since you have at least one current backup at the home or office, and one on the Internet, you are still in possession of the items with *real* value–your data, and peace of mind.

Mintz InfoTech, Inc.
OS X 10.11 Security Checklist

I have included the checklist that all of us at Mintz InfoTech, Inc. use when performing Security Checks for our clientele. This same checklist should be used to ensure your own system is fully hardened.

Passwords

Critical
- ☐ Strong account passwords
- ☐ All passwords recorded
- ☐ Any challenge questions and answers recorded

Optional
- ☐ Harden the Keychain with a different password than the user account password
- ☐ Harden the Keychain with a timed lock
- ☐ Synchronize Keychain across OS X and iOS devices through iCloud
- ☐ Synchronize Passwords across Android, iOS, OS X, and Windows devices with LastPass

System and Application Updates

Critical
- ☐ All OS updates installed
- ☐ All application updates installed
- ☐ Configure App Store to automatically install updates

Optional
- ☐ Install MacUpdate Desktop to automate application updates

User Accounts

Critical
- ☐ All users log in with non-administrative accounts
- ☐ Create an administrative account whose credentials may be used for administrator tasks
- ☐ Root user not enabled
- ☐ Guest user account enabled, no file sharing access to any folders

Optional
- ☐ Application Whitelisting with Parental Controls

Storage Device

☐ Enable FileVault 2 Full Disk Encryption

Sleep and Screen Saver

☐ Require Password after Sleep or Screen Saver

Malware

☐ Install Antivirus software (Avira for home use, Bitdefender for business use)
☐ Configure for automatic updates

Firewall

☐ Enable the Firewall
☐ Close unnecessary ports

Data Loss

☐ Time Machine active and encrypted
☐ Time Machine password recorded
☐ Carbon Copy Cloner backup active and encrypted
☐ Internet-based backup active (CrashPlan or CrashPlanPro recommended)
☐ Integrity test Time Machine backup monthly
☐ Integrity test Carbon Copy Cloner backup monthly

Firmware Password

☐ Firmware password enabled
☐ Firmware password recorded

Lost or Stolen Device

☐ Find My Mac active
☐ Guest User Log in enabled

When It Is Time to Say Goodbye

☐ Secure erase storage device

Local Network

Critical
☐ WPA2 with AES encryption for all Wi-Fi networks
☐ Strong password in use for Wi-Fi
☐ Wi-Fi password recorded
☐ No Ethernet hubs in use, only Ethernet switches
☐ Modems and routers power-cycled
☐ Modems and routers firmware updated

☐ Modems and routers checked for DNS Servers
☐ Modems and routers checked for Port Forwarding
☐ Modems and routers checked for DMZ

Optional

☐ MAC Address to Limit Wi-Fi Access
☐ Modems and routers checked for Port Forwarding and DNS

Web Browsing

Critical

☐ HTTPS Everywhere installed (if using Firefox or Chrome)
☐ Client educated on recognizing secure and unsecure web pages

Optional

☐ Private Browsing used
☐ DuckDuckGo search engine used
☐ Tor installed and configured
☐ Adobe Flash updated (if installed)
☐ Java updated (if installed)
☐ User educated on web scams

Email

☐ All email accounts using either SSL, TLS, or HTTPS
☐ User educated on how to recognize phishing attacks

Does the client need end-to-end email security?
If "No," then skip this section. If "Yes," as appropriate, set up with SendInc, S/MIME or GPG:

☐ Create a SendInc.com account for our client, and then educate client how to use SendInc.
Or:
☐ Acquire a Comodo Class 1 or 3 S/MIME certificate, install on computer, and then educate client how to use and have others do same.
Or
☐ Install GPG, and then educate client how to use and have others do same.

Apple ID and iCloud

☐ Create an Apple ID
☐ Implement Apple ID Two-Step Verification

Apple ID and iCloud Security

☐ iCloud account active on the computer
☐ Two-Step Verification enabled
☐ Two-Step Verification Recovery Key recorded

Document Security

Does the client need secure documents?
If "No," then skip this section. If "Yes":

☐ Educate how to password protect Microsoft Office documents
☐ Educate how to convert to .pdf, then how to password protect .pdf documents
☐ Educate how to create password protected disk images
☐ Download, configure, and educate how to use VeraCrypt

Instant Messaging

☐ Educate user that when instant messaging between OS X and iOS users with Facetime or Messages, all communications are secure.
☐ If instant messaging with Android, Windows or any OS other than OS X and iOS, install and educate how to use Wickr

Internet Activity

☐ Consult with user the comparisons between VPN and Tor/Tails to determine the best fit for their use
☐ As appropriate, install VPNArea VPN account and configure its software
☐ Educate the client how to use VPN software
  Or
☐ Create a Tails bootable thumb drive
☐ Educate the client how to use Tor/Tails
☐ Install LogMeIn Hamachi Mesh VPN

Audio and Video Communications

☐ Create and configure an OStel account

Index

Your Virtual CIO & IT Department

Mintz InfoTech, Inc.
when, where, and how you want IT

Technician fixes problems.
Consultant delivers solutions.

Technician answers questions.
Consultant asks questions, revealing core issues.

Technician understands your equipment.
Consultant understands your business.

Technician costs you money.
Consultant contributes to your success.

Let us contribute to your success.

Mintz InfoTech, Inc. is uniquely positioned to be your Virtual CIO and provide you and your organization comprehensive technology support. With the only MBA-IT consultant in New Mexico heading our organization, our mission is to provide small and medium businesses with the same Chief Information and Technology Officer resources otherwise only available to large businesses.

Mintz InfoTech, Inc.
Toll-free: +1 888.479.0690 • Local: +1 505.814.1413
info@mintzIT.com • https://mintzit.com

Practical Paranoia
Security Essentials Workshops & Books

This is an age of government intrusion into every aspect of our digital lives, criminals using your own data against you, and teenagers competing to see who can crack your password the fastest. Every organization, every computer user, every one should be taking steps to protect and secure their digital lives.

The *Practical Paranoia: Security Essentials Workshop* is the perfect environment in which to learn not only *how*, but to actually *do* the work to harden the security of your OS X and Windows computers, and iPhone, iPad, and Android devices.

Workshops are available online and instructor-led at your venue, as well as tailored for on-site company events.

Each Book is designed for classroom, workshop, and self-study. Includes all instructor presentations, hands-on assignments, software links, security checklist, and review questions and answers. Available from Amazon (both print and Kindle format), and all fine booksellers, with inscribed copies available from the author.

Call for more information, to schedule your workshop, or order your books!

Mintz InfoTech, Inc.
Toll-free: +1 888.479.0690 • Local: +1 505.814.1413
info@mintzIT.com • http://thepracticalparanoid.com

Review Answers

1. Vulnerability: Passwords

1. **Q:** What are the minimum number of characters recommended for a password?
   A: 14.

2. **Q:** What is one website that can be used to test the strength of a password?
   A: https://www.grc.com/haystack.htm

3. **Q:** In which system preference can the login password be changed?
   A: Users & Groups

4. **Q:** When changing a user login password, why is it best to do so only when logged in as that user account?
   A: This maintains synchronization between the user login password, and the user Keychain password. Changing the user login password in any other manner leaves the Keychain password intact.

5. **Q:** Where does OS X store most passwords?
   A: In the Keychain.

6. **Q:** What application is used to access the Keychain?
   A: The Keychain Access utility.

7. **Q:** What are two ways to harden the security of the Keychain?
   A: Change the Keychain password to be different than the login password, and automatically log off of the Keychain after X minutes of inactivity.

8. **Q:** What System Preference is used to synchronize the Keychain between a user's OS X and iOS devices?
   A: iCloud.

9. **Q:** What are the minimum OS X and iOS versions needed to synchronize the Keychain?
   A: OS X 10.9, and iOS 7.

2. Vulnerability: System and Application Updates

1. **Q:** US-CERT recommends installing updates within _____ hours of release.
   A: 48 hours.

2. **Q:** Name the three fundamental reasons for updates and upgrades.
   A: Bug fixes, monetization, and security patches.

3. **Q:** System and many application updates and upgrades can be configured from the _____ System Preferences.
   A: App Store System Preference.

4. **Q:** Apple and most 3rd-party application updates and upgrades can be automatically reviewed and downloaded using the _____ application.
   A: MacUpdate Desktop.

3. Vulnerability: User Accounts

1. **Q:** Name the six different types of user accounts available in OS X 10.11.
   A: Root, Administrator, Standard, Managed with Parental Controls, Sharing Only, and Guest.

2. **Q:** The maximum number of Root accounts available on OS X is _____.
   A: 1.

3. **Q:** By default, is Root enabled or disabled?
   A: Disabled.

4. **Q:** Which user account(s) may assume the powers of Root?
   A: Administrator.

5. **Q:** In what ways are Administrator accounts different than the Standard, Sharing, and Guest accounts?
   A: An Administrator account can create new user accounts, delete user accounts, modify the contents of restricted folders, authorize the installation or removal of applications and system updates, and take on the powers of root from the command line.

6. **Q:** How many Guest accounts are available on OS X?
   A: 1.

7. **Q:** Root may be enabled from the _____ System Preference.
    A: Users & Groups.

8. **Q:** The first user account to be created is a(n) _____.
    A: Administrator.

9. **Q:** Application Whitelisting can be enabled with _____.
    A: Parental Controls.

4. Vulnerability: Storage Device

1. **Q:** To disable access to USB and FireWire storage devices, the IOUSBMassStorageClass.kext and IOFireWireSerialBussProtocolTransport.kext files may be removed from which folder?
    A: /System/Library/Extensions

2. **Q:** Explain the fundamental difference between the original FileVault, and FileVault 2.
    A: FileVault encrypted the user's home folder on a user-by-user basis. FileVault 2 encrypts the entire volume.

3. **Q:** FileVault 2 may be enabled from which System Preference?
    A: Security & Privacy.

4. **Q:** Describe how to enable Target Disk Mode.
    A: Power on the computer, and then immediately hold down the T key.

5. **Q:** What does Target Disk Mode do?
    A: Fundamentally it deactivates the computing functions of the computer, leaving the Firewire and Thunderbolt storage functions active, turning the computer into an available storage device.

6. **Q:** Describe how to enable Single-User Mode.
    A: Power on the computer, and then immediately hold down the cmd + s keys.

7. **Q:** What does Single-User Mode do.
    A: Provides command-line access to the operating system and storage device prior to loading of the full OS.

5. Vulnerability: Sleep and Screen Saver

1. **Q:** Where can you configure requiring a password after sleep or screen saver?
   A: System Preferences > Security & Privacy > General tab.

6. Vulnerability: Malware

1. **Q:** Apple started to include system-level anti-malware beginning with OS X _____.
   A: 10.7.

2. **Q:** Name a website the independently researches and publishes anti-virus software effectiveness.
   A: http://av-comparatives.org.

3. **Q:** Name a few of the best anti-virus software for OS X in terms of both effectiveness and performance, according to this website.
   A: BitDefender, Kaspersky, AVIRA.

7. Vulnerability: Firewall

1. **Q:** The OS X firewall is enabled by default. (True or False)
   A: False.

2. **Q:** Where is the firewall enabled or disabled?
   A: System Preferences > Security & Privacy > Firewall.

3. **Q:** When selecting the firewall option to Block All Incoming connections, are all ports disabled?
   A: No. Ports needed for basic Internet services, such as DHCP, Bonjour, and IPSec, are left open.

8. Vulnerability: Data Loss

1. **Q:** Best Practices call for what backups?
   A: At least one full backup onsite, at least one full backup offsite, and one Internet backup.

2. **Q:** What application is used to format a storage device, and where is it located?
   A: Disk Utility, located in the /Applications/Utilities folder.

3. **Q:** What application can be used to create bootable clone backups?
   A: Carbon Copy Cloner.

9. Vulnerability: Firmware Password

1. **Q:** What is the name of logic board chip that can be password protected?
   A: EFI or Extensible Firmware Interface.

2. **Q:** How is the Firmware password cleared on Macintosh computers manufactured prior to January 1, 2010?
   A: Shut down the computer, remove or add RAM, power on and then immediately hold down the cmd-opt-p-r keys until the computer reboots.

3. **Q:** To create a Firmware password, you must be an administrator. (True or False)
   A: False.

10. Vulnerability: Lost or Stolen Device

1. **Q:** Find My Mac is enabled by default. (True or False)
   A: False.

2. **Q:** Should the Guest account be enabled when Find My Mac is active, and why?
   A: It should be enabled so a thief has easy access to an account, which will then have Find My Mac send location information.

3. **Q:** A lost Mac may be located via Find My Mac only with another OS X or iOS device. (True or False)
   A: False.

11. Vulnerability: When It Is Time to Say Goodbye

1. **Q:** The secure erase a boot device requires booting into _____.
   A: Recovery HD Mode.

2. **Q:** When erasing a storage device, the fastest option erases all directory information and data. (True or False)
   A: False.

3. **Q:** If a storage device is using FileVault 2 encryption, it can be securely erased by reformatting without encryption. (True or False)
   A: True.

12. Vulnerability: Local Network

1. **Q:** OS X client to OS X client communications are encrypted. (True or False)
   A: False.

2. **Q:** OS X client to OS X server communications can be encrypted. (True or False)
   A: True.

3. **Q:** The WEP Wi-Fi encryption protocol should be used whenever possible. (True or False)
   A: False.

4. **Q:** The WPA Wi-Fi encryption protocol should be used whenever possible. (True or False)
   A: False.

5. **Q:** The WPA2 Wi-Fi encryption protocol should be used whenever possible. (True or False)
   A: True.

6. **Q:** Of the two encryption algorithms–TKIP and AES–which should be used?
   A: AES.

7. **Q:** The network hardware that decodes and modulates the signal from your Internet provider to your cable or telephone jack is called a _____.
   A: Modem.

8. **Q:** The network hardware that allows hundreds or thousands of devices to interact between the local network and Internet is called a _____.
   A: Router.

9. **Q:** The network hardware or software that inspects data traffic between the Internet and local network devices is called a _____.
   A: Firewall.

10. **Q:** The network hardware that allows multiple devices to connect and interact with each other and the router is called a _____.
    A: Network Switch.

11. **Q:** The network hardware that allows tens or hundreds of wireless devices to connect to a network is called a _____.
    A: Access Point.

12. **Q:** The network connection speed between an OS X computer an Wi-Fi Access Point can be found by _____.
    A: Hold down the Option key while clicking the Wi-Fi menu icon.

13. **Q:** A _____ address includes a unique manufacturer code, and a unique device code.
    A: MAC.

13. Vulnerability: Web Browsing

1. **Q:** HTTPS uses the _____ encryption protocol.
   A: SSL.

2. **Q:** To ensure your browser goes to https even if entering https, install the _____ plug-in.
   A: HTTPS Everywhere.

3. **Q:** To ensure your browser doesn't store browsing history, passwords, user names, list of downloads, cookies, or cached files, enable _____ mode.
   A: Private.

4. **Q:** By default, any two people will have the same results for a given Google search. (True or False)
   A: False.

5. **Q:** By default, any two people will have the same results for a given DuckDuckGo search (True or False)
   A: True.

6. **Q:** TOR is based on the _____ browser.
   A: Firefox.

7. **Q:** It is OK to install browser plug-ins to TOR. (True or False)
   A: False.

14. Vulnerability: Email

1. **Q:** The attempt to acquire your personal or sensitive information by appearing as a trustworthy source is called _____.
    A: Phishing.

2. **Q:** Three common protocols to encrypt email between email server and user are _____, _____, and _____.
    A: TLS (Transport Layer Security), SSL (Secure Socket Layer), and HTTPS (Hypertext Transport Layer Secure.)

3. **Q:** OS X 10.11 Mail.app has separate settings for SSL and TLS. (True or False)
    A: No, only 1 setting.

4. **Q:** The encryption protocol used for web-based email is _____.
    A: HTTPS.

5. **Q:** Email encrypted with either PGP or GPG can be decrypted with either. (True or False)
    A: True.

6. **Q:** S/MIME Class 1 certificate is designed for business use. (True or False)
    A: False.

15. Vulnerability: Apple ID and iCloud

1. **Q:** In the event that your iOS device is stolen or lost, you should log in to _____ to remove that device from the verified list, so that no 2-step verification code will be sent to it.
    A: https://appleid.apple.com

2. **Q:** You must have a current email address in order to create an Apple ID. (True or False)
    A: False.

3. **Q:** The services that can be synchronized using iCloud are: _____.
    A: iCloud Drive, Photos, Mail, Contacts, Calendars, Reminders, Safari, Notes, Keychain. Non-synchronizing features are Back to My Mac, and Find My Mac.

4. **Q:** A mobile phone number that is capable of receiving texts is a requirement for iCloud 2-step verification. (True or False)
   A: True.

16. Vulnerability: Documents

1. **Q:** Microsoft Office for Mac version _____ and higher use strong AES encryption.
   A: 2011.

2. **Q:** Microsoft Office for Mac is limited to a maximum of _____ characters for the encryption password.
   A: 15.

3. **Q:** Adobe Acrobat 9 and higher use _____ encryption.
   A: AES 256-bit.

4. **Q:** Disk Utility can create encrypted disk images readable by both OS X and Windows. (True or False)
   A: False.

5. **Q:** VeraCrypt can create encrypted containers readable by both OS X and Windows. (True or False)
   A: True.

17. Vulnerability: Instant Messaging

1. **Q:** Instant messages sent via Messages between iOS and OS X is securely encrypted. (True or False)
   A: True.

2. **Q:** There are currently no cross platform secure instant messaging applications available. (True or False)
   A: False.

18. Vulnerability: Voice and Video Communications

1. **Q:** When using Facetime between iOS and OS X computers, the communications are fully secure. (True or False).
   A: True

2. **Q:** Skype is fully secure between any devices. (True or False)
   A: False.

3. **Q:** Google Hangouts has end-to-end encryption. (True or False)
   A: False

19. Vulnerability: Internet Activity

1. **Q:** VPN will encrypt all incoming and outgoing Internet traffic from the device it is installed on. (True or False)
   A: True.

2. **Q:** VPN will hide or change your Public IP address. (True or False)
   A: True.

3. **Q:** Viscosity.app requires being logged in with an Administrator account. (True or False)
   A: False.

4. **Q:** Chameleon.app requires being logged in with an Administrator account. (True or False)
   A: True.

5. **Q:** The software that can link multiple devices together into a VPN is named _____,
   A: Hamachi from LogMeIn.